D1461679

SUPPORT AND HOUSING IN EUROPE

Tackling social exclusion in the European Union

Bill Edgar, Joe Doherty and Amy Mina-Coull

The POLICY PRESS

JCSHR

FEANTSA

First published in Great Britain in September 2000 by

The Policy Press
University of Bristol
34 Tyndall's Park Road
Bristol BS8 1PY
UK

Tel +44 (0)117 954 6800
Fax +44 (0)117 973 7308
E-mail tpp@bristol.ac.uk
www.policypress.org.uk

© The Policy Press, 2000

ISBN 1 86134 275 6

Bill Edgar and **Joe Doherty** are Directors of the Joint Centre for Scottish Housing Research at the University of Dundee and the University of St Andrews. **Amy Mina-Coull** is a Research Associate at the Centre.

The contents of this book are based on research carried out by the national correspondents of the European Observatory on Homelessness, with the participation of research institutes and universities in 15 member states of the EU. This research was commissioned by FEANTSA – the European Federation of National Organisations Working with the Homeless – with the financial support of the European Commission (Directorate General for Employment and Social Affairs).

Cover design by Qube Design Associates, Bristol
Printed in Great Britain by Hobbs the Printers Ltd, Southampton

Contents

List of tables and figures

Tables

Figures

Foreword

Those working at grassroots level with homeless people have long argued that while the basic solution to homelessness is affordable housing, much more is needed to create sustainable homes.

Homelessness represents a combination of social dislocation and marginalisation. The experience of homelessness brings about a high level of complex needs, requiring access to adequate and appropriate housing together with psychosocial support in order to maintain social and residential stability. Effective strategies for tackling homelessness require a coherent and multidimensional approach at both national and European level. This should encompass comprehensive social welfare policies together with carefully targeted housing policies.

The last research report (Edgar et al, 1999) surveyed services for homeless people; this one looks specifically at the range of support offered to homeless people when they are given tenancies. It is now generally accepted that people require support if they are to climb out of the cycle of homelessness. The revolving door syndrome is a familiar one – homelessness, hostel, temporary accommodation in supported tenancy – and then back to homelessness. We all need help at some time in our lives and most of us are fortunate to have a circle of friends and families to call on. The social isolation of homeless people frequently denies them this option. If they are to be successfully reintegrated into the community – to sustain a tenancy, access training and obtain employment – then support in varying degrees is essential.

This report provides a detailed overview of the various innovative approaches being used across the European Union. It provides a more detailed understanding of the way in which the needs of homeless people are being met, and it examines the range of forms of provision and the factors which have stimulated their development. This study makes an important contribution to the policy debate on social exclusion – by considering the role of support in preventing homelessness. It analyses the organisational structures which enable the effective delivery of services to meet the housing and support needs of homeless people. With social inclusion a priority for the EU and its member states, and with homelessness one of the prime reasons for citizens being excluded, it is essential reading for all those involved from policy makers to service deliverers.

Finally, thanks are due to all those who made possible the production of this research report: the national correspondents of the European Observatory on Homelessness and their research institutes; the Directorate General for Employment and Social Affairs of the European Commission, the JCSHR and the FEANTSA secretariat.

John Evans
President of FEANTSA
May 2000

Acknowledgements

Our primary debt is to the national corespondents of the European Observatory on Homelessness. Their national reports provide the empirical basis for this report and were instrumental in sparking many of our ideas for the organisational framework. We therefore acknowledge our debt to and extend our thanks to the following correspondents: Robert Aldridge (UK), Tobias Børner Stax and Inge Koch-Nielson (Denmark), Alfredo Bruto da Costa (Portugal), Volker Busch-Geertsema (Germany), Pascal de Decker (Belgium), Henk de Feijter (Netherlands), Anne de Gouy and Julien Damon (France), Sirkka-Liisa Kärkkäinen (Finland), Heinz Schoibl (Austria), Jesús Leal Maldonado (Spain), Eoin O'Sullivan (Ireland), Monique Pels (Luxembourg), Ingrid Sahlin (Sweden), Aristides Sapounakis (Greece) and Antonio Tosi (Italy).

We would also like to acknowledge the key roles played by members of the FEANTSA secretariat in coordinating the project and in organising meetings of the Observatory correspondents in Brussels and Amsterdam; meetings which provided a crucial forum for the exchange information and the clarification of ideas. Finally we would like to express our thanks to Dawn Rushen, Editorial Manager at The Policy Press, for her efficiency and support in bringing this book to publication.

FEANTSA and the European Observatory on Homelessness

FEANTSA (the European Federation of National Organisations Working with the Homeless) is an international non-governmental organisation founded in 1989. FEANTSA currently has a total of 70 member organisations in the 15 member states of the European Union and other European countries. FEANTSA's mission is to engage in dialogue with European institutions and national governments in order to promote the development and implementation of effective measures to tackle the causes of homelessness. FEANTSA receives funding from the European Commission, is supported by the European Parliament and has consultative status at the Council of Europe.

The European Observatory on Homelessness was set up by FEANTSA in 1991 to conduct research into homelessness in Europe. It is composed of a network of national correspondents who collect information concerning homelessness and other relevant policy measures in the EU member states. Each year the Observatory produces a series of national reports on specific research themes and these are published as a European Report analysing transnational trends. The research of the Observatory is supported financially by the European Commission.

Contact address: FEANTSA, 1 rue Defacqz, B-1000 Brussels, Belgium; Tel 32 2 538 66 69, Fax 32 2 539 41 74, e-mail office@feantsa.org, website: http://www.feantsa.org

Coordinators and national correspondents of the European Observatory on Homelessness: 1998–1999

Coordinators

Bill Edgar, Co-Director of the Joint Centre for Scottish Housing Research (JCSHR), Director, School of Town and Regional Planning, University of Dundee, Perth Road, Dundee DD1 4HT, UK; Tel (44) (0)1382 345238, Fax (44) (0)1382 204 234, e-mail w.m.edgar@dundee.ac.uk

Joe Doherty, Co-Director of the Joint Centre for Scottish Housing Research (JCHSR), School of Geography and Geosciences, University of St Andrews, St Andrews, Fife KY16 9ST, UK; Tel (44) (0)1334 463911, Fax (44) (0)1334 46 39 49, e-mail jd@st-andrews.ac.uk

Amy Mina-Coull, Research Associate of the Joint Centre for Scottish Housing Research (JCHSR)

National correspondents

Austria: Heinz Schoibl, Helix-Forschung und Beratung, Mirabellplatz 9/3, A-5020 Salzburg; Tel (43) 662 88 66 23 10, Fax (43) 662 88 66 23 9, e-mail helix@salzburg.co.at

Belgium: Pascal de Decker, Sint-Denijslaan, 293, 9000 Gent; Tel (32) 9 220 59 26, e-mail pascal.de.decker@skynet.be

Denmark: Tobias Børner Stax and Inger Koch Nielsen, The Danish National Institute of Social Science, Herluf Trollesgade 11, 1052 Copenhagen K; Tel (45) 33 48 08 00, Fax (45) 33 48 08 33, e-mail Tob@sfi.dk or ikn@sfi.dk

Finland: Sirkka-Liisa Kärkkäinen, STAKES, PB 220, Fl-00531, Helsinki; Tel (358) 9 39 67 20 68, Fax (358) 9 39 67 20 54, e-mail sirkka-liisa.kärkkäinen@.stakes.fi

France: Anne de Gouy and Julien Damon, Association Habitat Educatif, 101 rue Talma, 94 400 Vitry sur Seine; Tel (33) 1 46 82 38 03, Fax (33) 1 46 82 38 55

Germany: Volker Busch-Geertsema, GISS e.v. (Association for Innovative Social Research and Social Planning), Kohlhöstrasse 22, D-28203 Bremen; Tel (49) 421 339 88 33, Fax (49) 421 339 88 35, e-mail giss-bremen@t-online.de

Greece: Aristides Sapounakis, Kivotos, Angelou Pyrri Street 9, 115 27 Athens; Tel (30) 1 770 33 57, Fax (30) 1 771 08 16, e-mail arsapkiv@mail.hol.gr

Ireland: Eoin O'Sullivan, Department of Social Studies, Trinity College, University of Dublin, Dublin 2; Tel (353) 1 608 2548, Fax (353) 1 671 2262, e-mail tosullivan@tcd.ie

Italy: Antonio Tosi, Dipartmento di Scienze del Territorio, Politecnico Milan, Via Bonardi 3, 20133 Milan; Tel (39) 02 239 954 17, Fax (39) 02 239 954 35, e-mail antonio.tosi@polimi.it

Luxembourg: Monique Pels, CEPS/INSTEAD, BP 48 L-4501 Differdange; Tel (352) 58 5855 536, Fax (352) 58 5560, e-mail moniquep@hermes.CEPS.lu

Netherlands: Henk de Feijter, Planologisch Demografisch Instituut, University of Amsterdam, Nieuwe Prinsengracht 130, NL-1018 UZ Amsterdam; Tel (31) 20 525 40 40, Fax (31) 20 525 40 51, e-mail H.J.Feijter@frw.uva.nl

Portugal: Alfredo Bruto da Costa, Portuguese Catholic University, rua Eiffel 4, 3 Esq, 1000 Lisbon; Tel (351) 21 796 89 45, Fax (351) 21 795 18 35, e-mail alfredo.bc@mail.telepac.pt

Spain: Jésus Leal Maldonado, Faculty of Political Sciences and Sociology, Universidad Complutense de Madrid, Campus de Somosaguas, E-28023 Madrid; Tel (34) 111 394 2644, Fax (34) 111 394 2646, e-mail 5050204@sis.vcm.es

Sweden: Ingrid Sahlin, Department of Sociology, University of Göteborg, PO Box 720, 40530 Göteborg; Tel (46) 31 773 53 92, Fax (46) 31 773 47 64, e-mail Ingrid.Sahlin@sociology.gu.se

United Kingdom: Robert Aldridge, Scottish Council for the Single Homeless, Wellgate House, 200 Cowgate, Edinburgh EH1 1NQ; Tel (44) 131 2264 382, Fax (44) 131 2254 382, e-mail robert@scsh.demon. co.uk

ONE

Introduction

This study examines the need for support to enable the successful reintegration of homeless people into mainstream housing, the extent to which the provision of support in housing is already occurring in the European Union, particularly as a solution for homeless people, and the problems and issues involved in its implementation. This report is based, in part, on the 15 national reports of the correspondents of the European Observatory on Homelessness. The brief for the national reports was designed to consider the role of supported housing in the prevention of homelessness, the reintegration of homeless people, and the provision of housing with support to people who would otherwise be homeless in each EU member state.

The background to the study is the development in many countries of the European Union over the last two decades, of designated 'supported accommodation', or of the provision of mechanisms of support to people in their own homes, without which they would be unable to live independently in the community. This development in policy has often accompanied the closure of large-scale institutional or residential establishments and temporary or emergency hostels for homeless people. The study is based on the premise that current approaches to dealing with homelessness are increasingly aimed at prevention, and the long-term reintegration of homeless people into mainstream housing. To the extent that reintegration is critical in the processes of social inclusion, the study reflects a key priority area expressed at EU and national levels.

Homelessness and approaches to homelessness

The complexity of the causes of homelessness make it difficult to achieve a single or consistent definition of homelessness. This has been discussed in detail elsewhere (Edgar et al, 1999; Avramov, 1996). The Council of Europe (1993) definition of homelessness provided a base definition, which has been adapted by FEANTSA as a working definition of homelessness which includes four main categories:

- rooflessness
- houselessness
- living in insecure accommodation
- living in substandard housing.

Each of these conditions raises issues about the inter-related need for housing *and* support to prevent homelessness and to reintegrate homeless people. *Rooflessness*, defined as rough sleeping, is the most visible form of homelessness. People with chaotic lifestyles or unsettled ways of living may be disproportionately represented among the roofless population. Successful resettlement for rough sleepers may be contingent as much on the availability of appropriate support as on the availability of temporary and permanent housing. *Houselessness* refers to situations where, despite access to emergency shelter or long-term institutions, individuals may still be classed as *homeless* due to a lack of appropriate support aimed at facilitating social reintegration. People who are forced to live in institutions because there is inadequate accommodation (with support) in the community to meet their needs are thus regarded as homeless. In this context, *homelessness* refers as much to the lack of housing as it does to the lack of social networks. *Living in insecure housing* (insecure tenure or temporary accommodation) may be a consequence of the inaccessibility of permanent housing. It may equally reflect the need for support to enable people to successfully hold a tenancy. The provision of appropriate support can be critical in helping people into permanent housing under their own tenancy. To some extent, the final category (*living in substandard housing conditions*) focuses greater attention on housing condition than on support needs. Nevertheless, support in this context may enable households to identify and sustain better housing. In each of these categories, support needs are related to access to the housing market as well as personal requirements for reintegration.

It is not sufficient simply to define the nature of homelessness in order to consider the role which support in housing may have in its prevention, or in the reintegration of homeless people. The process or trajectory of homelessness must be also understood in order to assess the contribution which supported accommodation can make. The process by which people become homeless as well as the duration of their homelessness are relevant factors in assessing the need for support

Figure 1: Supported accommodation and the trajectory of homelessness

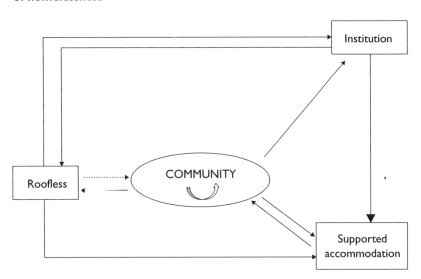

and the appropriateness of different forms of support provision in meeting the needs of homeless people. Figure 1 summarises three 'trajectories of homelessness' to illustrate the link between supported accommodation, social inclusion and homelessness.

Taking this approach we may determine that one route or trajectory to homelessness begins in institutional living and includes:

- people, for example with a mental illness or a learning disability, who have lived in psychiatric hospitals;
- young people who have lived in state or foster care during their childhood;
- people who have been in prison.

Reference has been made elsewhere to the scale and pace of institutional closure (see Ramon, 1996; Goodwin, 1990) and it is evident that this has not, anywhere, been matched by the provision of supported accommodation. The process of de-institutionalisation and community care has had an impact on the composition of homelessness. The closure of large psychiatric hospitals, for example, has been associated with an increase of the mentally ill among the users of services for homeless people (Fitzpatrick, 1998; de Feijter and Blok, 1999). Nevertheless, there are examples in most countries of projects where supported accommodation has been developed either in conjunction with particular hospital closures or to accommodate a specific institutional client group (for example ex-offenders).

A second trajectory begins on the street for the roofless population. Here, the route to supported accommodation is circuitous and begins at the emergency night shelter, moves to transitory accommodation, and thence to supported accommodation. The process is mediated by social work assessment and frustrated by a lack of facilities and adequate housing.

A third trajectory involves those people coming from within the community. An important component of this situation reflects the breakdown in family support. This will include, for example, older men who may be unable to cope following divorce or separation; it includes young people leaving the parental home (for a variety of reasons); it also includes women fleeing domestic violence. A second major component of this stream or trajectory, and an increasing one, includes those families who face eviction as a result of debt or anti-social behaviour. In some countries (for example Britain and France) such families may have a right to rehousing. However, in many instances families may need support to re-enter the housing market or to sustain a tenancy.

It has been argued elsewhere (Edgar et al, 1999) that there has been a changing perception of homelessness throughout the European Union. The analysis suggests that there is a shift occurring, within the member states, from a view which posits the nature and causes of homelessness in individual pathological explanations, towards socio-structural explanations. Paralleling this shift in attitude is a shift in policy responses from a focus on remedial treatment and control to responses aimed at prevention and reintegration.

This analysis suggests that current approaches to solving homelessness are aimed at the prevention of homelessness and repeat homelessness. Hence, increasingly, services are targeted, individualised, flexible and built around the provision of support to reintegrate people into mainstream housing. This realignment of service objectives has been associated with a shift from larger institutional forms of provision to smaller and more housing orientated forms of provision. It has also been associated with a widening of service provision to include not only the more traditional services aimed at emergency and crisis intervention, but also transitional (social, housing, financial) support aimed at permanent integration through suitable employment and housing. The nature of such innovation and the extent of its development within Europe is documented elsewhere (Edgar et al, 1999). Of significance for this report is the understanding that policies aimed at the reintegration of homeless people are perceived to be unsuccessful without the provision of adequate and appropriate levels of support. Evaluations of the Rough Sleepers Initiative in the UK (1996 and 1999) have, for example, highlighted the need for individualised support as a pre-requisite to successful resettlement, particularly for people with mental illness and those with unsettled ways of living. The recommendations of these evaluations have led to greater interagency cooperation to provide a coordinated package of both housing and support to rough sleepers.

The above discussion has suggested that the significance of support in housing may be understood with reference to three broad changes: changes in the understanding of homelessness (policy level), changes in approaches to dealing with homelessness (practice level) and changes in perceptions of the needs of homeless people (professional level). What is clearly absent from this analysis of the multilevel changes which have contributed to the emergence and growth of supported housing is a reflection of the views of homeless people themselves.

European socio-economic and demographic changes

Major economic and demographic changes have been taking place in the EU since the late 1970s. These changes have been well documented (for example Taylor, 1996). For the purpose of this study we draw attention to the impact of these changes on access to housing, the provision of support, and the growing demands for housing and support.

Economic changes have led to the restructuring of the labour market. Polarisation of the workforce between well paid permanent employment and low paid insecure or part time work has increased the risks of unemployment, poverty and social exclusion. Lone parents, families with children, persons living alone (particularly women) and the unemployed are most at risk of low income (European Commission, 2000a). Paralleling these changes in the labour market, national trends in housing have tended to favour free market rent policies and decreasing national commitments to the safeguarding of affordable housing. The combination of low incomes, rising housing costs, and restricted access to affordable housing, have placed a growing number of households at risk of homelessness.

Two demographic changes are particularly significant for our discussion: the ageing of the European population and changes in household structures. Between 1960 and 1998 the proportion of the population aged 65 and over has increased from 11% to 16% across the EU. The ageing of the population raises issues of care and support needs, particularly for those over 75. A recent Commission Communication (European Commission, 2000a) estimates that "up to 5% of people aged 65 and over are directly dependent on continuous social care and around 15% are partly dependent" (p 4). Elderly people are disproportionately represented among the poor in many member states. Their weak economic position increases their risk of homelessness while their increasing care and support needs may lead to inappropriate institutionalisation if adequate and appropriate housing and support provision is not available in the community.

Changes in household structure across the EU have been characterised by shrinking household sizes and an increase in the number of lone parent and single person households. As a result, the rate of household formation has accelerated despite relative stagnation in population growth. In most member states, the supply and nature of housing has yet to adequately meet the growing and changing demand. Moreover, new household types (lone parent household and single person households, especially elderly women) are particularly susceptible to low incomes raising issues about their ability to meet escalating housing costs.

European Union policies

Of the 23 directorates of the European Commission (EC), it is Directorate General for Employment and Social Affairs (formerly DG V) which is most closely associated with social policy and community care. Indeed, the research on which this study is based has been funded by this Directorate. The legal basis for Community intervention is restricted by the various Treaties to which the member states are signatories. The principle of subsidiarity has meant that the European Union is reluctant to override national sovereignty, especially in fields such as housing and social policy.

Since the early 1990s, the EC has increasingly taken an interest in two key areas of social policy: combating social exclusion and promoting the modernisation of social protection systems. The Treaty of Amsterdam reaffirms the joint competence of the European Community and the member states in the field of social policy and provides a legal basis for the Community's involvement in the fight against social exclusion. The Community's main role in social policy is to support and complement the activities of member states. The objectives of the EC's social policies are based on the Social Policy Agreement which, through the Treaty of Amsterdam, has been incorporated into the Social Chapter of the EC Treaty. These objectives, which include improving living conditions, have now been strengthened to encompass combating social exclusion, as articulated in Article 136 of the Treaty of Amsterdam. The Community's role in this area is defined by Article 137(2) of the EC Treaty, which provides for "measures designed to encourage co-operation between Member States through initiatives aimed at improving knowledge, developing exchanges of information and best practices, promoting innovative approaches and evaluating experiences in order to combat social exclusion". Insofar as this study considers the role of supported housing in promoting the social inclusion of homeless people, it makes a contribution to improving knowledge and exchanging information on measures to combat social exclusion at the European level.

Successive Commission documents (92/441/EEC, COM/97/0241, and recently COM/99/347) have focused on improving and modernising social protection systems in line with a broad European Social Model. One of the key objectives of the Concerted Strategy for Modernising Social Protection (COM/99/347) is to combat social exclusion and promote social inclusion by ensuring effective safety nets, focusing on prevention and contributing to comprehensive and integrated approaches involving relevant policies and institutions. This study makes a contribution to the dialogue on social inclusion by considering the role of supported housing in the prevention of homelessness and analysing the organisational structures which enable effective delivery of services to meet the housing and support needs of homeless people.

Social exclusion and homelessness

Combating social exclusion is a priority area for both the EC and member states. At the EU level, social exclusion is seen as a major economic and social challenge which could undermine social cohesion and economic productivity. The Commission recognises that despite prosperity and strengthened economies in the EU, "a significant number of Europeans still live in poverty and are subject to social exclusion on account of structural barriers" (European Commission, 2000b). To respond to this challenge, and in light of the strengthened provisions of the Treaty of Amsterdam, the Commission has proposed a new initiative to support member states to combat social exclusion. The initiative recognises the dual importance of adequate social assistance to meet the needs of those who are excluded as well as the importance of actively addressing the structural barriers which lead to exclusion (European Commission, 2000b).

Based on a conceptualisation of social exclusion in terms of poverty and low income, labour market reintegration and reform of social protection systems are perceived as the principle measures for tackling social exclusion. The active promotion of employment as a means of tackling social exclusion is discernible in all EU member states and particularly in those countries where social protection systems are heavily biased in favour of those in work. National policies are being implemented against a backdrop of continued economic restructuring and sustained high levels of unemployment, both of which impact disproportionately on low skilled, marginalised households, especially female headed households. EUROSTAT data shows that 18% of the EU population is living in relative poverty (measured as below 60% of national median incomes). While social transfers have prevented this level from rising to 26%, the persistence of poverty and its unchanged levels over the past 10 years underlines the limitations of current social protection systems in tackling the economic causes of social exclusion.

Homelessness is an extreme form of social exclusion. To the extent that poverty and low incomes are key underlying causes of homelessness, policies to promote labour market reintegration and improve social protection systems may decrease the risk of homelessness for some people. Indeed, supporting people to participate in the labour market, access training and participate in 'protected employment schemes' is central to supported housing provision in many countries.

However, homeless people are likely to be socially excluded on a number of platforms, of which labour market participation forms only one part. These can be roughly summarised with reference to economic exclusion, housing exclusion and exclusion from social participation. The personal support needs of many homeless people may mean that participation in the labour market is either wholly inappropriate or is, at best, a long-term rather than immediate objective. For these groups of people, adequate incomes from benefit systems will be critical to the process of social inclusion. Equally, based on the understanding that lack of permanent and appropriate housing is a key contributory factor in the process of social exclusion, reintegration into mainstream housing or appropriate supported housing is critical for successful social inclusion of homeless people. Finally, to the extent that social isolation and the disruption of social networks increase the risk of homelessness, supporting homeless people to re-establish or develop social networks may be fundamental to successful social inclusion. Social inclusion for homeless people thus extends beyond the EU priority areas to encompass housing inclusion and development of social networks.

Supported housing

By its very nature, supported housing is difficult to define. Supported housing can take a variety of forms which are distinguished by the relationship of the housing provision and the support provision, by the form of financing, or by the organisational arrangements in place for the management of the housing and support frameworks. Thus supported housing may be viewed as a continuum ranging from self-contained mainstream housing with minimal support (referred to here as support in housing) to, at the other extreme, shared accommodation with high levels of support. Supported housing may be either mainstream housing where a planned programme of support is provided, or it may be a specific form of housing which has been funded, built or designated for the purpose of providing an integrated package of housing and support (often for a specific client group). Supported housing is thus defined by the aim, degree and focus of the provided support, not by the physical housing situation. The support implied is, in this context, *organised (personal or social) support* whose aim is to (re-)integrate people into the community and/or normal housing, prevent homelessness, or optimise the normality of a housing situation for people who have difficulty managing in mainstream housing. The aim of the provision is to enable people to *live independently* in the community.

Whichever form supported housing takes, it will involve three key dimensions: the provision of *accommodation*; the provision of *support*; and the existence of an *organisational arrangement* for managing and funding this provision. Each of these dimensions shapes the nature of the provision, its responsiveness to individual needs and the outcomes achieved.

It is evident that a number of short-hand terms are in use to describe situations where support is provided to enable people to live independently in the community. In this report we distinguish between 'support in housing', and what may be interchangeably referred to as 'supported housing' or 'supported accommodation'. Support in housing denotes situations where support is provided in mainstream housing on a needs–led basis with the intention of eventually decreasing or terminating the support while allowing the individual to remain in the dwelling. By contrast, 'supported housing' or 'supported accommodation' refers to situations where the dwelling is designated for the purpose of providing an integrated and individualised package of housing and support. Whether this provision is intended to meet the needs of the individual on a permanent basis or for a transitional period, the arrangement can be said to have been designated for this purpose because of the existence of a particular management and funding arrangement required for its facilitation. In these situations, occupancy of the accommodation is dependent on acceptance of a support package and would terminate should the support no longer be required. Because the majority of supported housing in the member states falls within the second category, the terms 'supported housing' and 'supported accommodation' will be widely used in this report. 'Support in housing' will only be used to refer to those specific situations where the provision is not designated.

It is to be expected that different welfare systems will interpret the issues of social exclusion differently and hence the groups of people to whom policies are directed will vary. However, we can identify a wide range of groups who may require support in order to live independently in the community or who may be marginalised in society to a degree which requires specific forms of support to redress their social exclusion. These can include:

- older people (especially frail older people)
- people with learning disabilities
- people with mental health problems
- vulnerable young people
- vulnerable (young) single parents
- people with a physical or sensory disability or multiple disabilities
- people with a drug/alcohol addiction
- people with HIV/AIDS
- ex-offenders
- women fleeing domestic violence
- immigrants and asylum seekers
- people who are homeless or at risk of homelessness.

Not all people in these groups will require support in order to sustain normal housing in the community. For many people in these circumstances, their vulnerability could lead to social exclusion unless there is adequate and appropriate support to ensure their inclusion.

De-institutionalisation and community care

It is possible to discern a number of common trends occurring throughout Europe in the last two or three decades in relation to the provision of health and social services. First, there has been extensive criticism of traditional (residential) institutions. This has coincided with a shift from a medical model of disability to a social model of disability. Hence, criticism has centred on the medical model – treating people as patients based on a therapeutic regime leading to a passive role for those being treated – combined with social and spatial exclusion of vulnerable people from the rest of society. Secondly, this criticism coincided with economic pressure against expensive large-scale institutional provision of care and health services. These twin foci of concern fuelled the development of initiatives aimed at caring for people within the community. In some countries 'community care' has been enshrined in legislation, while in others it has shifted the approach and focus of treatment in more traditional settings. Whichever form it has taken, the principles of community care have sought to establish the rights of the individual to self-determination, privacy, autonomy and inclusion and have sometimes been summarised in the twin concepts of empowerment and normalisation.

These trends indicate several important areas for discussion in this report. First, given that these trends reflect criticism of traditional forms of provision of health and social services, and have led to community care approaches, the relationship between social service agencies and housing agencies in the provision of supported accommodation is critical to the nature and relevance of this approach to the prevention of homelessness. Second, the need to provide both housing and support requires coordination, both between housing and social services, and between public sector purchasers of services and voluntary sector providers; in addition, it requires coordination of capital funding and revenue funding. Thirdly, it raises issues in relation to the user perspective with regard to changing professional roles and attitudes as well as to perceptions of risk in dealing with challenging behaviour in shared accommodation or in normal housing situations.

Structure of the report

The first two chapters of this book set out the context for the study. The nature of social exclusion and issues of citizenship related to policies of reintegration of homeless people are discussed in Chapter 2. Chapter 3 examines the principles of community care and the nature of de-institutionalisation which has been occurring throughout Europe. The following two chapters discuss the findings from the national reports of the correspondents of the European Observatory on Homelessness in relation to the structure and organisation of supported housing. Chapter 4 considers the nature of supported housing and develops a typology for understanding the relationship between the accommodation dimension and the support dimension. Chapter 5 examines the governance issues in the provision and delivery of supported housing in each of the member states. Chapter 6 focuses on the central concern of this study by assessing the contribution of supported housing to the prevention of homelessness and the reintegration of homeless people. Because of the importance of user involvement in the development and implementation of policies for homeless people, Chapter 7 considers the issues related to the user perspective and reflects on the lack of progress involved. Chapter 8 identifies the key trends evident in Europe, the issues related to the potential for the transfer of experience, and the need for further research.

TWO

Social exclusion, homelessness and support in housing

✗

Introduction

In the conclusion to *Services for homeless people* (Edgar et al, 1999) we argued that the persistence of homelessness throughout Europe is related to the failure of traditional policies, largely derived and shaped in the immediate postwar decades, when faced with the changed economic and demographic circumstances of the last quarter of the 20th century. Recent reappraisal by academics and practitioners of the dimensions of European homelessness have demonstrated their complexity and multifaceted nature, as exemplified in the diverse composition of the homeless population and in the complex and varied nature of the causes of homelessness (see for example, Neale, 1997 and Somerville, 1998). Such re-formulations reflect a shift in perspective from one which viewed homelessness as an attribute of poverty to one which sees homelessness as a dimension and expression of social exclusion. Solutions to the problems of homelessness are now understood to require more than the redistribution of resources; complex problems require complex solutions which, in the case of homelessness, focus as much on the social circumstances and the welfare of homeless people as on the materiality of their living conditions.

The aim of this chapter is to provide background and context for our detailed examination of the provision of supported housing in Europe. To this end we first examine the emergence of an increasing concern on the part of the European Community with social issues. In seeking an understanding of disadvantage and deprivation (including homelessness) there has been a discernible shift in the perspective of the EC from a focus on 'poverty', to a focus on 'social exclusion'; that is, from a sometimes narrow concern with issues of resource distribution to a recognition of the multifaceted nature of disadvantage and the marrying of issues of resource deficits with the relational social dimensions of deprivation. The second section of this chapter moves to an explicit consideration of European homelessness as a facet of social exclusion and considers the role of supported housing in the alleviation of the problem.

Social exclusion – history of a concept

To the extent that social cohesion, and its corollary social inclusion/ exclusion, were of interest to the EEC when the Community was founded in 1957, they were considered restrictively in economic terms, as matters of market integration, free trade and the movement of labour. In the intervening decades the social and political attributes of cohesion have come to be recognised by the Community and have, albeit slowly, increasingly been considered in policy debates. This broadening of horizons is the result of two interrelated developments. First, an understanding and acceptance that economic decisions have negative, as well as positive, social and political consequences; that is, they impact unevenly across European regions and through European society. Second, the Community has expanded from a base in relatively homogeneously developed countries with continental welfare regimes, to embrace liberal, social democratic and, most recently, formative regimes of southern Europe[1]. The European Community is now characterised by an altogether greater diversity in which social and spatial, as well as economic, uneven development is clearly manifest. As the Community moves towards ever closer economic integration, and contemplates further expansion into Eastern Europe, an explicit concern with social and political issues has become increasingly apparent; talk of a 'Social Europe' and the social clauses of the 1997 Amsterdam Treaty are symptomatic (Hantrais, 1995; Pinder, 1998). Yet, in spite of this growing sensitivity to the social, the economic focus of the Community remains privileged. Attempts to develop European-wide social policies have been frustrated by the legal limitations of EU competence enshrined in the 1957 Treaty and by the outright hostility of some member states. Both these obstacles were clearly seen in the recent ruling of the European Court of Justice, following an action initiated by the UK, which confirmed that in the field of social policy only 'non-significant' actions – defined as those that do not interfere with policy arrangements of member states – can be legally executed by the EU.

The shift in Community perspective from an exclusive concern with the economic to one which also recognises the importance of the social, can be dated to the mid-1970s. Prior to this time, the Community's interest in social issues was a direct and explicit off-shoot of economic policy, with attention squarely focused on the regulation and promotion of labour mobility between member countries. The European Social Fund, for example, was, from its foundation in 1962, directed primarily at projects designed to facilitate such mobility and at the formulation of bilateral agreements intended to guarantee social security rights for workers moving across country borders. In a complementary manner, the European Regional Development Fund focused on capital investment and on the promotion of industrial expansion and labour demand with the objective of preventing depopulation and decline in peripheral regions.

Following the recession of the early 1970s, a series of European-wide studies demonstrated a spectacular rise in the number of people earning less than 50% of their national average incomes[2]. These studies also enumerated changes in the composition of the poor, drawing a distinction between the 'new poor' (the long-term able-bodied unemployed and those on permanently low wages) and the 'old poor' (elderly people, sick and short-term unemployed); changes which reflected both the impress of globalisation on Europe and the impact of profound social and demographic transformations. The problems of the 'new poor' were of particular concern because many were excluded from employment-related benefits, thereby calling into question the effectiveness of hitherto comprehensive poverty protection programmes and placing a greater reliance on inadequate and informal measures of assistance (Alcock, 1993, p 44). These stark indicators of persistent and growing poverty helped spark a discernible change in the focus of European research; they provided the backdrop to the sequential embrace of the language of poverty and of social exclusion by the European Commission in its policy deliberations.

From the mid-1970s, European social research embarked on a series of investigations of the relationships between economic cycles and standards of living, of the uneven impact (socially and geographically) of economic growth and decline, and of deprivation and the redistribution of wealth. This research was matched at the policy level by a growing interest in social as well as economic planning and, more tangibly, in the initiation of a range of community programmes designed to respond to problems of poverty. For example, 1974 saw the commencement, as part of a social action agenda, of a three-part poverty programme. The first programme (1975-80) comprised a small number of pilot schemes and studies in community development. The second (1984-89) established local action research projects throughout the 12 member states, supplemented by statistical and attitudinal work by Eurostat. The third, and most influential of the programmes, Poverty 3 (1989-94), was designed to foster economic and social integration of the least-privileged groups. This involved 39 action research projects working directly with poor people. Paralleling these poverty initiatives, the use of the European Social Fund became more interventionist; it grew to 6% of the Community's budget and its resources were increasingly directed at assisting member countries with the social problems of unemployment by providing for job training and job creation (European Commission, 1991, 1991a; Alcock, 1993, p 44). Yet, notwithstanding these developments, Alcock, among others, has judged that the European Social Fund's targeting of social issues through the 1980s was primarily designed as a "compensatory device to facilitate the achievement of the broader economic objectives" (Alcock, 1993, p 354). In a similar vein, it can be argued that the limited impact of the poverty programmes (the models of best practice they identified were largely ignored) reflected not only underfunding, but also a continuing and overriding concern with the economic to the detriment of the social. While such judgements about the tangible 'on-the-ground' objectives and impacts of the European Social Fund and the poverty programmes are undoubtedly reflective of reality, it is nevertheless the case that at least symbolically the poverty programmes, and especially Poverty 3, were extremely important in raising the political profile of deprivation and poverty and their links with social exclusion (European Commission, 1994, 1994a; Berghman, 1995, p 19).

With its origins in French sociological research, the concept of social exclusion was first brought into the political arena by French Socialist governments of the 1980s. Parallel, but not identical, concepts of 'new poverty' and 'underclass' emerged in Britain and the USA, respectively, at about the same time. In Silver's account (1995, pp 63-4), social exclusion in the French political tradition referred "to all those categories of people – mentally and physically handicapped, suicidal people, invalids, abused children, substance abusers, delinquents, single parents, multiple problem households – who were unprotected under the social insurance principles of the time". During the 1980s the concept came to embrace further categories of social disadvantage and its use was augmented to indicate "the way in which societies and economies systematically marginalise some and integrate others and distribute rewards which both include and exclude" (Rodgers, 1995, p 44). By the mid-1980s, in the French usage and increasingly in the European usage of the term, social exclusion referred not just to employment issues, but also to the growing instability of social relations arising from the apparent erosion of family life and the loosening of class solidarity with the decline of trades unions.

A tangible marker on the road to the European adoption of the terminology of social exclusion was the formulation in 1988 of the 'Community Charter for Fundamental Social Rights for Workers'. Introduced as an attempt to heighten awareness and to stimulate national action on poverty and exclusion, the Charter included references to equal opportunity, sex discrimination and the rights of older people. However, as its name suggests, the focus was very much on employment rights, reflecting the traditional and continuing concerns of the EC with economic issues and the labour market. Yet, when it was proposed to incorporate the Charter into a Chapter of the Maastricht Treaty, vigorous objections were raised, particularly by Britain. The proposed Social Chapter of Maastricht gave voice to concerns about improving living standards, promoting health and safety of workers, and combating social exclusion through labour market integration and equal pay. As such it did not embody revolutionary new proposals. Indeed it could be argued that the provisions reflected much of what was actually happening as, for example, in the use of the European Social Fund. Nevertheless, by formal inclusion in the Treaty, the Chapter gave concrete expression to obligations which several member states were unwilling to shoulder. A diluted version of the Charter was eventually accepted as a protocol to the Treaty. While this fell short of the original intentions, the acceptance of the protocol was indicative of a growing concern with poverty and social disadvantage on the part of most member states in the run up to monetary union. In 1989 the Council of Ministers passed a resolution calling for action to combat social exclusion, and in 1990 set up an Observatory to monitor national trends and policies in this field[3]. These concerns were also manifest in debates in DG V and DG XII[4] as a result of which the objectives of the structural funds were amended to include an explicit commitment to combat social exclusion and social exclusion research was incorporated within the fourth framework.

In a separate, but parallel and influential development, in 1994 the Council of Europe commissioned a substantial pan-European study of social exclusion among its 41 member countries, entitled 'Human Dignity and Social Exclusion' (Corden and Duffy, 1998; Room, 1999, pp 166-74). The Council of Europe, unrestrained by the economic orientation of the Community, had already demonstrated an early concern with social issues. The Council's 1961 Social Charter, for example, spelt out a number of fundamental rights for workers and citizens of Europe, explicitly referencing the rights of the family, mothers and children to social, legal and economic protection. These concerns were reinforced and strengthened in a 1996 revision of the Charter which came into force in July 1999. This revision brought together all the original clauses and eight new clauses. The new clauses include the right of protection against poverty and social exclusion, protection for the rights of women, children and disabled people and the right to housing (Article 31)[5].

The recent explicit incorporation of the terminology of social exclusion in the clauses of the 1997 Amsterdam Treaty reflects its final acceptance as the common language of debate about social issues in Europe. The overt, Europe-wide adoption of the language of social exclusion at this time reflects a confluence of political expediency and conceptual exigency. France had long advocated the adoption of the term 'social exclusion', no more so than during the Presidency of Jacques Delors (see Wendon, 1998). This advocacy itself reflected a long standing French unease with regard to the use of the Anglo-Saxon concept of 'poverty', an unease initially expressed at the launch of the European Commission's poverty programmes in the mid-1970s (Room, 1992). When disquiet about the appropriateness of the term 'poverty' was expressed by some other member countries, particularly Germany and Britain, which, with guaranteed minimum incomes, claimed to have eliminated the problem of poverty (Berghman, 1995, p 16), political and ideological obstacles to the adoption of the terminology of social exclusion evaporated. The political acceptability of the term coincided with a growing recognition on the part of researchers and policy analysts that the problems of deprivation and disadvantage in Europe of the 1990s were no longer adequately understood in terms of the concept of 'poverty' and that social exclusion seemed to offer a potentially new and enlightening basis for conceptualisation.

Definition: between rhetoric and reality

The European Observatory on National Policies to combat Social Exclusion has provided a succinct and representative definition of social exclusion:

> The process by which individuals and groups become isolated from major societal mechanisms, which produce or distribute social resources ... the condition of alienation from one or more of the main mechanisms of the labour market, the family and other informal networks (kin, friends, community, the state). The socially excluded can therefore be taken to be individuals who for some reason show displacement, whether temporary or permanent, from those institutions. Their link to these mechanisms is either weak or in extreme cases non-existent. (Room, 1992, p 103)

This definition highlights the inclusivity and expansiveness of the concept and hints at its complexity. Defined as both category and process (as noun and verb), social exclusion is undoubtedly a complex, even at times a chaotic, concept. As a category it potentially includes all who experience some form of deprivation and can appear as little more than a "synonym for disadvantage" (Room, 1999, p 171). As a process it seems to lack precision and focus. The processes of exclusion are implied rather than enunciated and appear to be as numerous as the categories which are excluded. In seeking to explain everything, it is in danger of explaining nothing. Capable of multiple interpretations, social exclusion is open to use and abuse for political and ideological ends, in that its meaning can be tailored to specific and particular political contexts; as Silver has astutely observed, "the power to name a social problem has vast implications for policies suitable to address it" (Silver, 1995, p 61). Social exclusion has proved to be a politically malleable concept, attractive to the governments of many EU member states; it has been adopted, for example, with particular alacrity in Blair's 'Third Way' Britain and in Schröder's 'Die Neue Mitte' Germany.

However, for all its equivocation and complexity, social exclusion has proved to be more than an ideological tool for rhetorically inclined politicians. Both Atkinson (1998) and Room (1999), for example, argue that under the influence of social exclusion the debate on poverty and deprivation has moved on significantly. It has been used insightfully by researchers and constructively by practitioners; it has been used in a variety of social policy contexts as diverse as employment, health and housing and at a variety of scales, from the local community to the national level, and has been applied in the context of both developed and underdeveloped countries (see for example, Rodgers et al, 1995; Parkinson, 1998; Byrne, 1999). As Gore observes: "[t]he emergence of the term [social exclusion] reflects [a successful] attempt to reconceptualise social disadvantage in the face of major economic and social transformations" (Gore, 1995, p 3).

Transformations in European economic structures and sociodemographic composition over the past 20 years, reflecting the impact of the latest phase of globalisation, have had a major impact on manifestations of poverty and deprivation. De-industrialisation, technological change and fragmentation of the labour market have combined with demographic and social changes – an ageing population, a decline in 'traditional' family structures, an increased rate of household formation, and increased levels of migration, especially of refugees – to create the conditions for sustained high levels of unemployment, including an increasing incidence of long-term unemployment, deepening social inequalities and intensifying social polarisation. These changes have been accompanied by varying degrees of marginalisation of some groups and individuals from the civil, political and economic structures of society. The concept of 'social exclusion', in encapsulating the impact of these changes, has provided an analytical framework in which the multifarious and changing dimensions of deprivation and disadvantage can be encompassed.

Social exclusion recognises that disadvantage is a composite condition, combining the material with the non-material, financial hardship with exclusion from institutions and other social relationships[6]. Used descriptively, social exclusion has a lot in common with relative poverty. However, it goes beyond both the economic and social aspects of poverty to embrace political rights and citizenship and issues such as participation and social identity. While it captures the multidimensional character of deprivation and disadvantage, a social exclusion approach also recognises that these overlapping dimensions are not always or necessarily congruent; exclusion on some dimensions may not necessarily mean exclusion on all other dimensions[7]. Graham Room (1999), in a recent examination of the way in which social exclusion has been employed by researchers and policy analysts, has identified several features of social exclusion which, he argues, in combination demonstrate its advantages over more conventional poverty approaches. These features include its dynamic, community oriented and relational view of the nature of disadvantage and deprivation (see also Atkinson, 1998; Corden and Duffy, 1998, p 109).

For Room, the dynamic characteristics of a social exclusion approach are to be seen in the movement away from comparative statistics towards a consideration of factors "which can trigger entry [to] or exit [from]" conditions of deprivation and towards an understanding of how "the duration of disadvantage shapes how it is experienced". Room cites the findings of the European Community Household Panel as an example of the successful adoption of such an approach (Room, 1999, p 168). Social exclusion, in comparison to conventional cross-sectional studies of the incidence of poverty, also explicitly recognises that deprivation and disadvantage are not just issues of the absence of individual or household resources. Social exclusion links the absence of resources with deficits in community facilities and services: dilapidated schools, remote shops, poor transport, and the absence of supportive and cohesive social networks. Room argues that community networks in particular are vital in enabling disadvantaged people to gain control over their lives and as such are an essential ingredient in combating exclusion and aiding integration. In Room's assessment, the relational nature of the concept of social exclusion further distinguishes it from poverty. Social exclusion moves beyond a consideration of the distribution of disposable resources to examine issues such as inadequate social participation, lack of social integration and lack of power and, importantly, recognises that the manifestation of these features is very much determined by the overall societal context in which they occur (Room, 1995, p 5). As Somerville has cogently observed, social exclusion is socially (and we can add politically) constructed, that is, "it is produced by combinations of economic, social and political processes operating at particular times and places" (Somerville, 1998, p 762). Social exclusion, in recognising the contextual nature of deprivation and disadvantage, is a 'pivotal concept' which "aims less to identify the contours of empirically observed reality than to highlight the relationships between processes, between macro and micro mechanisms, between individual and collective dimensions" (Yépez, 1994, quoted in Gore, 1995, p 15).

Room concludes his comparison of poverty and social exclusion by making a distinction between the 'continuity' perspective of the poverty approach and the 'catastrophic discontinuity' of social exclusion (Room, 1999, pp 171-2). Drawing a comparison with Wilson's (1987) interpretation of the underclass in the USA, Room argues that social exclusion carries with it "the connotation of separation and permanence: a catastrophic discontinuity in relationships with the rest of society" (Room, 1999, p 171). 'Catastrophic discontinuity' refers to a condition in which "people who are suffering such a degree of multidimensional disadvantage, of such duration and reinforced by such material and cultural degradation of ... [their] neighbourhoods ..., that their relational links with the wider society are ruptured to a degree which is to some considerable degree irreversible". Room continues, "[w]e may sometimes choose to use the notion of social exclusion in a more general sense than this: but here is its core" (Room, 1999, p 171).

Room is sensitive to the possibility that the identification of such a catastrophic discontinuity or cleavage between the 'included' and the 'excluded' contains the risk of presenting the 'included' society, if not as an homogeneous, undifferentiated entity, at least as a consensus society, free of tensions, conflict and divisions. It is this issue among others which exercises Hadjimichalis and Sadler (1995) and Kleinman (1998) in their critiques of social exclusion. In emphasising catastrophic discontinuity, social exclusion, they argue, serves only to reinforce the ideology of consensus politics by camouflaging the inequalities of power relationships in the wider society. Further, by emphasising a cleavage between the 'included' and the 'excluded', social exclusion approaches draw attention to the behaviour of the excluded, encouraging a 'blame-the-victim' diagnostic, a pathological explanation of disadvantage and deprivation, thereby detracting from an examination of the obstacles and barriers to inclusion put up by mainstream society. These criticisms are pertinent, and clearly represent tendencies which need to be monitored in policy analysis and policy formulation. However, they are not inherent in the social exclusion approach. The counter view – and one which is entirely compatible with a more subtle engagement with the concept of social exclusion – is in Room's words,

> ... that society is a battle ground of different social groups (based on background, ethnicity, economic interest, gender, age etc) seeking to maintain and extend their power and influence, in a zero sum struggle with other groups whom they seek to exclude. Exclusion is the result of this struggle rather than a label to be attached to the casualties of some impersonal process of urban-industrial change. (Room, 1999, p 172)

Social exclusion – convergence and diversity[8]

The relational characteristics and analytical value of social exclusion are well demonstrated in Silver's paradigmatic analysis of the concept. In her threefold typology, Silver accommodates both the multiplicity of meanings associated with the concept and the diversity of political and philosophical contexts within which social exclusion is embedded.

> Each of the three paradigms [solidarity, specialist, and monopoly] attributes social exclusion to a different cause, and is grounded in a different political philosophy: republicanism, liberalism and social democracy.... Each provides an explanation of multiple forms of social disadvantage – economic, social, political and cultural – and thus encompasses theories of citizenship and racial-ethnic inequality as well as poverty and long term unemployment. (Silver, 1995, p 61)

In the solidarity paradigm, society is portrayed as a moral community with a core of shared values and rights; exclusion is seen as the breaking of a social tie, a failure of the relationship between society and the individual. In this paradigm, the concept of citizenship is especially emphasised, in which individual political rights and duties are balanced by a moral obligation on the part of the state to aid the inclusion of the excluded. The specialist paradigm, on the other hand, is underpinned by Anglo-American liberalism, in which society is seen as structured around the division of labour and composed of individuals with rights and obligations. Social exclusion can occur as the result of choices made by individuals or result from discrimination against individuals; it can also be the product of market failures or non-enforcement of rights. In the monopoly paradigm society is viewed as inherently conflictual, with a contested hierarchy of different groups controlling resources. The concept of exclusion here focuses on the notion of social closure, a process by which one group, sharing a common culture and identity, monopolises access to rewards and resources, thereby closing off opportunities to outsiders.

Complementing Silver's work, Christine Cousins has articulated a fourth 'neo-organic' paradigm. Developed from Silver's 'organic' notion of social exclusion, this paradigm perhaps lacks the careful articulation of the other three, but is distinguished by 'the pursuit of a social order based on groups, which may be vertical, functional or primordial, that is regional, religious, ethnic or linguistic' (Cousins, 1998, p 130). Exclusion occurs because some of the groups that comprise civil society are privileged over others; a privileged position that may be reinforced by state intervention. The 'neo-organic' paradigm is also characterised by exclusion based on membership of the core sectors of the labour market which secures access to social assistance; for those without membership there are only weak or no benefits.

Silver and Cousins argue that these paradigms provide a schema both for understanding how social exclusion is differently manifest in the countries of the EU and an explanation of variable policy responses.

Different ways of thinking about exclusion will lead to different ways of acting against exclusion. Silver is hesitant in attributing paradigms on a country-by-country basis. Rather, as ideal types, the paradigms are seen by Silver as contested concepts in a national discourse. In France the national debate is between solidarity and the monopoly paradigms; in Britain and Scandinavia the debate is between social democracy (monopoly) and liberalism (specialist). Diametrically opposed policies are suggested by different paradigms of exclusion: the monopoly paradigm suggests the need for the effective extension of regulation, the specialist paradigm the abandonment of regulation, the solidarity and organicist paradigms the building up of institutions to establish partnership and concentration (Rodgers, 1995, p 256). Such policy differences are well demonstrated in the different approaches to social exclusion adopted by individual EU countries. Silver and Wilkinson, for example, conclude from their comparative study of social exclusion in France and Britain that,

> ... French insertion policies have different emphases than the British. Most French policies purportedly serve both social and economic purposes, in line with the ideology of solidarity, whereas British programmes emphasise economic 'enterprise'. French income support is more permissive in accepting social as well as economic insertion activities, whereas British benefits are accompanied by more coercive requirements to move towards economic insertion alone. (Silver and Wilkinson, 1995, p 308)

Employment training in Britain was judged by Silver and Wilkinson to be "more punitive and oriented towards the private sector than the French". The French government has intervened to "combat exclusion from both the demand and supply sides of the labour market", while the principal insertion strategies in Britain, in contrast, "have targeted the most disadvantaged groups and areas, providing legal remedies for insuring the quality of local public services and reintroducing excluded groups through full integration through co-ordinated, cross departmental initiatives" (Silver and Wilkinson, 1995, p 308).

As Silver and Wilkinson's study indicates, comparative analyses of national policies designed to combat exclusion, demonstrate a variety of circumstances and strategies across Europe, from state 'interventionist' tendencies to state 'neglect' tendencies, from laissez-faire, neo-liberal programmes to more community-based strategies. Such differences reflect varying trajectories of economic growth, political practices and cultural traditions inherited from the past; variations captured by and manifest in paradigms of social exclusion. While a diversity of approaches towards social exclusion remains the predominant characteristic, there are signs of some, albeit limited, convergence in European social policies; as Sykes cautiously concludes, "though it is premature to decide which particular form it might take, some sort of transnational European social policy framework does seem to be evolving alongside national systems" (Sykes, 1998, p 263). He cites the emergence of uniformity in immigration policies and the widespread adoption of 'Welfare to Work' programmes as examples (see also Mitchell and Russell, 1998; James, 1998). Yet along with other commonalities of welfare service delivery in Europe – the assumption of a regulatory and enabling role by the state, the increasing involvement of the voluntary sector and the emergence of state/private sector management partnerships – it can be argued that these policy developments have emerged by default as much as by design; that is, in that they are concerned primarily with labour mobility and reinsertion into the labour market, they are but a byproduct of economic objectives rather than the direct outcome of a concern to comprehensively deal with problems of social exclusion. If this is a correct assessment, then the effectiveness of such default policies in contributing to an alleviation of social exclusion is open to question, for, as has been frequently observed, social exclusion may have as much to do with marginalisation *in* employment as exclusion *from* the labour market (for example see Hadjimichalis and Sadler, 1995, p 239). As a multifaceted and relational phenomenon, social exclusion is as much about citizenship rights and entitlements as it is about employment: the right to equality before the law (civic citizenship), the right to participation in the political process (political citizenship), and entitlement to equality of living standards and quality of life (social citizenship). These rights may be enhanced, but are not guaranteed, by inclusion in the labour market[9].

These issues reflect a tension at the heart of European economic and social policy. In the pursuit of economic integration, and particularly in attempting to meet the criteria for monetary union, EU countries have moved to reduce taxes, cut public expenditure and reduce public debt. The consequence of the pursuit of such economic objectives is the 'targeting' and restricting of social provision. Economic gain leads to social debt in that the privileging of the economic throws up new problems and exacerbates existing problems of social exclusion. As Hadjimichalis and Sadler observe, the processes of social exclusion (or marginalisation in their vocabulary):

> ... must be understood in their totality, in terms of their integral
> links to the current phase in European integration and not as separate,
> fragmented phenomena. The poor, the marginalised, are not simply
> those who stayed behind, who were bypassed by progress and who
> remained in, on or around the social, cultural and spatial margins of
> Europe. They are the losers in a zero-sum game of European
> integration, in which everybody hopes to gain, but in reality the
> winners will be few. (1995, p 240)

The claim that the economic competitiveness of the EU cannot be
sustained against a background of high unemployment, poor health,
increasing poverty and low educational achievement (Chapman and
Murie, 1996, p 310) may underestimate the degree and level of social
exclusion that a successful economy can tolerate, but whether or not
economic objectives are threatened by social exclusion, there is an issue
here which, for reasons of social justice, needs to addressed. The social
clauses of the Amsterdam Treaty, albeit a disappointment in their
restrictiveness, are a recent concrete demonstration by EU member states
of both a recognition of and an increasing willingness to address the
tension between economic goals and social outcomes. However, the
ability of the European Commission and European Parliament to
effectively and directly intervene is still constrained by their limited
competence with regard to social policy formulation. Dealing with the
manifold symptoms of social exclusion – apart from those directly
manifest in the labour market – has, therefore, required an indirect
approach on the part of the EU itself. This is nowhere more apparent
than in relation to those aspects of social exclusion related to housing
and homelessness. The founding treaties of the EU (the Treaty of Rome,
1957, the Single European Act, 1987 and the Maastricht Treaty, 1993)
make no mention of housing. Consequently, the EU has no competence
to intervene in housing policy or to fund directly the provision of
accommodation. However, as Chapman and Murie (1996) have
observed, with the growth of interest on the part of the EU in the social
impact of economic policies, housing gets drawn in on the back of
concerns with social exclusion, and has benefited indirectly from the
availability of structural funds for tackling such issues as urban
regeneration, training and job creation. In the field of housing, more so
perhaps than in relation to other aspects of social exclusion, subsidiarity
applies; responsibility for housing policy is principally a matter for national
and local authorities[10].

Homelessness and social exclusion

> Homelessness is perhaps the most extreme manifestation of social
> exclusion, representing the denial of a fundamental requirement of
> social integration: adequate shelter. (Fitzpatrick, 1998, p 198)

While the identification of homelessness with social exclusion is entirely
appropriate, to focus on absence of shelter, as Fitzpatrick does in the
above quotation, is to artificially narrow the equation and not even to
its essentials. Seen as a facet of social exclusion, homelessness is more
than a bricks and mortar issue, a point well reflected in a recent
FEANTSA report which sees homelessness as representing a combination
of social dislocation and marginalisation (FEANTSA, 1999, p 11). With
the Europe-wide acceptance of the relevance of the terminology and
concept of social exclusion, there has emerged an understanding of
homelessness as a multifaceted problem, linked to issues of long-term
unemployment and citizenship. A social exclusion perspective draws
homelessness into the European debate on social and welfare policy,
recognising that homelessness is as much about social relationships and
personal welfare as about the material conditions of housing
circumstances. Solutions to the problems of homelessness that provide
for successful integration, involve explicit consideration of issues of social
participation and of personal security, control and empowerment, as
well as of provision of adequate shelter.

Just as a place in the labour market does not in itself guarantee a
solution to the problems of social exclusion, so the provision of shelter
does not guarantee the successful social integration of homeless people.
As Somerville has recognised, housing itself (other than by its absence)
is implicated in social exclusion:

> Housing can be analysed as a set of social relations, including
> characteristic networks and patterns of activity.... Housing processes
> can be understood as processes which either promote social inclusion
> or contribute to social exclusion. Social exclusion through housing
> happens if the effect of housing processes is to deny certain social
> groups control over their daily lives, or impair enjoyment of wider
> citizenship rights. (Somerville, 1998, p 772)

Housing is implicated in social exclusion in several ways: through the
production process and through the exclusionary effects of both tenure
and location (Somerville, 1998). Shortfalls in the production of affordable

housing, through market 'failures' or planning 'strategies', can deny certain, especially poorer, groups access to appropriate shelter. Additionally, the production of inadequate or inappropriately designed housing restricts access by people with disabilities, thereby ensuring the continued "isolation of many disabled people and their dependence on others for carrying out basic care services" (Somerville, 1998, p 772). Different tenure types have different exclusionary implications. Access to owner occupation is based on credit worthiness criteria which have the effect of keeping out poorer, less well paid sections of society. Access to social housing, based on criteria of need, is generally more accessible to poorer families, but can neglect sections of society such as young single people whose needs are perceived to be less pressing. Social housing allocations can also be discriminatory with restricted access to certain ethnic or 'immigrant' groups or those judged to be undeserving because of the attribution of some social stigma such as 'problem family' due to debt arrears or anti-social behaviour. The location of housing can also operate in an exclusionary manner, most obviously in relation to those communities which monitor residence and operate a covert and sometimes overt system of vetting residents. At the other end of the social scale, location can contribute to exclusion in that a community or neighbourhood is branded as a 'ghetto' or 'sink estate' in which residents are effectively trapped and experience prolonged and often extreme forms of social isolation; what Marcuse in the context of the United States social policies has labelled 'homes for the homeless' (Marcuse, 1996). To add complexity to this analysis of the relationship between housing processes and social exclusion, Somerville (1998, p 777) observes that homelessness in some extreme circumstances is the *solution* (albeit temporary) to exclusion, as in cases of women escaping domestic violence who flee the family home to find protection and 'inclusion' in a safe refuge.

The linking of homelessness with social exclusion has brought about a reappraisal of the problems of homelessness and a concomitant reappraisal of the strategies and policies needed to deal with these problems. There is now wide recognition in Europe that a response to homelessness through an expansion of traditional welfare and housing services is both impracticable and undesirable. It is impracticable in that there has been a retrenchment of the welfare state in reaction to unprecedented changes in European economic and sociodemographic structures. Rapid increases in long-term unemployment have combined with demographic transformations, such as a rapidly ageing population, to create a fiscal crisis for the welfare state which has inhibited the expansion of state welfare services, including those for the homeless. The appropriateness of traditional state welfare services for homeless people has also been questioned on the grounds that, with their traditional emphasis on institutional control and containment, and on transitory and emergency provision, they have lacked an involvement with or commitment to long-term, multifaceted solutions to homelessness identified by a social exclusion perspective. As a consequence of these developments there has been a retreat of the state from the direct provision of services to the homeless and, as elsewhere in relation to social and welfare policy, the assumption by the state of an enabling and regulatory role. Paralleling this changing role of the state, there has been a (re)emergence of civil society in the form of voluntary agencies (NGOs) as alternative providers of welfare services. These changes in the respective roles of the state and civil society reflect, in part, the resolution of the discourse, referred to above, between the various paradigms of social exclusion identified by Silver. The retreat of the state from the direct delivery of European welfare services reflects the impact of the specialist paradigm, driven by a neo-liberal economic philosophy, on alternative paradigms. In each case and in each country, solidarity, monopoly and organicist paradigms have retreated in favour of specialist tendencies[11].

While the retreat of the state has created gaps and left demand unfulfilled, it has also opened up opportunities for the new providers. Untrammelled by past practices and traditions, they have the opportunity to develop innovatory practices informed by a social exclusion perspective. From this perspective, the problems of homelessness require the development of complex, multifaceted solutions which provide, in addition to adequate housing, care and support tailored to individual need. The best of these innovations take into account not only the provision of shelter, but also the extent to which, by assisting in the development of social networks (occupational, political and cultural), they have an impact on the everyday lives of homeless people, allowing them to cohere and integrate with mainstream society or some identifiable and supportive community. One such 'innovatory practice' has been the emergence of the concept of 'supported housing' in the past 15-20 years. In its most complex manifestation, supported housing embraces many of the objectives of those policies designed to alleviate problems of social exclusion: normalisation of living circumstances for vulnerable groups and tolerance of diversity in the context of independent living, as well as the development as far as possible of individual and group capacities and capabilities, leading to empowerment and the ability of people to exercise choice and control over their living circumstances. The following chapters explore these issues.

Notes

[1] See Edgar et al, 1999, Chapter 2, for an elaboration of this regime typology.

[2] Between 1975 and 1985 the numbers rose from 44 to 55 million – see Hyde and Ackers (1997, p 354).

[3] The 'European Observatory on National Policies for Combating Social Exclusion' (European Commission, 1993); this Observatory was in existence for the 1990-94 period only.

[4] The remit of DG V was employment, industrial relations and social affairs and it was responsible for the anti-poverty programmes; DG XII's remit was science, research and development.

[5] With a view to ensuring the effective exercise of the right to housing, the Parties to the Charter undertake to take measures designed: (i) to promote access to housing of an adequate standard, (ii) to prevent and reduce homelessness with a view to its gradual elimination and (iii) to make the price of housing accessible to those without adequate resources. With the 'right to housing' now enshrined in the revised social charter of the Community, the absence of a decent home (homelessness) becomes explicitly (as opposed to implicitly) a recognised dimension/measure of social exclusion (FEANTSA, 1999, Newsletter No 6).

[6] Eurostat responded to this multi-dimensionality in the European Household survey launched in 1995.

[7] Room reminds us that many of the classical studies of poverty involved an explicit awareness of multidimensionality; for example, Townsend, 1981, Coates and Silburn (1970) and the UK Social Science Research Council programme on 'Transmitted Deprivation' detailed in Rutter and Madge (1976). In drawing comparisons between a poverty approach and a social exclusion approach, Room cautions against 'collective amnesia' (Room, 1999, p 171). The adoption of social exclusion does not mean that we should ignore past research nor that we cannot learn from past policies designed to deal with disadvantage.

[8] This heading is partly derived from Sykes and Alcock (1998).

[9] See also Bauman's (1998) arguments re consumer society vs work society and the problems of labour force integration.

[10] Chapman and Murie identify three ways in which the EU demonstrates responsibility for housing but which fall short of formal policy intervention: First, by encouraging dialogue between member states for the exchange of experiences and the sharing of good practice. This has resulted in a series of reports by the European Commission on housing issues (for example European Commission, 1993) and periodic meetings of European housing ministers. Second, through the impact of various pieces of legislation and regulatory guidelines with regard to such issues as public procurement, health and safety, technical standards and consumer protection on the way housing is provided and managed. Third, by the establishment and financial support (through DG V for the most part) of series of pan-European networks which focus on housing: CECODHAS (European Liaison Committee for Social Housing), OEIL (the European Organisation of Unions for Integration and Housing of Young Workers), FEANTSA (European Federation of National Organisations working with the Homeless) and EUROPIL (the European Federation for Social Assistance and Integration through Housing). The primary roles of these organisations is as providers of information and they perform an important function in lobbying the Commission and Parliament on behalf of housing and related issues. See also, Kleinman, 1996, Chapter 5.

[11] The nature and degree of retreat has of course varied from country to country. For example, in Sweden while neo-liberal policy dominates economic policy, there has been considerable resistance to specialist/neo-liberal tendencies in relation to welfare, with some evidence of a re-establishment of social democratic policies (*Herald Tribune*, 4-5 October 1999).

THREE

Care in the community and de-institutionalisation

This chapter provides a context for understanding how policies of supported housing have developed in Europe. The discussion is arranged around three main themes. First, the process of de-institutionalisation and the development of community services and the principles underlying care in the community are articulated. This discussion establishes the context in which care services are increasingly delivered within the community, where people live, rather than in institutional settings. Second, based in part on the national reports of the correspondents of the European Observatory on Homelessness, we examine the community care framework in the 15 member states of the European Union, in order to provide a context for the development of supported housing. This consideration highlights the primacy of the family as care provider in those countries with formative welfare policies (mainly those countries of southern Europe). The chapter therefore concludes with a consideration of the role of the family in the provision of support, since this may help to explain the absence of formal (state-promoted) structures of supported housing.

De-institutionalisation

De-institutionalisation has been perhaps the most significant development in the way services for people with care needs have been organised in Europe in the last 25 years. The shift from traditional forms of institutional care to new models based on community services is attributed by Ericsson and Mansell (1996) to a shift in thinking occurring during the late 1960s (Kugel and Wolfensberger, 1969). The development of community based services for people with care needs can thus be said to have begun in the early 1970s throughout Europe, though the nature and speed of such change occurred more swiftly in some countries than in others depending on the nature of the welfare regime involved. The emergence and development of community based services provided the basis for a wider criticism of institutional forms of service provision, in the face of which programmes for the refurbishment and development of institutions were almost inevitably replaced by policies of institutional closure. Since the early 1980s, as community based services have developed, the pace and scale of institutional closure, in most countries and for most client groups, has accelerated.

The factors underlying de-institutionalisation are described in detail elsewhere (Ericsson and Mansell, 1996; Wolfsenberger, 1992; Seligman, 1992). For the purposes of this study we may summarise these factors as:

- *Care/professional:* the shift in professional attitudes and the development of new models of care provision based on a broad consensus that "large institutions were not compatible with disabilities, and the (recognition) that people with the most challenging needs could live successfully in the community" (Castellani, 1996). The development of effective psycho-therapeutic drugs for suppression of dysfunctional behaviour also facilitated the shift from a medical model of treatment to a social model where care is delivered to people living in the community.
- *Economic/political:* a combination of financial factors based, on the one hand, on the realisation of the high costs required to improve and refurbish older institutions, and the difficulty of meeting high specification standards of service quality within existing budget and staffing constraints and, on the other hand, increased public sector pressure arising from decentralisation and expenditure restraint.
- *Social/community:* the increasing role of NGOs, the increased effectiveness of lobbying by families and disability groups, high profile scandals and court cases in some countries, combined with the development and improvement of community services throughout the 1980s, created the climate for both de-institutionalisation and institutional closure.

It is important for the purposes of this study to highlight two important aspects of the process of de-institutionalisation. First, the closure of institutions has nowhere been completed and complete closure is probably neither achievable nor desirable. For example, people with mental health problems will continue to need specialist centres which cater for those whose behaviour can not be accommodated in the community and for those who continue to need periods of 'hospitalisation' and treatment. Further, with regard to single homeless people, there is evidence in Europe of the re-emergence of institutional forms of provision in response to the decline in social rented accommodation and related housing market imperfections (for example in Germany and in Sweden: see Busch-Geertsema, 1998, and Sahlin, 1998). Secondly it is important to remember that, while much of the literature on de-institutionalisation has tended to focus on the learning disability client group, both the process of de-institutionalisation and its implications for the development of community support services are different for other client groups such as frail older people, people with mental health problems, young people leaving care and single homeless people.

This shift, from institutional care to models based on the delivery of care services in the community, is about more than simply a change in the locus of the delivery of care. Underlying the trend is a change in perception and social attitudes which reflects the acceptance of everyone's rights – to be included in society, to freedom from discrimination and to exercise control over daily life. These rights are articulated in the community care principles of independent living, normalisation and empowerment.

Community care principles

The principles which underpin the development of support services in the community rather than in institutions or residential establishments can be associated with a shift in perception from a medical to a social model of disability. The principles imply the removal of the social and structural constraints which limit the quality of life of those with support needs, either by removing the obstacles to their ability to live independently, or by safeguarding their rights by addressing the factors which may stigmatise, discriminate or exclude them from participation in society. Basic notions of social inclusion, human rights and citizenship are central to community care (Wolfsenberger, 1992; Emerson, 1992; Pace, 1987; Engberg, 1982). Using these basic notions we can identify three main community care principles – independent living, normalisation and empowerment.

The principle of enabling people to live *independently* in the community focuses our attention on the concept of 'dependence', since independent living can only be facilitated if the factors leading to a person's dependency can be addressed. Townsend (1964, 1981), in a study examining the dependency factors in older people, defined dependency in three related dimensions which he described as:

- social: resulting from social isolation and lack of contact
- physical: resulting from mobility difficulties
- psychological: resulting from mental confusion or dementia.

The nature and severity of dependency in each of these dimensions can vary for different individuals and for the same person over time. Townsend proposed a scaling index to assess when the severity of dependency on any one or a combination of these dimensions would hinder the person's ability to live independently without support. While Townsend applied this definition of dependency to older people, the concept is readily applicable to other groups. A range of dependency scales has been developed for different client groups, and there is an extensive literature which assesses their accuracy and usefulness in different medical and care contexts. For our purposes it is sufficient to note that people may be assessed as having high, moderate or low levels of dependency. The feasibility of delivering care services in the community is clearly greater for people with low or moderate dependency levels while, traditionally, residential or institutional accommodation has provided the setting for the delivery of care to people with high dependency needs. However, as the pace of institutional closure continues, and as appropriate housing and support services develop in community settings, people with high levels of dependency are, in many countries, increasingly being accommodated in more normal housing environments (subject always to financial constraints and political will).

According to Means and Smith (1994, p 72) "the campaign for *normalisation* and ordinary life principles is primarily associated with professionals attempting to act in the interests of people with learning disabilities". Emerson (1992) demonstrates how the concept of normalisation originated in Denmark and was further developed in North America and subsequently in Britain (see Nirje, 1969). Emerson (quoting Bank-Mikkelsen, 1980, p 56) traces the origin of the concept to the Danish 1959 Mental Retardation Act, which defined the aim of services as being "to create an existence for the mentally retarded as close to normal living conditions as possible". The definition of the concept was later elaborated to include "making normal, mentally retarded people's housing, education, working, and leisure conditions. It means bringing them the legal and human rights of all other citizens"

(Bank–Mikkelsen, 1980, p 56). Thus, the notion that 'mentally retarded people' should enjoy patterns of life and conditions of everyday living which are as close as possible to the lifestyles enjoyed by non–disabled citizens, grounded the concept in basic human and civil rights rather than medical or scientific justification. This understanding of the concept could be encapsulated as an 'equal but separate' approach, protecting the rights of disabled people whether they live in the community or in totally segregated environments.

The concept of normalisation was later developed by Wolfenberger (1972, p 28) to include the establishment or maintenance of "personal behaviours and characteristics which are as culturally normative as possible". This normative approach introduced into the definition of the concept the consideration of the impact of services on the 'social image' of service users as well as the impact of services on the 'personal competency' (capability or capacity) of service users. In later work (Wolfenberger and Thomas, 1983) this normative aspect of the concept of normalisation focused on three aspects of service delivery:

• the physical setting of the service
• the way a service supports relationships between people
• the way a service structures people's activities.

The concept of normalisation, having developed within this disability framework, can thus be understood to have several related aspects:

• *quality of life:* associated with the debate about the quality of service delivery (normally in institutional and residential settings);
• *lifestyle:* related to the rights of people with support needs to enjoy the lifestyle experienced by non–disabled citizens;
• *valorisation:* the need to develop socially valued roles for people with disabilities or support needs which prevent their stigmatisation or exclusion.

The concept of normalisation underpins the community care principle of independent living. However, it does not necessarily imply that all people (no matter what their level of disability or support needs) can be fully integrated in the community in normal housing. Thus the concept of normalisation should not be confused with the objectives of reintegration or resettlement of people into the community. The principles of normalisation as outlined above can clearly be applied to institutional and residential establishments as well as to the delivery of care services to people living in the community.

In a recent review, Mallander et al (1998) have suggested that normalisation has two strands. One aims at normalising the living conditions for disabled or excluded people, the other at normalising the behaviour and lifestyles of these people.

Normalisation of living conditions often implies a compensation for dysfunctions and difficulties caused by disabilities or chronic illness, for instance, physical adaptation of dwellings in order to facilitate independent living for people who use wheelchairs, or practical help with tasks they can not handle because of frailty or physical illness or disability. This kind of 'normalisation assistance' is mostly optional and involves little or no conflict of interest between the receiver and the provider, except for the costs and frequency of the help. Here, the concept of 'service' has the same meaning as for independent people who want help with various tasks or activities in their everyday lives.

Figure 2: Typology of target groups for supported accommodation

		Normalising lifestyles	
		Yes	No
Normalising housing conditions	Yes	1 Learning disability	2 Physically disabled Young people Vulnerable single parents Domestic violence
	No	3 Alcohol/drug abusers Mentally ill Ex-offender	4 Frail older people HIV/AIDS

Source: Adapted from Sahlin (1999)

Normalisation oriented towards an individual's lifestyle and behaviour is more controversial. The demand is often derived from the social authorities or the support service provider, as when social workers want to promote their clients' working ability in order to reduce the welfare budget. A conflict of interest is common when social authorities aim at controlling, for instance, the everyday life of alcohol and substance abusers, or that of youngsters who escape school and parental surveillance. Clients sometimes perceive even the long-term benefits from the measures as unclear and uncertain. In other words, the normalisation of behaviour may imply some degree of social control rather than emancipation.

Sahlin (1999) uses this dichotomy to suggest a typology of supported living arrangements (Figure 2). Sahlin describes the aims of normalisation for each of the groups in Figure 2 in the context of municipal responsibility in Sweden. For the first of these groups, those with learning disabilities, the principal objective is that of normalisation following the closure of psychiatric institutions. The second category includes people who require either adapted housing and/or support to make the transition to normal housing. The aim and practice of support for people in the third category, she suggests, reflect the fact that these people alternate between institutional care and normal housing; the aim of support being to influence behaviour. Although drunkenness was decriminalised in Sweden in the 1970s, people in this group are still susceptible to control by the criminal justice system in the absence of support. Normalisation is oriented more towards lifestyle and everyday routine rather than towards housing conditions *per se*. In the fourth group, there may be no explicit normalisation aims but there is a local responsibility for service and support to facilitate independent living.

All of the groups in Figure 2 may be homeless or at risk of homelessness in the absence of appropriate support in the community. Using FEANTSA's working definition of homelessness (see Chapter 1) it is perhaps most appropriate to identify the roofless and houseless in the dimension of normalising lifestyles, and those in insecure housing situations located in the dimension of normalising housing conditions. While the typology is limited, it is useful in distinguishing the purpose of support and the needs of different groups of people. It could be further enhanced by mapping onto it the responsibility for support provision.

The third community care principle, referred to earlier, is *empowerment*: a process by which people are supported to take control over their daily lives and to exercise choice. Empowerment thus refers to the acquisition by individuals of the power to take decisions in matters relating to themselves, in relation to their daily lives and in relation to their self-development. In a few member countries of the EU empowerment is an attribute of citizenship rights and entitlements, which are protected by the state through legislative guarantees. These rights and entitlements ideally include the right to equality before the law (civic citizenship), the right to participation in the political process (political citizenship) and entitlement to equality of living standards and quality of life (social citizenship) (see Marshall, 1950). In practice such rights and entitlements are unevenly distributed, with particular sections of society, such as homeless people and those living in institutions, being particularly neglected or excluded. The principal of empowerment implies, therefore, that the successful (re)integration of homeless people and effective community care requires not just the provision of support for specific individual needs (important though this is) but equally the restoration of universal citizenship rights to facilitate the fullest level of societal participation by the formerly excluded. Empowerment is also about the exercise of more mundane, day-to-day choices and decisions – about place of residence, about working, shopping and recreation, about friendships. The ability to exercise control over decisions affecting these aspects of life are, as Sen (1985) has argued, not necessarily guaranteed by the granting of rights, nor even by the provision of resources, if the specific capacities and functionings of individuals are not addressed. A person-centred programme of care in the community and of rehousing requires that these issues, as well as the clinical needs of clients, be directly tackled in the development of support and care packages. In this context the concept of 'normalisation of behaviour' becomes a constructive and emancipatory, rather than a manipulative and controlling process. The principle of empowerment further implies that the ability of individuals to exercise effective control over decisions which affect their daily lives is not an acquired 'once-and-for-all' characteristic, but an outcome of an ongoing process of reciprocity and negotiation between support and housing providers on the one hand, and clients on the other; it is as much about the process of provision as about the resources that are provided.

The provision of care services in Europe

The aim of this section is to describe the development of care services in the European Union in order to provide a framework for understanding the particular forms of supported housing which have emerged in the individual member states. Comparison of European social care services is described in detail elsewhere (Munday and Ely, 1996). The lack of comparable data on social care services at the European level which renders impossible valid data-based comparisons is well understood (Munday, 1993). Equally, the diversity of experience within the member states of the European Union, ranging from Nordic models of social welfare provision to close-knit family and community structures prevalent in parts of southern Europe, has been mapped by authors in the social field in areas as diverse as childcare and care of older people (Greengross, 1992; Jamieson, 1990).

The extent to which European welfare states are converging towards a model where the market takes care of those in employment, while the less privileged groups in society remain the responsibility predominantly of local institutions, either in the form of municipalities or private charity, is a matter of debate (Abrahamson, 1992; Kahn and Kamerman, 1976; Munday and Ely, 1996; see Kleinman, 1998 for a review of the convergence debate in the context of housing policy). Three different lines of argument are discernible in the literature. Kahn and Kamerman suggest that economic and industrial development are important determinants of social welfare policies and provision, such that countries with higher standards of living have more highly developed social care services than do poorer countries. Munday and Ely, on the other hand, argue that especially since 1976 (when Kahn and Kamerman were writing) right-wing political and economic ideologies have been greater determinants of changes in welfare policies. It is clear also that demographic change, particularly the ageing of the European population and the strong trend towards smaller families, will have implications for the provision of care and the responsibilities of families and the state in this regard (Greengross, 1992). Ely and Samà (1996) argue that, faced with increasing need and limited state resources, all countries are rapidly adopting policies of welfare pluralism in social care, emphasising the contribution of families and non-governmental organisations while reducing the role and direct contribution of central and local government. The study identifies the following significant features of welfare pluralism:

- the state draws on the resources of all sectors;
- non-financial resources for welfare are given increasing recognition in policy and practice;
- contractor provider arrangements between enabling authorities and the non-profit sector;
- emergence of a for-profit role in care services;
- informal care.

Ely and Samà conclude, however, that in spite of such convergence, it is unlikely that a common model of service provision will emerge, since "underlying systems of social protection and financing and organising service provision are too divergent, as are the expectations of the public in the different countries" (Ely and Samà, 1996, p 122).

Abrahamson (1992) proposes a simple model based on the understanding that resources can be obtained from the three spheres of the market, the state and civil society, with the welfare of the individual being "dependent upon the extent and combination of his/her relation to these three spheres" (1992, p 6). In terms of social policies in Europe, the market and the state have, over time, been increasingly emphasised to the detriment of the sphere of civil society. In describing the institutional organisation of social policies, Abrahamson argues (see Figure 3) that the market dominated in most western European countries because of the emphasis on social insurance systems, while the public sector dominated in eastern Europe; in contrast institutions of civil society, such as the family and the church, become more dominant in southern Europe.

Figure 3: Institutional organisation of welfare

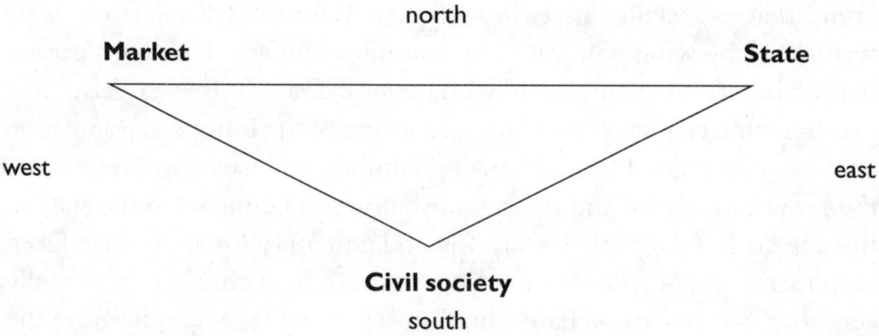

Source: Abrahamson (1992)

It has been a common feature of the literature, following the seminal work by Esping-Andersen (1990), to group the countries of Europe into four distinct welfare regimes (see Edgar et al, 1999 for a review, and Chapter 2 for a discussion in the context of social exclusion). However, in the context of this study we revert to a simpler threefold classification in order to reflect the social policy context within which supported housing has emerged. First, we consider a group of countries where the process of de-institutionalisation has had a long history, and has tended to be the main policy framework within which supported housing has developed. These include Denmark, Finland, Germany, the Netherlands, Sweden and the UK. Second, we consider countries where policies of social inclusion and reintegration have formed the backcloth to the emergence of supported housing, developed in relation to social protection legislation and related stakeholder responsibilities. This group of countries includes Austria, Belgium, France and Luxembourg. We include Italy in this group even though it has features in common with the other two groups (for example, a long history of de-institutionalisation and a strong involvement of charitable welfare provision). Third, we consider countries where de-institutionalisation may itself be weak or where the role of the family, and civil society, is dominant providing a strong informal care sector. Here we include Greece, Ireland, Portugal, and Spain.

De-institutionalisation countries

Denmark

Denmark has recently experienced a radical change in social legislation with the replacement, in 1998, of the 1976 Social Assistance Act by three new bills which now constitute the central elements of social assistance and social policy. This change represents the culmination of the development of social policy during the last 20 to 25 years which has been characterised by three main tendencies: decentralisation, the emergence of social assistance as a civil and universal right, and de-institutionalisation.

While the 1976 Social Assistance Act represented the culmination of the creation of a universal welfare state in Denmark, the 1980s saw a change in government (the replacement of a social democratic coalition government by a conservative/liberal coalition) and a reconsideration of the nature of welfare state service delivery. This reconsideration reflected a crisis in legitimacy and financing. As in other countries, the public sector was heavily criticised for being expensive and expansive, and the crisis of legitimacy was resolved by restraint in expenditure. These arguments continued, with different nuances, into the 1990s when a social democratic government again came to office. The amending legislation introduced in the three new social bills of 1998 represent the most concrete outcomes so far.

What characterises this process towards a new legislation might be described as a period of social experiments whose main features might be summarised under the following headings:

- from universalism towards targeted services;
- from free access towards users' payment for services;
- from institutions towards supported housing for different disadvantaged groups;
- from dominance by professionals towards user involvement;
- from confidence in the ability of the state to solve all problems towards a re-vitalisation of civil society/the voluntary sector;
- from passive income support towards activation.

The legislation introduced in 1998 builds on earlier legislation introduced in 1995. An important aspect of the Social Assistance Act of 1995 was the introduction of the obligation on municipalities to provide shelter for single people as well as families. The legislation also required local authorities, both in the regional counties and in the municipalities, within three months of a person's admission to a section 105 institution, to evaluate the needs of the person in regard to housing arrangements and/or social support. This evaluation had to be carried out together with the user her/himself, the intention being to provide a basis for individually tailored action, thus providing the users with a better basis for reintegration.

One of the changes introduced by the 1998 legislation was the abolition of the term institution:

> ... the previously used concept of institutions in areas concerning adults is abolished thus making it possible for the municipalities and the regional counties to organise the provision of measures with respect to the individual, independent of the type of dwelling in which she or he is living. (Børner Stax et al, 1999, p 29)

This represents a clear separation of housing arrangements from related support measures. Instead there shall, ideally, be an evaluation of individual needs for support, and measures directed towards these needs shall then be provided regardless of the individual's housing circumstances. The law is thus not prescriptive of the type of housing within which support can be funded.

The legislation makes it the responsibility of the regional counties to "ensure the necessary number of places for temporary shelter in housing arrangements for people with special social problems who are not capable of staying in their own dwelling, and who have needs for a housing offer and for activating support, caring and subsequent support" (Børner Stax et al, 1999, p 12). On the other hand, it is the responsibility of the municipality to ensure that there exist measures directed towards the provision of assistance, caring, and general support as well as towards the possibilities for rehabilitation of persons that are in need due to physical or mental disabilities or special social problems. The comments accompanying the legislation make it clear that these regulations governing support provision are to be seen as "one step further in the direction of equalising the possibilities for and treatment of people with physical and mental disabilities or persons with special social difficulties independently of housing arrangement" (Børner Stax et al, 1999, p 13).

Finland

In 1973 the government in Finland began to draw up a national housing programme, and for the first time representatives of the Ministry of Social Affairs and Health were invited to take part. This led to the creation of a taskforce in 1974 to address the housing needs of special groups (Saarenheimo and von Hertzen, 1996). The proposals by the taskforce were based on the assumption that the provision of housing for special needs groups should, as far as possible, be located among 'normal' people in the 'normal' housing stock. However, those people with particular difficulties which prevented them from living independently should be provided with supported dwellings where it would be possible to provide a varying degree of care and supervision depending on the needs of the occupant (Valtakunnallinen asunto-ohjelma vuosille, 1976).

The Finnish Social Welfare Act of 1982, which regulates municipal social services, created a new rubric of 'housing services' which included supported accommodation. The National Board of Social Welfare issued guidelines in 1985, under the Social Welfare Act, to govern the provision of housing services by municipalities, which included sheltered housing, supported housing and the adaptation of dwellings for older people and disabled people. These guidelines also included, for the first time, other vulnerable groups and their needs.

In addition to the Social Welfare Act, other legislation refers to the provision of support and care services in relation to housing or to supported accommodation. The Child Welfare Act (1983), for example, obliges municipalities to arrange housing for families and children who are affected by child welfare measures and includes young people under the age of 21. Similarly, it is a statutory responsibility for municipalities to provide service housing for disabled people under the Act on Services and Assistance for the Disabled (1987). The Mental Health Act (1990) requires supported or service housing associated with rehabilitation to be made available to persons suffering from a mental illness or other mental disability.

As in many other countries, responsibility for social and health services has been decentralised to the municipal tier of government, although Finnish municipalities have considerable autonomy about how to organise these services. Also, as in other European countries, there is an increasing trend in Finland for municipalities to discharge their statutory responsibilities by purchasing services from independent voluntary organisations (see Kärkkäinen, 1999). Nonetheless, in most municipalities supported housing is still arranged as part of ordinary support services.

Germany

Social care in Germany is part of a comprehensive system of social insurance in which there are three sub-areas: social insurance, public assistance and compensation, and welfare (Busch-Geertsema, 1999). Public welfare is governed by laws at the federal level, with variations between the *Länder* in the levels and methods of financing benefits and social services. The role of the federal government is mainly restricted to planning, coordination, funding and legislation. A few social services are provided by the *Länder* but most are provided by local government. Public welfare can be divided into two forms: 'subsistence help' and 'help in particular conditions of life'. The latter includes help to integrate people with disabilities, help for homeless people and ex-prisoners, and services to integrate older people into the community. The centrality of the principle of subsidiarity in the German constitution ensures a substantial independent sector in social welfare.

During the last decade supported housing has been the subject of debate in many sectors of social services. There has been a trend to expand the provision of 'supported housing' services for frail older people, vulnerable young people, people with learning disabilities, people with physical disabilities, people with mental health problems, people with drug or alcohol dependency, people suffering from AIDS and ex-offenders as well as homeless people. As early as 1984, an important amendment was made to the Federal Welfare Act which laid down a priority for open forms of support. A subsequent amendment in 1996 gave greater emphasis to this provision, requiring that necessary support be given as far as possible outside residential establishments, homes or similar institutions.

Supported housing was often introduced, not so much as an alternative to accommodation in residential establishments, but rather as a complementary or interim step between accommodation in residential homes and normal housing. Many large-scale institutions, for example, set up 'external residential groups' (*Außenwohngruppen*) to complement their service. The level of provision of supported accommodation for older people remains relatively small (an estimated 30,000 places in 1998) compared with residential institutions (an estimated 660,000 places) (BMFSFJ, 1998, p 94).

There is a strong emphasis on work with children and young people in German social services. In this sector, housing is part of pedagogical support and efforts to achieve the social integration of young people (Muenstermann, 1996). Although the first types of shared housing for vulnerable young people began in the 1960s, it is only since the mid-1980s that there has been a discernible trend to decentralise and individualise such support. Places in traditional homes have been reduced and places in shared supported housing, external residents groups belonging to institutions (*Außenwohngruppen*), and self-contained housing combined with the provision of support and care (*betreutes Einzelwohnen*), have been created. The Welfare Act for Children and Young People, which was fundamentally reformed in 1991, explicitly provides not only for pedagogical support, but also for other forms of supported housing (section 34, *Kinder und Jugendhilfegesetz*). In this context, people under 27 years of age have a legal right to support in developing their personality and leading an independent life. Although supported housing has a high status in this sector of social work for vulnerable young persons, places in homes are still predominant, not least because of the difficulty of acquiring adequate housing during a period of housing shortage.

As in other European countries, there has been a series of reforms in the German psychiatric sector since 1970. However, in practice, large-scale institutions are far from being abandoned or reduced. Recommendations by an expert commission of the Federal Government in 1988, that a self-contained way of living in the familiar home setting should be considered as a priority aim, have yet to be fully realised. Thus, compared to the 95,000 places in homes and residential institutions, there are only 18,300 places in supported shared and self-contained housing for people with mental health problems or learning disabilities.

The Netherlands

The continuing process of restructuring and decentralisation in the Dutch administrative system has meant that the 12 provinces in the Netherlands have increased their responsibilities (especially in relation to planning, budgeting and coordination), that the four big cities have some of the powers of the provinces as well as their municipal powers, and that the municipalities are responsible for the provision of many social services (but not residential care). However, there are differences in the degree of decentralisation for different client centred services (for example in relation to young people, older people and homeless people). It is thus often difficult to know who is responsible for what in social services (Munday, 1996).

According to the 1994 Dutch Welfare Act, care services should be efficient, effective and client-centred (de Feijter and Blok, 1999). In the social shelter and care sector, responsibility for policy formulation, monitoring, research and coordination of policies lies with the National Department for Health, Welfare and Sports (VWS). With the introduction of the TWSSV (the temporary law on stimulating social innovation) in 1994, responsibility for implementation and funding in the field of social shelter and care (including innovation and quality monitoring) were decentralised from central government to the (48) municipalities which were obliged to maintain service levels and to guarantee access on a national level. It has long been the tradition in the Netherlands for social care services to be provided by independent non-governmental (not-for-profit) organisations. The Federatie Opvang, as the national umbrella agency for organisations for social shelter and care, is responsible (under the direction of the Department of Health, Welfare and Sports) for the development of a system of client registration, quality control and models of funding.

The main goals of decentralisation, according to Rekenkamer (1997), were to ensure a supply of services that is adjusted to the changing demand for shelter and care and strengthening of prevention and aftercare by way of an optimal cooperation on a local level between the social shelter and care sector and other complementary forms of care and services (1997, p 14). Van der Meijden (1994) summarises the aims of decentralisation of care services specifically in relation to homeless people as:

- promoting a return to normal life;
- stimulating supported living by social shelter and care institutions;
- shifting the emphasis from residential care to prevention, ambulatory care, day care and reintegration projects.

He further suggests that, to achieve these aims, it is necessary to develop:

- coordination between national and local governments and between welfare (paid for by the national budget) and health (paid for from insurance);
- coherence between housing, mental health care, care for elderly people and social security;
- networks between shelters, labour offices, social services, housing associations and ambulatory services.

Not surprisingly, there is evidence from recent research to suggest that such coordination and integration of services has yet to occur to any extent in practice and that in particular the integration between housing and social affairs on the one hand and the care sector on the other hand is poorly developed (FO, 1998, p 13).

Sweden

In Sweden, the 1982 Social Services Act provides the cornerstone defining citizens' rights and (municipal) responsibilities for ensuring that support is provided to enable the individual to live an independent life. The Act also applies to those who have only 'social' problems (Norström and Thunved, 1998, p 104). The Act of Support and Services (1994) is a bill of rights for people with disabilities, including physical disabilities and learning disabilities. The novelty of this legislation, most relevant for those at risk of homelessness, is the inclusion of a 'third circuit' of persons including people with mental health problems and people who, for reasons associated with alcohol or substance abuse, have disabilities which hinder their functioning in society (Norström and Thunved, 1998, p 317). In 1998 more than 44,000 people received support under this legislation, the majority (88%) of whom were people with a learning disability (NBHSS, 1998).

The deregulation of public housing allocation during the 1990s has meant that by 1998 only 6% of municipalities have housing agencies which give precedence on waiting lists to homeless applicants (NBHBP,

1998, p 62). Sahlin (1993, p 59ff) argues that one outcome of this situation is the creation of a secondary market resulting in the increased segregation and isolation of clients in category houses and in flats subleased by social authorities on special terms (including possible immediate eviction). While 43% of municipalities in 1998 had a "special programme in order to acquire housing for households who, because of alcohol or substance abuse or other problems, were not accepted as tenants" (NBHBP, 1998, p 9), 80% reported difficulties in acquiring housing for those households.

The most common form of support housing in Sweden is group housing (Sahlin, 1999). General advice and guidance to the municipalities by the NBHBP (1994, pp 8-10) establish norms for such housing which draw on the principles of normalisation described above. These guidelines include:

- The physical setting:
    › accommodation shall be adapted to the individual's needs; number of residents should not exceed six (four for people with a learning disability);
    › group housing units shall be localised in an ordinary residential house;
    › several group housing units should not be located together.
- The way a service supports relationships between people:
    › shall provide opportunities for community, of being together and of participating in activities in the community.
- The way a service structures people's activities:
    › support to promote personal development and active participation in society;
    › support should aim to provide a normal pattern of life in a homely environment;
    › provide opportunities for an active life outside the group home.

United Kingdom

In the UK, the National Health Service and Community Care Act (1990) introduced changes which transformed the planning, provision and delivery of health and welfare services. The Act gave social work authorities the lead role in community care planning, with responsibility for assessing needs, managing care packages and contracting the delivery of services. Social work authorities were intended to retain purchaser functions while provision became part of a mixed economy of care, with services increasingly provided by the voluntary and private sectors. The original intention of the legislation was to facilitate the movement of people from long-stay hospitals and institutions. To promote this, funds were transferred from the Department of Social Security to local authorities to contribute to the support of people within their own homes. However, the legislation has encountered substantial problems in its implementation and has been much criticised, especially with regard to the housing contribution – or, more specifically, the funding of the housing contribution. It has been argued (Petch et al, 1996) that considerable shortfalls in the provision of appropriate accommodation pose a serious problem in the implementation of community care.

It is in this context that governmental concern has focused on the distinction between housing support and social care, and between social care and healthcare. Much of the debate has been around the issue of who pays. Aldridge (1999) argues that "so far the debate in the UK has not progressed to identifying a means by which there is a seamless continuum of funding for an individual's support needs, whether those needs are for housing support, emotional support, personal care costs, social care costs or medical support costs" (1999, p 9). Until a recent court ruling, in 1997, established that housing benefit could only be used for the maintenance of the fabric of the building, it was possible for a range of social and personal support facilitates to be financed by this means. This court ruling created a climate of uncertainty and blighted the development of new projects.

In December 1998 the government published a consultation document (*Supporting people*) which proposed the introduction of a new form of funding for supported accommodation from the year 2003. The fact that this is a joint report by eight different government departments, led by the Department of Social Security, is an indication of the complexity of the way supported accommodation has developed across the UK. In its analysis of supported accommodation in Britain the report found that the current funding streams are complicated, uncoordinated and overlapping. It further found that no one has responsibility for ensuring the quality or adequacy of support. The report states that there has been no strategy to coordinate the work or expenditure of the various departments involved in making provision for support services. For service providers, time, energy and resources are diverted from service provision into constructing complex funding packages and managing a wide variety of funding streams. Residents may have their options limited or skewed because of the kinds of service which are funded, and those which are not.

Because of the way in which funding streams have developed, services tend to focus on tackling problems after they have arisen, through crisis intervention rather than on prevention. As a result, there is concentration in supported accommodation on high cost, highly intensive support projects. This lack of low intensity preventative support can result in individuals being directed into projects where they receive a higher level of support than they require. Alternatively they may not receive support, fail their tenancy, and then require high intensity and high cost intervention.

A further funding issue relates to whether, and how much, service users should pay for support services. A principle in the UK is that healthcare is available free of charge at point of use. Social care is generally 'means tested', as is housing support. The point at which social care becomes healthcare is therefore very important, and could have a significant impact on health budgets, or conversely on service users' own means/resources. The issue is not clearly defined in the UK. For example, where a person with mental health problems is supported in accommodation, it is arguable how far the funding should relate to a preventative health budget, to what extent it is concerned with social support needs, and to what extent funding is related to his or her ability to sustain a tenancy, that is to say, their housing-related costs.

Despite the intention to streamline supported accommodation funding there are two principal weaknesses in the proposals. First, it is the intention to transfer funding from the demand-led base of housing benefit to cash-limited local authorities. In a cash-limited system, where funding essentially is rationed, there is the danger of creating an hierarchy of vulnerability, where one need is set in competition with another. Secondly, the proposals do not resolve the artificial barrier which exists in the funding regimes between 'housing support' and 'personal care'. A welcome principle, however, is the move towards an individual needs based system. The intention is to provide a supported accommodation package which is tailored to the individual's needs. This is in line with many of the welfare services trends across the EU.

Reintegration countries

Austria

The Austrian system of social care is well developed, regulated and funded for specific target groups, namely elderly people, mentally ill people, people with disabilities and, to a lesser extent, young people and women escaping domestic violence (Schoibl, 1999). For these target groups, social care provision is delivered either in therapeutic communities, shared flats (most common) or self-contained dwellings (most recent). These community based services have been established as an alternative to institutional care and inspired by small scale and individualised ideologies. Their development has been complemented by a process of professionalisation, the evolution of a professional culture, and the construction of integrated systems of care in all Austrian regions.

By contrast, social care provision for homeless people is fragmented and unregulated, lacks a legislative framework, and is vulnerable to insecure funding mechanisms. Reforms of traditional institutional services for homeless people have been largely driven by service providers themselves. The shift from large-scale hostel and asylum type provision to smaller-scale shared living arrangements began during the 1980s in response to social work criticism of standards and developments in service providers' understanding of the problems faced by homeless people.

The service-led nature of these reforms has both advantages and disadvantages. On the one hand, providers with close working knowledge of their clients may be well placed to develop responsive support services in smaller structures which meet client needs. Since the early 1990s, a new trend towards specialisation of services for homeless people has emerged. The established pattern of providing undifferentiated support to a wide range of target groups by generic staff is being replaced by specialist orientation towards specific target groups of homeless people, with individualised support to meet defined needs delivered by qualified staff. On the other hand, the absence of overall guidance, legislation and regulation has given rise to widely disparate approaches, differentiated pace of development and lack of coordination. Until recently, interagency cooperation has been largely based on individual case work with little or no coordination of overall provision even within specific towns or cities. This situation has adversely affected homeless people's access to services and service providers' ability to link up with the most appropriate local care and support providers.

The concept of 'supported housing' is widespread in Austria despite a lack of consensus on its definition, aims, nature, organisational or operational structure. The term is used to refer to a range of provision with different approaches, methods and standards. The only commonality between these forms of provision is the simultaneous offer of accommodation and support. Broadly speaking, two categories of supported housing can be identified: group homes or shared supported housing and supported single or family housing in self-contained flats. While this categorisation distinguishes between different housing forms, there is no corresponding categorisation with regard to working methods, standards, underlying principles or funding mechanisms. As a result, wide variation in support provision exists, based not on individual needs but on service provider perspectives. These run a gamut from total control to high levels of individualisation and empowerment. Moreover, there is little evidence of interchange of ideas or experiences between providers operating in different sectors. Supported housing for homeless people has developed in virtual isolation from provision for more mainstream target groups.

Since the 1990s, two developments have been occurring in relation to supported housing for homeless people. The first of these has been a rethinking of the nature and aims of support provision, spurred on by interagency dialogue and partnerships between homelessness services and public or private sector social housing providers. As a result, professional concepts of individual support aimed at independent living are emerging. These are represented in new standards relating to support provision and staff qualification, although there is currently no system for enforcing or regulating these standards. The second development has been the recognition of the need for localised integration of existing structures to provide an interlinked chain of reintegration. As yet, this new concept has not been fully realised in any single town or city.

The Austrian social safety net is divided between an insurance-based social security system and a social welfare system. Social security is regulated and administered by the federal state while social welfare systems are governed, regulated and administered wholly by the nine different *Bundesländer*. The general federal laws governing social security (the ASVG) fail to mention either access to housing or housing costs. Responsibility for supporting households in distress and providing subsidies towards housing costs lies with the provinces, through their social welfare systems (*Sozialhilfegesetz*). Although the *Bundesländer* are obliged to provide the assistance required, most provincial laws on social welfare explicitly exclude specific target groups (for example foreigners) and specific areas of need (for example financing of rent arrears) from their benefits systems. Furthermore, the complexities of social welfare systems, lack of adequate information and advice services on welfare benefits, and differences and restrictions relating to access, hinder access to welfare benefits for those most marginalised. In some *Bundesländer*, welfare benefits do not adequately reflect the real costs of housing which, due to the mismatch between supply and demand, have been steadily rising.

In 1975, ÖROK, the Austrian authority responsible for regional planning, stated that: "The provision of the population with housing has to be guaranteed in a way that the location and quality of accommodation enable both private sphere and social development of the single individual in the residential area." The fundamental targets laid down by ÖROK have been largely integrated into the regional planning laws of the *Bundesländer*. These stress the need to eliminate shortcomings in the housing stock by means of socially oriented and spatially differentiated housing policy. In real terms, however, insufficient housing subsidies, difficulties in accessing subsidised rented dwellings, and regional variations in tenancy legislation have rendered such targets ineffective for vulnerable households. Schoibl argues that these shortcomings of the provincial social welfare systems illustrate the low priority accorded to tackling homelessness in Austria.

Belgium

In Belgium, the combined effects of demographic changes and growing unemployment and employment insecurity have, in the past few years, been key contributory causes of housing insecurity. By 1997, the number of people living on subsistence level income had risen to 80,000 with many more households facing financial difficulties despite the apparent drop in the official unemployment rate. This suggests that the processes for social exclusion and marginalisation are continuing for a specific part of the population despite multilevel approaches to combat poverty.

Measures aimed at combating poverty can be seen in a number of key policy areas: labour market policies, housing policies, education policies, social care policies and social welfare policies. The multitiered social security safety net differentiates between unemployed workers at the top end of the spectrum whose entitlement to benefits is directly linked to their last earnings and the long term unemployed who have dropped several 'floors' in benefit levels over time.

Since the late 1980s and early 1990s, more specific policies to combat poverty have taken shape and been targeted at those most in need. Thus special projects for specific groups who did not get enough money or recognition in the mainstream provision of welfare work were conceived and funded. In 1994, a general report on poverty was prepared as a response to the elections which saw the rise of extreme right wing parties. The report which linked poverty to existing policies has been a strong stimulus for the emergence of more specific policies to combat poverty. These policies have led to a number of measures and sub-measures in most domains and at most government levels, with a characteristic transfer of responsibilities from central to regional government and a further decentralisation towards the individual. In general, these measures are characterised by their target/outcome orientation and their integrated way of thinking. On the other hand, it may be argued that the measures which also stem from the need to more effectively target public expenditure are creating a third circuit which, in the long term is unlikely to lead to social cohesion. De Decker (1998) cites Vranken et al (1997, p 30) who argues that:

> ... these measures are too weak to row against the stream of economic transformations and processes of globalisation, processes which are, at the same time, strengthened by processes of individualisation, a trend that is the consequence of rising insecurity. (Vranken et al, 1997, p 30)

Overall, access to social housing in Belgium is becoming increasingly difficult for the poorest part of the population and those most at risk of social exclusion. This is because eligibility rules for access to social housing have altered and draw more on the 'good tenant/low risk' philosophy than the 'affordable housing for all' principles. The difficulties of accessing permanent affordable housing of decent quality may be creating a ghetto of marginalised people living in a secondary housing market – supported housing. If the aim of supported housing is to eventually 'pass through' wherever appropriate to more independent living, then the means for achieving that independence must be available.

France

In France, the links between social care provision and housing policy date from the 1950s, when support was offered to households living in transitional housing while awaiting rehousing in permanent accommodation. Early provision of supported housing was based on an educative model to enable households to develop the skills required to sustain mainstream tenancies in the newly constructed mass housing. This socioeducative model, which dominated until the early 1980s, has been progressively displaced by conceptualisation of social care in terms of mediation in accessing and maintaining housing.

The 1980s and 1990s saw the introduction of successive measures, directives and legislation targeted specifically at those most marginalised in society. These measures have increasingly encouraged a rapprochement between social care and housing policy through integrated policies, cross over ministerial and departmental responsibilities, and the evolving role of professionals and key agencies. Starting with the law of 19 November 1974, successive legislation explicitly recognised the support and care needs of marginalised households. The directives of 4 July 1977 and 25 July 1979 defined the aims of socioeducative action linked to housing (ASEL) in terms of social, economic and cultural insertion through personalised support to families. The circular of 21 February 1990 further elaborated the operation and purpose of the ASEL by linking the provision of support to the eventual accessing of permanent, independent housing in good condition. To achieve this outcome, four key types of support were identified (de Gouy and Damon, 1999):

- assistance in budgeting
- information
- maintenance and improvement of housing and common areas
- improvement of neighbour relations, participation in social life and integration within the community.

A further circular of 23 March 1990 recognised the important role of the ASEL in successful rehousing. The support provision can be of varying intensity depending on the extent of individual problems and of different natures depending on need.

The *Loi Besson* (31 May 1990) introduced the right to housing and remains one of the key legislative instruments in the field of public and social action for households in need. The *Loi Besson* created and consolidated a wide range of pre-existing measures. Notably, it established the *fonds de solidarity pour le logement* (FSL) in each *departement*. The FSL's primary purpose is to finance the provision of social care in access and maintenance of housing. Under the *Loi Besson*, the aims of social care are redefined as follows:

- assistance to identify housing need and housing options (information, search for solutions);
- practical support to sustain a tenancy (housing management support);
- social support towards integration within the community, the city, the neighbourhood and so on.

For the first time, the *Loi Besson* required the *departements* to assume co-responsibility for developing and implementing housing plans in their area. The *departements*, who are the key players in the planning, regulation and coordination of social action, had no formal competence in housing. By enabling them to share responsibility for housing planning, the *Loi Besson* created a direct localised link between housing and social care.

Cumulatively, the measures introduced during the early 1990s were based on two key concepts:

- the *parcours residentiel* (the route to housing) – support to identify and meet housing need for those in temporary accommodation;
- *accompagnement social* (social support) – incremental process of individualised support for individuals and families to enable them to eventually access and sustain long-term housing.

These two concepts were partially integrated in the *Loi Besson*, which decentralised responsibility for planning and organisation of both housing and social care. One of the critiques of the *Loi Besson* has been its marginal recognition of the important role of the associations in providing both the social care and the means of accessing permanent housing through mediation on the housing market. This gap is being addressed in the new law to combat social exclusion (29 July 1998), in which associations are recognised as key and equal partners in the delivery of social care services linked to housing.

Italy

The supply of supported accommodation in Italy occurs within a welfare and social policy system that was traditionally characterised by two principal traits. The first is the insurance nature of the social protection system, which means that there is no comprehensive protection system defined on a national/universalistic basis. While relatively broad welfare protection is afforded to 'workers' and to categories such as minors, elderly people, handicapped people and disabled people, protection is scarce and uncertain for other adults (Negri and Saraceno, 1996). 'Unprotected' adults are entrusted to the social assistance system, a system which as a rule is separate from the main body of social protection policies, and is heavily characterised by its discretionary nature and measures largely aimed at emergency situations. There is, therefore, scarce protection for groups in society who may be particularly vulnerable to social exclusion. This framework also places emphasis on the initiatives of local administrations (municipalities) and of the voluntary sector (associations, NGOs), and results in considerable variance of policies from area to area (Tosi and Ranci, 1999).

The second trait is the massive assignment of responsibility for care to families. This, on the one hand, is a well-known aspect of the insurance welfare state model, while on the other hand, it reflects an ideological philosophy which attributes a fundamental role to the family in the supply of protection and care for the weaker members of society. This set up, based on a strong complementary relationship between state and family, has made it possible to attenuate the polarisation of society for many years, but today is suffering from the growing limits of the capacity of the family system to supply welfare protection. This is an aspect of the crisis of the historical 'Italian model of welfare' (Tosi and Ranci, 1999).

The process of de-institutionalisation of mental health services in Italy has been described as a model (Ramon, 1993). The process was one of gradual closure of hospitals, which involved residents in the running of the hospital, in decision making and in introducing a style of living that is more similar to that existing outside. This includes getting to know the community, while the community becomes involved in activities inside the hospital.

Housing policies are also found wanting from a social welfare perspective. The supply of social housing is scarce and based on allocation criteria that are not wholly rational, while social housing policies are not targeted to the needs of marginalised groups and groups in extreme poverty, as well as being poorly integrated with general social welfare programmes (Censis, 1993). The development of policies in this direction would in any case be made difficult by the extremely small size of the rental sector and by the absence of a non-profit sector that is sufficiently well established to perform social housing functions.

The insurance nature of the system means that marginal populations receive little protection, and that for them the limits of the social services assistance system are particularly accentuated by its separation from the main body of social protection policies, its discretionary nature, and the emergency approach of many measures. The homeless provide a good example of the position that marginalised populations occupy in this type of system. In the absence of full social rights for the homeless (Tosi and Ranci, 1994), it is inevitable that intervention is distinguished by broad powers of discretion and variability as well as by the prevalence of emergency thinking aimed above all at providing stop-gap measures for the most visible and serious situations. The separate and residual nature of this intervention constitutes the inevitable corollary of a social welfare protection system that recognises the homeless as its 'customers' only in particular and circumscribed cases.

There have been significant developments in public sector housing, above all at regional and local authority level. Various regional governments have introduced innovations to their public sector housing system in an attempt to take account of new phenomena of housing exclusion and social exclusion. Marginal groups nevertheless continue to encounter difficulty with access to public sector housing, and the effectiveness of the system continues to remain limited by the irrationality of the allocation criteria (classification by category) and still more by the insufficient quantity of the supply.

The gap between public sector housing provision and public social services provision translates into the limited effectiveness of the housing supply and difficulties in developing prevention and social reintegration programmes for marginal or excluded populations.

Important developments are currently in progress both at local and national level. A set of legislative measures has been, or are being, approved at national level which could substantially change the conditions of social policies with appreciable results in the supported accommodation field. The main measures are as follows:

- Parliamentary bill 'measures for the creation of an integrated system of social assistance action and of social services', currently before the Commission for Social Affairs of the Chamber of Deputies.
- Law on immigration 6 March 1998, N 40.
- Reform of the Law on rents: this provides for (in addition to a system of tax benefits) support for those suffering most hardship by means of a 'National Fund for the support of access to rented accommodation'. This fund has a budget of 1,800 billion Lire (€613 million) for the three-year period 1999-2001 and is to be used to subsidise rent payments.
- Law to institute a minimum (re)insertion income. This constitutes the great change in progress. It fills a large gap in the welfare protection system. For the time being, however, it has only been introduced

experimentally, involving, for the next two years, 40 local authorities (most in the South), and to be implemented within budget limits (500 billion Lire – €258 million).

Luxembourg

Luxembourg is characterised by its generous social welfare system and has been shown to be at the head of all other member states not only in its absolute level of benefits but also in terms of the relationship between benefit levels and purchasing power (Observatoire Européen des Politiques Familiales, 1994). While enviable, this situation has more recently contributed to a philosophy of non-intervention/inaction in service provision by the state. Moreover, eligibility for this generous benefit system is based on a number of stringent conditions including very lengthy residence requirements which, by definition, exclude foreign residents and immigrants (10-year minimum residence). Pels (1999, p 10) summarises this situation as follows: "la législation est donc généreuse quant aux montants accordès, mais restrictive en termes d'accès aux droits" [the legislation is therefore generous in terms of actual benefits but is restrictive in terms of eligibility and access to rights].

Since 1986, Luxembourg has operated a *Revenu Minimum Guaranti* (*RMG*), which has proved a significant step in combating social exclusion through the provision of minimum income levels for those who may be unemployed or unable to work. For the first 10 years of its operation, access to the *RMG* was limited to those who had resided in the Duchy for a minimum of 10 years and were at least 30 years old. After several changes to the legislation, the government, in 1996, rescinded the 10-year residence requirement for certain classes of people, notably EU and EEC citizens and political refugees. The minimum age has also been reduced from 30 to 25. The *RMG* has also been made accessible to persons without a fixed abode.

One of the central axes of housing policy in Luxembourg is increasing the size and availability of the affordable housing stock through the rehabilitation and renovation of vacant properties and houses in need of repair, the promotion of 'buy to let' options and new construction within environmental guidelines. The 7th programme of construction is designed to combat the current shortage of affordable housing through the construction of nearly 5,000 units of which nearly half are destined for sale, a very small proportion destined as construction land and the remainder intended for rent (social). Housing policy encourages access to housing by means of subsidies for self-build, purchase, renovation and improvement. There are no direct housing benefits to offset the costs of renting and *RMG* does not take into account the real costs of housing.

Supported housing has been well developed in Luxembourg for a number of years. Initial provision was introduced at the same time as reception centres and aimed at providing social, professional and family reinsertion for people in need. By the mid-1980s, reception centres and foyers were beginning to recognise the need for an intermediary form of provision between total care in hostels/reception centres and independent living in self-contained housing. The need for such provision was particularly acute for young people leaving care. One of the key obstacles for a range of homeless or potentially homeless groups was access to affordable housing in good condition. Long waiting lists and high entry costs exclude low/no income households. The aims of supported housing were thus to provide intermediary housing solutions with support to meet individual needs. Supported housing in Luxembourg is organised through an integrated network of agencies enabling efficient access and appropriate matching of needs to service provision.

Civil society countries

Greece

The Greek constitution states that the provision of accommodation to people who are homeless or housed in unsuitable conditions constitutes a special task for the state. A legal framework for the provision of social housing to people of low income does exist. Nevertheless, there is no statutory obligation on local or central government institutions to provide suitable accommodation and support to individuals or social groups defined as 'vulnerable' (Sapounakis, 1999).

Social housing provision in Greece does not target poorer families, but is rather directed at low to middle income workers who have met a number of established criteria, including length of residence in the area and level of contributions to the Workers' Welfare Organisation (OEK) fund over a period of time. Social housing is provided through a combination of loans to pay for houses constructed specifically for this purpose by social construction companies on behalf of the (OEK) or through rent subsidies for similar houses. Over the past decade, waiting lists for access to this type of housing have increased considerably due to a combination of increased demand and a slower pace of construction due to financial problems.

Greece has limited social welfare and housing provision, and the family plays a central role in supporting those members who cannot otherwise support themselves. Co-habitation of parents and adult children is also still very common in Greek families, about a third of older people live in the same household as their children. This is partly the result of financial necessity, since few young people are able to afford independent housing. However, it also reflects the importance of the extended family as the dominant form of family organisation even today. In most Greek families, adult children would not be expected to leave the family home before marriage, and elderly relatives would normally return to live with the younger generation, especially after the death of a spouse. However, as houses become smaller in size and family bonds gradually slacken, co-habitation in this fashion is often replaced by financial assistance to those in need. Social changes, and the gradual loosening of family bonds, suggest that family solidarity, although still strong, may not have quite such a central role in Greek society in the future. A number of other significant changes have been occurring in Greek society over the past decade to test traditional family roles. These include:

- the influx of Greek repatriates from the former USSR and other areas;
- the influx of new economic migrants, asylum seekers and other immigrants;
- growing awareness of the conditions of the Romani population;
- the loosening of family ties with growing urbanisation and economic insecurity;
- the ageing of the population;
- deinstitutionalisation for people with mental illness.

These changes are placing new pressures on central and local governments to intervene in social welfare and housing, not least because the threat of homelessness appears to be rising as a consequence of rising housing prices fuelled by a disproportionate ratio of supply to demand and the inaccessibility of social housing. To date, such interventions have been limited both in scope and in geographic spread, although awareness of the problems has been heightened through a number of highly visible campaigns and, to some extent, European intervention in the field of deinstitutionalisation.

Ireland

Two interrelated developments have shaped the evolution of arrangements for the provision of welfare in Ireland. These, according to O'Sullivan (1999), are the increasing autonomy and capacity of the state to pursue and implement its welfare policy goals and the decline to the Catholic Church as a large-scale welfare provider. The capacity and autonomy of the state in terms of welfare provision has largely been shaped by its relationship with the voluntary sector. While the construction of social services provision over the last quarter of a century, despite its late development, has expanded rapidly (O'Cinneide, 1993), the widespread involvement of voluntary agencies in welfare provision has meant that the ability of the state to pursue policy objectives "unfettered by the demands of vested interest groups (has) continued to be circumscribed" (O'Sullivan, 1999, p 12). Although the capacity of the state to direct welfare policy has strengthened, this has occurred more through its increasing regulation of voluntary agencies rather than the development of comprehensive state-based service provision. Boyne (1998) argues that voluntary agencies have continued to provide welfare services, not because they are the most cost-efficient, effective and empowering form of provision, but because they represent a powerful interest group. This inherited structure of voluntary management and organisation of service delivery has influenced the interactions between state agencies and voluntary agencies and between central state and local state agencies, according to O'Sullivan. Thus an important feature of welfare provision in Ireland has been the dominance of voluntary agencies in the provision of many services, with the state largely confined to acting as financier. In the face of increasing demand and the diminished capacity of non-state welfare providers, the state has had few options but to increase its level of direct welfare provision in recent years. Despite this shift, the policy has been for the state to achieve a degree of regulation over non-state welfare providers, who have traditionally operated with great autonomy, rather than to become a large-scale provider of services.

Portugal

In Portugal, the Ministry for Employment and Social Security is responsible for social care services and social policy generally. However, in comparison with other European countries, social care is relatively underdeveloped, with a strong dependence on the independent sector. It has been estimated that there were over 2,000 independent not-for-profit social care institutions in 1992 (Marques and Bras Gomes, 1993 quoted by Munday, 1996). Portugal presents the only case in Western Europe of a government actively attempting to deter de-institutionalisation for people with a mental illness (Ramon, 1996). Although qualitative changes in approach to the problems of homelessness occurred from the late 1980s, mainly from general institutional provision to individualised support and assistance, this was not comprehensive and was generally experimental in nature. The traditional institutionalised approach continues to be the predominant type of assistance provided to most needy individuals and families and to the homeless in particular (Bruto da Costa, 1999).

Spain

The evolution of social services and social assistance in Spain has meant that, although there is a national legal right of all citizens access to social services, the competencies over strictly social services affairs are devolved to the Autonomous Communities. Thus each region develops its own social services laws. Municipal authorities also have responsibility for social rehabilitation and development. While the national legal framework guarantees rights to social services, assistance is targeted at specific groups including: the family, children and young people, older people, physically disabled people, offenders and ex-offenders, drug addicts, ethnic minorities, the homeless, immigrants and refugees. The decentralisation process of social assistance has allowed the development of two types of social services, primary care social services and specialist care social services. Primary care services include information and orientation services, home provided aid and other mechanisms to support community, alternative lodgings, and prevention and social insertion of people at risk of social exclusion. The delivery of this primary social care is through social service centres. However, the importance of private institutions and voluntary agencies is also significant in service provision. State action designed for "the Improvement of Social Solidarity and Co-operation" complements social protection benefits by promoting community initiatives and voluntary associations. The diversity of practice specific to each municipality, and the importance of the role of private and voluntary institutions, hinders "the task of systematising a 'support in housing' typology with precision" (Leal Maldonado and Laínez, 1999, p 15).

The role of the family

The role of the family may be changing in the face of new work patterns, the emergence of a new gender balance arising from the increased participation of women in the labour force, and from changing social values, ageing of the population, and the increased mobility of people in the enlarged labour markets of Europe. This section considers the role of the family in the provision of care, since this will help to explain the nature of support services both in countries with well developed formal systems of care and in countries which depend on the informal support provided by the family.

The family has recently re-emerged as an issue of consideration in welfare state analysis. Feminist critiques have argued that male-centred welfare state theory inaccurately describe women's relationships to the welfare state because women's work is often unpaid family labour. Furthermore, although it remains the lynchpin of welfare state reform, the family has become problematic as a result of demographic and social changes which have meant that the stable one-earner family is increasingly atypical as a result of the growth of one-person households, divorce and co-habitation. Hence families which have either more than one earner or a single parent are increasingly the norm. In this context the role of families, and particularly women, in the provision of 'informal' care is changing. This change can be expressed in a more structured manner by reference to the degree to which families can absorb social risks. Esping-Andersen (1999) uses this approach to discuss degrees of *familialisation* or *de-familialisation*. *De-familialisation* refers to the degree to which the family's welfare and caring responsibilities are relaxed, either through welfare state provision or through market mechanisms. A de-familialising system seeks to unburden the household and diminish the individual's welfare dependence on kinship. A familialistic system, on the other hand, is one in which public policy assumes or insists that the family must carry the principal responsibility for their members' welfare. Such systems are often influenced by religious (Catholic) teaching and the principle of subsidiarity which limit public intervention to situations where primary social networks fail. Indeed, in Germany the principle of subsidiarity in the Federal Welfare Act places an emphasis on the family, and only when family and voluntary support is no longer sufficient does the state step in.

Evers (1993, p 3) suggests that, in the period following the crisis of the welfare state, "the concept of dominant state-centred welfare has corroded and lost its hegemony". In all European countries, he argues, there is acceptance that the four spheres of the market, the state, the voluntary sector and the family should all have an active role in social policy, and that the important controversies are now about the respective roles, responsibilities and limits of these spheres. Thus, while the role of the family as the main source of support may be changing (especially in the more traditional cultures) in the face of social and economic changes, the family still has an important role to play in support provision in all welfare systems. Indeed, the shift from 'welfare states' to 'welfare pluralism' suggests a greater responsibility for the family. Esping-Andersen (1999), however, has argued that postwar welfare states never fully absorbed the family caring burden, being principally confined to healthcare and income maintenance, and that only a handful of contemporary welfare regimes pursue a *de facto* reduction of the family's welfare burden. In Britain, for instance, where the role of family support is largely unrecognised by the state, carers' organisations suggest that the value of such family care could be as high as £3.5 billion (€5.8 billion) each year. These organisations argue that without the informal support sector both low level support and more intensive support services would simply be unable to meet demand.

There is considerable evidence that, in all countries, women are the main providers of informal care within the family. Yet it is apparent that, in the face of new work patterns leading to the increased participation of women in the labour market, ageing of the population, and the increased mobility of people in the labour market, the role of women in the family as informal care providers is under threat. The ability of the family to provide support to its members also relies on intergenerational capacity. Here again the ability of younger family members to support an older person, or of older people to care for their grandchildren is threatened by a variety of factors including an increased labour mobility (affecting the spatial propinquity of the generations) and a lack of suitable larger, affordable housing.

Esping-Anderson's (1999) description of familialistic regimes, and Abrahamson's (1992) description of models of welfare, would suggest the primacy of the family in support provision in those countries with more formative welfare systems and more weakly developed provision of supported housing (for example, the Mediterranean countries). Greece is a clear example of a country where the family plays a crucial role in filling the gap left by the absence of a well-developed welfare system, a role which extends to the provision of care and support. Sapounakis

(1996) suggests that, with regard to housing, a stable system of family solidarity has developed over time which helps family members in need. The recipients of such help, which include the extended as well as the immediate family members, are those in greatest need; for example, newly married couples, elderly people and disabled people. Direct housing provision is still common for newly married couples, in the form of a 'dowry' from the bride's family. Although the institution of the dowry has been abolished in the legal sense, it remains a strong element in Greek society. Where the family is unable to afford to purchase or build a house or flat, assistance will be given to rent accommodation. These close family bonds are manifest to all family members facing insecurity of tenure. We have already commented on the fact that co-habitation of parents and adult children is still very common in Greek families. This reflects the importance of the extended family as the dominant form of family organisation.

While the importance of the role of the family may provide a partial explanation for the weaker development of formal mechanisms of supported housing in countries such as Greece, Ireland, Portugal and Spain, this in itself it is not a sufficient explanation. Equally, if the role of the family as support provider is weakening, as this analysis suggests, then the need for more formal mechanisms of support in the community will become more apparent.

FOUR

The emergence of supported housing

This chapter considers the nature and emergence of supported housing in the European Union. The chapter begins with a discussion of the relationship between support and housing and suggests a fourfold typology as a framework for the examination of the relationship between accommodation and care provision. Employing the threefold classification of European countries introduced in Chapter 3, there follows an examination of the development and form of provision of supported housing in EU member countries. The conclusion identifies common trends and themes across Europe and suggests a tentative framework for understanding the diversity of approaches to supported housing.

The nature of supported housing

The process of de-institutionalisation, driven by the principles of normalisation, which has been occurring throughout Europe since the 1970s, has led to the emergence of community models of care delivery. Services for people with support needs can now be provided to people either in an institutional setting, in their own home, or in 'intermediate' settings such as supported accommodation or 'special needs housing'. The factors which have led to de-institutionalisation suggest that home, as a place to receive care, has significant advantages compared to institutions. The availability of affordable, appropriate and flexible housing is thus a *sine qua non* for the effective delivery of care services in the community. Inadequacies in the provision of appropriate mainstream housing, as much as inadequacies in the provision of support, can lead to people entering or returning to institutional care or drifting into homelessness.

It is possible to distinguish between two situations in relation to the origins of supported housing:

- where the housing provides the setting for the delivery of personal care or therapy (ie 'institutional' forms of care can be delivered successfully in the community);
- where support is provided to enable someone to live independently in the community (ie to prevent institutionalisation).

With regard to the latter situation, where support is provided to enable someone to live independently, further distinctions can be made on the basis of the purpose for which the support is provided. First, support designed to facilitate the reintegration of people through the acquisition and maintenance of the skills needed to sustain an independent life; second, support provided for the purposes of rehabilitating people with challenging behaviour, anti-social behaviour, chaotic lifestyle or personal care needs from, for example, addiction; and third, support designed to prevent homelessness through the delivery of care in the community for people who might otherwise be institutionalised. In each of these situations support may be required by the person either for a transitional period while they adjust to independent living, or it may be needed permanently because of their dependency or disability, or it may be required on a flexible basis to meet fluctuating needs.

The type of support which a person may require can be classified in relation to three broad elements:

- *housing and domestic:* this includes 'enhanced housing management' support (maintaining a tenancy), help with housework, everyday activities;
- *counselling and skills:* this includes support in developing skills to live independently, as well as counselling to deal with specific problems such as substance abuse, or relationship problems;
- *personal and healthcare:* this includes personal care, such as bathing and dressing, as well as medication.

This analysis further suggests that the nature of support and the purpose for its provision is likely to be different for different client groups. It follows that the nature of the housing provided will differ according to the needs of the client group, the life course stage of the clients, the nature and level of support provided and the overall purpose (and duration) of the provision. The relationship between housing and care in all of these situations is summarised across four perspectives in Table 1. The elements in the matrix are intended to illustrate the shifts which may occur across the continuum in each of the three dimensions of

Table 1: Housing and care perspectives

	Community support	Intermediate support	Institutional support
Accommodation perspective	• Shared housing • Self-contained housing	• Residential accommodation • Staffed group homes • Supported accommodation	• Institutional accommodation • Hostel accommodation
Support perspective	• Transitional support • Visiting, floating • Flexible/individualised • Irregular • Housing, skills	• Transitional or permanent support • On premises • Planned/and flexible • Up to 24 hours • Housing, skills, personal care	• Permanent support • On premises • Planned/prescribed • 24 hour • Skills, personal care
Management perspective	• Multiagency • Funding linked to social protection and housing subsidy	• Multi-agency • Mixed funding	• Single agency • Funding linked to care provision
User perspective	• Full tenancy rights • Personal control over daily decision	• Limited tenancy rights • Limited personal decision making	• No tenancy rights • Professional control over daily decisions

institutional, intermediate and community support. Clearly, there will be overlap along the continua in each of the dimensions as one moves from institutional to community settings.

From an accommodation perspective it is possible to perceive different dwelling forms ranging from purpose-built, larger and more institutional forms of accommodation to smaller, ordinary shared or self-contained housing involving more homely living environments. Where accommodation acts as a locus for the delivery of care, at the institutional end of the spectrum, then the care will be focused more on personal or healthcare and be permanent or prescribed in nature. Where support is provided as an aid to enable a person to live independently in the community then both the nature and intensity of the support will diminish and become more focused on the housing rather than the lifestyle needs of the individual, and should also become more targeted on individual needs rather than be prescribed by the form of provision. As we move away from the purpose-built, designated and institutional forms of provision, the need to ensure the separation of support and housing will lead to a multiagency approach to enable the provision of 'supported housing'. This will involve both housing and social work agencies, probably public and voluntary sector agencies as well as more disparate (and possibly complex) forms of funding. This shift is also likely to involve the attribution of personal rights which will include normal tenancy rights as well as rights of decision over the form of support and the choice of provider. A dilemma which is evident across each of the perspectives identified in Table 1 is that, as the responsibilities become more diverse and complex at the community end of the spectrum, so the risks and uncertainties become greater. This may indicate both a threat to the sustainability of such housing and support provision and the potential to control as well as liberate the individual.

Defining supported housing

It is possible to envisage, theoretically at least, different configurations of supported housing depending on the purpose of the support, the requirements of the individual and the 'trajectory' of the individual into homelessness. Table 2 identifies four such configurations.

Table 2: The scenarios of supported housing

	Purpose of provision			
	A	B	C	D
Accommodation	Permanent	Permanent	Transitional	Transitional
Support	Permanent	Transitional	Permanent	Transitional

The first scenario A describes the situation of designated supported accommodation: the accommodation is intended to be the individual's permanent home and support is planned on a permanent basis to enable the individual to live as independently as possible in that dwelling. This situation arises both in purpose-built supported accommodation and in situations where an individual is allocated permanent 'ordinary' (pre-existing) housing with a planned programme of support. In the latter case, the occupancy of the dwelling may be conditional upon the receipt of support.

The second scenario B identifies the circumstances of people who have temporary support needs. The accommodation they occupy is intended to be their permanent home and their occupancy of it is not dependent on receiving support. Hence the terms 'ambulant personal support for people living in dwellings' (Germany), 'ambulatory coaching projects' (Netherlands), and 'floating support' (UK) are variously used to describe these situations. This is often perceived as the ideal model of provision and is referred to as 'support in housing'.

The third scenario C reflects situations where permanent support is needed and a shift to the delivery of care services from an institutional to a community base. Where supported accommodation is provided in the process of de-institutionalisation, transitional accommodation may be provided for an individual in a variety of situations. This occurs while assessment is taking place, or while the individual undergoes a period of transitional support and training prior to being allocated permanent accommodation. In these circumstances, it is expected that the individual will always require some support in order to live independently in the community. However, the intensity and type of support required may change over time. The support is offered in a situation where a 'chain of care' (Finland) or 'staircase' of support (Sweden, Netherlands) exists, providing a continuum from high levels of support to lower levels of support. This is often referred to as a 'continuum of care'.

The fourth scenario D describes situations where there is a need for (short-term) transitional accommodation and support. During a person's life course, there may be periods of transition when the individual moves from one stage of life circumstances to another. Some people require temporary accommodation and support in order to facilitate this period of transition. For example, young people leaving care may require a temporary period of support while they acquire the necessary life skills to live alone. It is often the case that the acquisition of such skills is best obtained in specialist accommodation or in situations where the mutual support of others is available. This scenario can also occur in a personal crisis or emergency situations such as relationship breakdowns, or periods of instability as a result of pregnancy in the case of vulnerable young women, for women fleeing domestic violence, as the consequence of substance abuse, or for asylum seekers.

It is to be expected that the details of supported housing provision will be different across Europe depending on the particular social welfare system involved, and the process or stage in de-institutionalisation and implementation of community delivery of care services which has been achieved in each country. The statutory definitions, where these exist, and the practice of relevant aspects of support provision will now be considered as a complement to the generic and theoretical definition of supported housing elaborated earlier.

The provision of supported housing in Europe

In Chapter 3 we suggested a threefold classification of countries in Europe which can be used to understand the emergence of supported housing and to help explain the differences in the nature and form of provision. This classification is employed here to examine the nature and definition of supported housing and to consider the factors which have been significant in its emergence and development.

In those countries where the process of de-institutionalisation has progressed furthest, and where the principles of normalisation underpin social welfare systems, the definition of supported accommodation is likely to be enshrined in housing, social welfare or community care legislation. In these circumstances the understanding of the nature and purpose of supported housing will have been influenced by the process of de-institutionalisation and reflect the needs of the particular client groups most affected by that process, such as people with learning difficulties and people with mental health problems. For example, where de-institutionalisation has been the driving force in the provision of supported housing, we may anticipate that issues of rehabilitation and integration will be paramount. Further, where statutory definitions exist, we may expect responsibilities to be identified for provision and for funding and the role of the state, either as a provider or an enabler, will be more apparent. These characteristics are dominant in the first group of countries in our classification: Denmark, Finland, Germany, Netherlands, Sweden and the UK.

Denmark

In Denmark, the new social assistance legislation introduced in 1998 (see Chapter 3) provides a statutory framework in relation to supported housing. In particular, the legislation has relevance to the classification of marginalised groups, the de-institutionalisation of measures directed to people with support needs, the classification of types of dwellings related to measures of social support and, finally, the span of social measures available. The legislation refers to 'people with special social problems', which is taken to include homeless people, and makes separate reference to people with mental disabilities and people with physical disabilities.

An important innovation in this legislation is the removal of the term 'institution' and hence the intention to de-institutionalise measures for the socially excluded. This would appear to be a significant shift from the Social Assistance Act of 1995 which allowed the municipalities to establish shared dwellings for people accommodated in accordance with Section 105, and provided the municipalities with the possibility of linking support (professional or voluntary) to these dwellings. This suggests that the recent legislation introduces more flexible funding arrangements through the separation of housing and support.

It remains the responsibility of the regional counties to "ensure the necessary number of places for temporary shelter ... for people with special social problems who are not capable of living in their own dwelling, and who have need of housing ... and support" (Section 94). In this way, the legislation recognises a distinction between the acute needs, temporary needs and permanent need for support and housing. However, it is not prescriptive about the form of accommodation within which these needs are met.

Paragraph 73 of the legislation makes it the responsibility of the municipality to ensure that measures exist to provide for the "assistance, care and general support as well as towards the possibilities for rehabilitation for people who are in need due to physical or mental disabilities or special social problems". Guidance under the legislation defines the nature of support quite broadly. The aim of the social support is to enable the individual to live independently in a moderately protected environment. The types of support to be provided include counselling and guidance with regard to ordinary daily functions such as cleaning, personal hygiene and budgeting, supporting the individual to participate in occupational and leisure activities, helping the individual to establish contact with his/her surroundings, family and friends as well as more formal contacts with relevant specialist support services.

This legislative framework, both from the 1995 and 1998 legislation, thus provides for a form of supported accommodation which is "somewhere in-between an institution and taking care of oneself in their own home" (*Folketingets forhandlinger*, 1995, p 2449). Significantly, it also provides for a de-coupling of housing and support arrangements, providing equality of treatment regardless of the form of accommodation the person occupies. It is apparent, however, that the municipalities will have to realise their responsibilities under the legislation to provide dwellings, whether single or shared, if the intentions of the legislation are to be realised.

Finland

In Finland, supported housing has a long history dating back to 1976 when a taskforce suggested that "Members of special groups with physical or social difficulties preventing them from living completely independently should, however, be provided with support dwellings where it is possible to provide a varying degree of care and supervision depending on the needs of the occupant" (Valtakunnallinen asunto-ohjelma vuosille, 1976). This would be achieved mainly within the confines of general housing policy. Since the mid-1970s, when the shift towards community services began, several traditions have emerged in supported housing which differ in terms of their approaches to and definitions of supported housing. Two distinct situations are identified, where:

- *Supported housing is rehabilitative in nature:* aimed at people discharged from institutions who need help in adjusting to life in the community. Rehabilitation homes and support homes provide care of a therapeutic nature. The intention of the accommodation is to be transitional between institutional and community living. The care is of an institutional nature and the principles of normalisation, related to the ability to control one's daily life, is limited. This accommodation is seen as part of a 'care chain'.
- *Supervised dwellings:* this accommodation is intended for people who, because of their way of life, are thought to need supervision, guidance and rehabilitation with regard to their housing.

The term 'supported housing' is still used in Finland, even though it is recognised that the term 'support in housing' is more appropriate, since "a considerable percentage of the housing in which support is provided is in practice intended only for temporary supported housing use" (Kärkkäinen, 1999, p 8). When the person no longer needs support, s/he needs to move elsewhere. Supported housing in this situation is regarded as part of a chain of services which, in the case of a homeless person, begins with shelters and emergency services.

Efforts to regulate and control supported housing have been made through legislation since the early 1980s. The Social Welfare Act (1982) uses the term 'housing service'. Housing services, of which supported housing or support in housing is one part, are provided for people who, for some special reasons, need assistance and support in acquiring a home.

Legislation in the 1980s, although only 'skeleton laws in content' (Kärkkäinen, 1999), aimed at eliminating homelessness. However, since homelessness was viewed as a social issue, as an issue of solidarity, the 'houseability' of those in need of housing was seldom questioned in the official debate surrounding this legislation. It was assumed that, by providing suitable housing services, a suitable home (or place in care) could be found for all homeless people. In practice, at the local level, those in need of housing are assessed to determine whether they can cope in an ordinary independent dwelling or whether they need supported housing.

Germany

In Germany, there is no national definition of supported housing to be found in welfare legislation and the term is thus used for a wide range of approaches focused on the needs of different client groups. It is assumed that permanent support is needed for older people and people with a physical disability, while young people and homeless people will require support for a transitional period in their lives. Given the absence of a legal definition, regulations have been developed by financing bodies (for example by the Bundesarbeitsgemeinschaft überörtlicher Träger, which is an association of public bodies responsible for financing specific social services on the *Länder* level under the Federal Welfare Act), which state that:

> Supported housing combines an independent way of living in rooms which are privately rented and can thus be used as one's own responsibility with systematically organised regular advice and personal support by professionals. It takes place in single dwellings or in shared dwellings. Contrary to support in homes, the persons concerned, assisted by outside persons, manage everyday matters and decide on their way of living independently and on their own responsibility. Responsibility of professionals covers only the professional's carrying out of personal support and does not include

any authority to give directives to clients concerning their personal way of living. (BAG üö TR, 1995, p 10)

The term 'supported housing' is criticised because it implies that the support is linked to the dwelling rather than the individual and that tenancy of the dwelling is dependent on receiving the support. The term 'ambulant personal support for people living in dwellings' is therefore favoured (BAG Wohnungslosenhilfe, 1998, p 29).

Some institutions in Germany have developed 'external residents groups' as a way of moving people on into the community in a planned and phased manner. These 'decentralised stationary accommodation' projects may therefore be considered to be supported housing, even though the residents do not have a tenancy contract and the respective institution can give directives which affect the residents' daily way of living. Hence supported housing has often been introduced not so much as an alternative to accommodation in residential establishments, but rather as a complementary step between accommodation in institutions and in 'normal' housing.

The definition of support used distinguishes between designated or planned programmes of support related to specific accommodation and general, community-based, advice and support centres/services. Thus support "must have a binding character as well as a certain intensity and continuity" (Busch-Geertsema, 1999). For example, *Bundesländer* guidelines on supported housing for single homeless people (people with an unsettled way of living) schedule a ratio of staff to client ranging from 1:12 to 1:20. However, the intensity of support is acknowledged to range from intensive individual support limited in time (ratio of staff to client of 1:2.5) to housing-related advice services (ratio of staff to client of 1:50).

The definition of supported housing contained within the Federal Welfare legislation reflects the community care principles of normalisation, empowerment and independent living. However, flowing from this basic model there exists a range of mechanisms for linking support and housing which involve specific funding and management arrangements. The legal basis for financing support further differs for the various target groups. Support for vulnerable young people is regulated by the Welfare Act for Children and Young People (*Kinder und Jugendhilfegesetz*: KJHG), whereas support for most other target groups falls under different sections of the Federal Welfare Act (*Bundessozialhilfegesetz*: BSHG). However, the Welfare Act does not give an exact definition of supported housing. Equally there are considerable differences of definition between *Bundesländer*, as well as difficulty in distinguishing supported housing from, on the one hand, stationary institutions and residential homes, and, on the other, from private rented housing with low-intensity support for residents from ambulant advice and service centres.

The Netherlands

In the Netherlands, it is possible to identify two forms of provision: supported living projects (where support is needed permanently) and 'ambulatory' coaching projects (where support need is transitional). The former cater mainly for people leaving institutional care. The latter target people who have difficulty maintaining their independence and thus run the risk of eviction and homelessness.

We have already described (in Chapter 3) how social care services in the Netherlands have, for a long time, been provided by independent non-governmental organisations. The *Federatie Opvang*, as the national umbrella agency for social shelter and care organisations, is responsible (under the direction of the Department of Health, Welfare and Sports) for the development of a system of client registration, quality control and models of funding. The following definition is used by Federatie Opvang (1998, p 2), the national federation for organisations for homeless people: "Supported housing is a function which aims at coaching people to (more) independent housing, whereby support is available on the basis of a client's needs, restricted to some hours per week".

Sweden

In Sweden, since the late 1990s, the goal of homelessness policy is no longer articulated in terms of providing homes (*bostad*) but of providing housing (*boende*), which connotes a collective arrangement under the surveillance of, and sometimes with support from, the authorities (Sahlin, 1998).

The Social Service Act (valid from 1982 but recently revised) includes a number of paragraphs which are relevant for people in need of supported accommodation. Under this legislation, the municipality "has the ultimate responsibility to see that those who are staying within the municipality get the support and help they need" (para 3) – referring to emergency help, including the provision of temporary night shelter for people who would otherwise sleep rough. The sixth paragraph of the Act states that individuals who cannot satisfy their needs themselves or by other means have, under certain conditions, the right to assistance for maintenance and for living ('other assistance'). This help should be designed in a way that increases the individual's ability to lead an independent life. The assistance includes social welfare, work or training as prerequisites for welfare and 'other assistance' as help provided in the home and housing with special services for disabled individuals.

The Social Service Act (para 21) obliges the local social services authority to ensure that those people who "encounter severe difficulties in their ways of life" get the opportunity to live in the community. This obligation includes ensuring that people are "housed in a way that is adjusted to [their] need of special support".

This obligation also applies to those who have only 'social' problems as well as disabilities (Norström and Thunved, 1998, p 104). Moreover, the municipality is also obliged to organise outreach activities in order to keep itself informed about the situation of people with physical and mental disabilities and plan its measures for these groups.

In 1994, an Act of Support and Services for people with disabilities (LSS) was passed by the parliament to replace and extend the 1986 Law on care of the mentally disabled. The novelty of this legislation, most relevant for the risk of being homeless, is the inclusion of a 'third circuit' of people, namely, the mentally ill and, according to the intentions of the Act, people who for reasons such as alcohol or substance abuse, have disabilities which hinder their functioning in society (Norström and Thunved, 1998, p 317). The measures for special support and special service specified in the Act (para 9) include advice and other personal support which requires trained personnel; help through 'personal assistants'; "housing through foster care or in housing with special services for children and youth who should not remain with their families"; daily activities for adults who have no work and are not involved in education; and "housing with special service for adults or other specially adjusted homes for adults". This concept covers all kinds of housing needed by the disabled individual. Examples include apartments adjusted for wheelchairs, service housing with normal tenure and group housing which is staffed day and night, where all kinds of practical support is offered (Norström and Thunved, 1998, p 323).

The most common form of supported accommodation in Sweden is group housing. Over the last decade very specific and detailed norms concerning group housing have been established (NBHBP, 1994, p 8): group housing should be located in an ordinary residential house and have access to various services; several group housing units should not be located adjacent to each other; the number of residents should not exceed six (four in the case of people with a learning disability). Equally, the aim of support has been specified as aiming to provide for the residents' personal development and active participation in the society; a normal pattern of life and a home environment; influence and the right to respect for their own demands and interests and possibilities for an active life (also outside the home) with opportunities to meet existing friends and to develop new friendships (NBHBP, 1994, p 10).

Supported accommodation is thus defined according to several dimensions, such as the target groups and their perceived needs, the aim and amount of support, the provider of the support and the characteristics of the dwelling. Changed legislation and the redistribution of responsibility in the 1990s have implied that the municipalities, and within them the social authorities, are assigned ever more of the obligation to house and care for groups in need of support and services. Although the old distinctions are still preserved to some degree, for example with separate departments handling people with learning disabilities or mental illness, older people and people with physical disabilities, there is a corresponding tendency towards a convergence in the discourses about support and services for the different target groups.

The traditional coupling, prior to de-institutionalisation, of providers of support with target groups remains in special housing provision. Such associations are being maintained, as clients belonging to the 'same' category are gathered in the same housing unit under the lead of the same organisation/department. People who are regarded as having a learning disability, a mental illness, frail older people, substance abusers, alcoholics, and battered women live in separate housing units and/or are the subjects of separate projects.

United Kingdom

Supported accommodation in the UK is also extremely diverse. However, there are a number of dimensions which appear to be common to definitions of supported accommodation in England (National Housing Federation, 1996) and in Scotland (Edgar and Doherty, 1996). The three dimensions are: the physical character of the property, the social environment (the degree of intervention and regulation) and the place of the project in wider community networks (Munn, 1996). The last category relates, for example, not only to the number of official partner organisations, but also to how much use is made of services in the wider community and how much residency in the project is part of a process leading to settlement/resettlement.

An operational definition of supported accommodation has been developed for the Scottish database of supported accommodation (Edgar and Doherty, 1996): "Housing designated for the specific purpose of accommodating individuals requiring some form of support in order to live independently in the community" (p 2).

This operational definition is based on three principles. The main purpose of supported accommodation is to provide housing that enables people to live independently. Residents will normally have some occupancy rights through a tenancy agreement, an occupancy agreement or equivalent, which establishes their rights in relation to the agency which owns or is responsible for managing the dwelling. Designated accommodation is housing provided for the specific purpose of housing individuals who require some level of support to remain in the community. This normally means that either or both capital and revenue funding arrangements have been entered into for the specific purpose of providing such accommodation. People living in the housing provided require an appropriate level and type of support. Support is part of a planned programme of care delivered as part of the project, although the precise nature and level of support varies between projects.

A small but growing proportion of supported accommodation is provided under a different model commonly known as 'floating support' where the two elements of housing and support are explicitly separated such that the support can, theoretically, float off to another client in another home (Douglas et al, 1998).

Munn (1996) suggests an adaptation of the Scottish definition towards a model utilising the three dimensions described above, which represent a continuum in which individual projects can be plotted. It does not ascribe positive or negative values to a particular placing on the continuum, but begins to make description methodical.

It is also true to say that most supported accommodation in the UK is relatively modern, developed in the last 15 years, and that the concepts of support are constantly evolving. The evolution is partly in response to changing funding regimes and partly in response to changing ideas of best practice. It is also the case that practice has been developing since the implementation of the Community Care legislation in 1990, described in Chapter 3, which provides the funding and regulatory framework for supported accommodation. Approximately half of all supported accommodation is registered with local social services

Table 3: A continuum of supported housing

	Minimal regulation and intervention	Moderate regulation and intervention	High regulation and intervention
Ordinary housing	Floating support	Supported tenancy or flat	Live-in carer or support
Housing of unexceptional style and location	Group living	Residential care	Nursing home
Institutional building	Night shelter	Large-scale hostel	Hospital

Source: Munn (1996)

authorities, although the current system of deciding on which projects should be registered has been criticised for its inconsistency. Two thirds of accommodation (approximately) is provided by housing associations with the remaining accommodation provided either by other voluntary sector organisations or by local authorities directly. The evolving nature of supported accommodation reflects the resolution of this tension between, on the one hand, the separate funding streams for accommodation and support, and, on the other, the regulation of quality control for vulnerable groups.

In the second group of countries in our classification, although the process of de-institutionalisation has been deep and had an equally long gestation, the emergence of supported housing has been characterised by a lack of formal legislative framework. Rather, its development has tended to develop from practice-based innovation, through a bottom-up approach, or has been associated with the development of policies of reinsertion and social inclusion. There is also a tendency for variation in practice to result from distinctive administrative, or federal, structures of government.

Austria

In Austria, the lack of federal legislation on homelessness and on the regulation of supported housing is an underlying reason for the absence of a national definition of supported housing. The term 'supported housing' is commonly used to describe a wide range of methods, approaches and standards in provision and has generally been derived through a 'bottom-up', service-led evolution of supported housing provision. This lack of cohesive definition and understanding of supported housing may be attributed to two interrelated characteristics of the Austrian social welfare system. Decentralisation along provincial lines of responsibility for housing, for social welfare and for the organisation and delivery of services for homeless people is a key feature of the Austrian social welfare system. As a result of this decentralisation, an uneven development of services has occurred both between provinces and within provinces themselves. The extent to which supported accommodation provision has developed has therefore been largely driven by the development of existing homelessness services in particular areas and by a combination of political will and organisational structures which are as much localised as they are provincialised.

Despite the widespread differences in the description of supported housing services, however, one can say that, as a common denominator, all supported housing services bring together a combination of housing provision and support delivery albeit to varying extents and in different forms.

Working from the premise that defining supported housing in Austria is really a matter of understanding the nature of existing services, two broad categories of supported housing may be distinguished:

- residential housing or living in shared flats with provision of more or less individual support (may be called individual support in shared housing);
- single flats for single people or families with provision of individual support (supported single or family housing).

Such a distinction may further be explained as a continuum from quasi-institutional living to living arrangements which most closely resemble mainstream living. For some client groups, a relatively clear progression along the continuum may be possible while, for others, direct access to more independent living may be the norm and, still for others, progress along the staircase may be impeded for a number of reasons which are elaborated in Chapter 6.

Support provision is also widely varied with a strong emphasis on counselling which is closely linked to obtaining access to employment or, at least, some means of survival. Employment re-training and protected job markets are an often-cited feature of supported housing projects in Austria.

Belgium

The growth of supported housing in Belgium can be explained with reference to four developments. First, the professionalisation of services placed greater emphasis on the individual and on concepts of independent living although, over time, the notion of 'independence' has to be redefined. Second, the 'small-scale' ideology shifted thinking from large hostel provision to more homely autonomous living. Third, the ideology of emancipation emphasised the individual's potential rather than their limitations and saw them as active participants rather than passive recipients. Finally, in the absence of an effective housing policy, and given the failure of social housing to meet the needs of homeless families, welfare workers have been increasingly involved in finding both housing and support solutions for their clients.

Although supported housing exists in all three Belgian administrative regions it is only legally recognised in Flanders. The 1991 general law on Welfare Work in Flanders officially recognised and created the funding framework for six working methods for the provision of services to homeless people. Among these, supported housing is defined as a combination of support and housing to enable homeless people who cannot live independently to live as independently as possible in the community. The nature of the support is determined by individual need and the duration of the provision may be short, medium or long term. The concepts of individualisation, normalisation and integration are key features of the definition.

In Wallonia, supported housing, although not officially recognised, has generally grown out of the work of the reception houses, who recognised the need for more independent forms of living. The existing provision can be characterised by its organisational links and physical proximity to reception centres. In general, supported housing in Wallonia tends to be small-scale shared housing environments where support is provided by the reception centres and where there is an expectation that access will be gated by the reception centre itself.

Thus, in Belgium, supported housing may be seen as part of a continuum of provision lying between institutionalisation and independent living. It may be defined according to a number of axes:

• the integral link between housing and support both at the organisational and at the implementation levels;

- the form of the accommodation which should be small-scale and, preferably, self-contained, be purpose-built or purpose-adapted and be separate from reception houses;
- the ethos of the support provision which should be oriented towards the individual, provided by the welfare worker and organised and delivered through joint working between the welfare worker and the client;
- the means of access which should generally avoid the gating principle;
- the community-based location of the provision;
- the professional and autonomous working methods of the support team.

France

France lacks a clear semantic and legislative definition of supported housing. In fact, the emphasis seems to be on social support (*accompagnement social*) and its link to housing provision. Thus the term is often used in collaboration with the notion of 'mediation' for the purpose of supporting the individual to achieve social and economic reintegration (or reinsertion). Result-based orientation has often mitigated against long-term provision of supported housing with a preference for shorter-term mediation.

The delivery of supported housing is through a multidisciplinary team approach which combines more traditional housing providers (associations, habitation à loyer modérés [HLM], and private landlords) with welfare workers and employment/training schemes.

The identification and assessment of support needs may come from a range of sources including landlords themselves, who may request support for certain tenants in order to prevent eviction. Thus the form of supported housing may vary from the provision of support in existing and non-designated housing to special housing with support projects. There is also evidence of innovative schemes where housing permanence is guaranteed against a backdrop of flexible and diminishing support provision to mirror individual need.

Concepts of choice, freedom and individualisation are paramount although supported housing may also be construed as a coercive tool by which landlords can safeguard against rent arrears through the forcible imposition of the acceptance of support as a prerequisite for continued occupation.

Italy

In Italy, there is no term which directly corresponds to 'supported accommodation'. There are various terms, however, which designate forms of accommodation to which some form of support is associated. The terms relate to a specific type of provision or to a particular target group, for example:

- *cenrti di accoglienza:* reception centre for marginalised groups or transitional shelters for specific groups of people;
- *alloggi protetti:* protected accommodation or transitional housing associated with social reintegration plans;
- *communità-alloggio:* community lodgings or sheltered housing for people at risk.

These terms imply an accent on social services and reveal the location of the resource as being mainly in the social welfare field rather than housing. An important distinction is made between intervention aimed at people who are socially excluded (serious *marginalisation*) and intervention aimed at people at risk of marginalisation. This distinction relates to two different functions of support: rehabilitation and prevention. For people who are seriously socially excluded intervention may have different objectives – emergency/containment and integration/reintegration; support is multidimensional and is probably provided in special purpose accommodation (ie purpose-built). For people at risk of marginalisation support is sectoral, that is to say, limited to a particular aspect, and the philosophy is of an integrated approach.

It is suggested (Tosi and Ranci, 1999) that the classification of supported housing can be differentiated by considering different target groups since the relationship between the accommodation and the support is determined by the particular risks of each group. For some groups (for example women fleeing domestic violence, vulnerable young people) the accommodation dimension is important because it is a condition for the protection and development of an integration programme or because risk is strongly determined by housing difficulties. For other groups (for example single homeless people, people with drug or alcohol dependencies) the support dimension is more important because reintegration is understood to be determined by lifestyle factors. In the Italian context, the scale of both legal and illegal immigration and asylum seekers introduces a particular category of people in need of support and housing insertion. Table 4 summarises this understanding.

Although the provision of supported accommodation is widespread in the Italian system, it is hardly defined (as such) in the institutional system, at least for certain types of target population and functions. Two traits above all determine the status of supported accommodation: the poor, non-universalistic protection provided for adults in difficulty or marginalised and the gap between housing and social services which distinguishes the entire system.

The latter distinction is clearly reflected in regional legislation. What is termed 'housing assistance' or 'for housing need' is often defined by special regulations, separate from those on social services, which in many cases makes no provision for social work support for users or for a systematic link between housing assistance and the demands of social work provided by other offices. Review of this regional legislation identifies a diversity in approach (Kazepov, 1996, quoted in Tosi and Ranci, 1999). It is possible to distinguish between, on the one hand, provision for emergency accommodation and support (for example, in Trento Province, Toscana, Calabria and Sicilia) and, on the other, social assistance for 'adults at risk of serious marginalisation' (legislation in Piedmonte, Emilia Romagna and Marche, see Tosi and Ranci, 1999).

Much of the possible action that can be taken regarding 'the emargination of adults' falls within the area of supported accommodation. However, the accommodation supply is referred to by terms such as 'transitional accommodation', 'mini-apartments', 'apartments', 'protected accommodation'. These facilities are aimed at integration or reintegration, in the case of those already marginalised, or at the prevention of processes of (further) social drifting for at-risk cases.

People offered transitional accommodation provided by local authorities, directly or by contracting out to third sector associations, often include the following categories: women, single mothers either expecting or with children, young people or minors (at risk), elderly people, and people released from residential institutions. It is important to remember that elderly people and minors at risk receive better and more systematic institutional protection and this is also reflected in the field of supported accommodation; this reduces the margins of discretion available to local agencies with regard to standards and forms of provision.

Table 4: Classification of supported accommodation

Target	Objectives	Support	Accommodation
Persons in difficulty/at (high) risk of marginalisation	Protection Prevention of further drifting Social/housing insertion Social/housing insertion of tenants of public housing Housing insertion	Social accompaniment, benefit payments, work insertion Social accompaniment, benefit payments, work insertion etc Mediation and guarantee on the rental market (Social accompaniment)	Special accommodation Ordinary housing Public housing Ordinary housing
Serious marginalisation/ no abode	Social reintegration (personal independence) Improvement of quality of life Social reintegration	Social accompaniment: individual reintegration plan ('Light') social accompaniment Social accompaniment Individual reintegration plan, relating to specific risks	Transitional shelters/ housing Shared dwellings Shelter type accommodation Transitional accommodation Shared dwellings Special purpose structures Ordinary housing
Foreign immigrants	Temporary accommodation Housing and social insertion at the arrival stage Housing insertion	Support for housing and social insertion: advice and social accompaniment Support to deal with specific or additional difficulties that immigrants meet Mediation activity etc (Social accompaniment)	Special purpose structures: 'First reception' centres

Source: Tosi and Ranci (1999)

Luxembourg

In Luxembourg, supported housing is perceived as an intermediary step between direct access, emergency shelters with communal living environments and more independent forms of living in self-contained housing. There is no official recognition of supported housing as a model of provision although generous funding from relevant ministries (such as the Ministry for the Family) of non-governmental organisations who provide housing with support suggests that the model is widely accepted.

Three forms of housing are common: communal housing (larger forms of sharing), small shared housing and self-contained housing. In all of these, however, duration of stay is limited since the housing is designated as supported housing and hence individuals must move on when they no longer need support. The nature and level of support also varies widely but can be characterised, at least in the smaller-scale provision, by its emphasis on meeting individual needs, providing choice and encouraging independence.

The final group of countries may be characterised by the fact that de-institutionalisation has not proceeded with the same pace and extent as in other European member states (with the possible exception of Greece where the process of reform of psychiatric hospitals was initiated prior to their admission to the EU). The countries do not, therefore, have a formal legislative or policy framework within which models of supported accommodation or supported housing could emerge and hence they are characterised by a relative absence of the models of accommodation which are in evidence elsewhere in Europe. In these countries the importance of the role of the family in care provision and of the voluntary (especially church-based) organisations may also account for the relative lack of development of innovation in relation to supported housing as a mechanism to prevent homelessness or institutionalisation of vulnerable groups in society.

Greece

Greece has neither a legal definition of homelessness nor a consistent definition of supported housing. However, since the mid-1980s, a growing political, administrative and public awareness of the dimensions of homelessness coupled with EU supported changes in institutional care for people with mental illness have led to the emergence of target-group specific supported housing provision. The purpose of this provision can be characterised as both preventative and rehabilitative, although the principles of choice, individualised support, integration and independence are in their infancy.

The scale and nature of supported housing provision is client-group specific with small-scale shared housing being the principal form for people leaving institutional care and elderly people, while larger-scale temporary provision is the primary model for homeless people. The lack of long-term options for rehousing or resettlement suggests that the role of supported housing as an intermediary step in a staircase towards permanent housing is as yet undeveloped.

Ireland

In Ireland, according to O'Sullivan (1999) supported housing is a 'strange' concept with 'limited applicability'. Homeless people and vulnerable people in need of shelter and support have traditionally been taken care of within family structures or by confessional organisations and agencies associated with the Catholic Church. As demographic and social change impinge on Irish society the state has taken greater cognisance of housing issues, but has paid little or no attention to provision of supported housing. It has been left to voluntary organisations to fill in the gaps left by the erosion of traditional forms of provision. Supported housing in Ireland, to the extent that it exists at all, has been in the form of short-term, localised provision and has rarely been evaluated.

Portugal

Supported accommodation is a recent practice in Portugal, which has largely emerged through the innovation in practice among voluntary organisations working for the homeless. Since homelessness is largely an urban phenomenon, it appears to be more a concern of local authorities rather than national government. Hence, there is no integrated or coherent strategy aimed at enabling people to live independently in the community. Approaches to homelessness have, historically, been both sectoral and localised and have lacked the integration of services implied by the concept of supported housing. The projects, which are described in later chapters, are evidence of very recent signs that public policy has recognised the importance of supported accommodation as one measure to solve the problem of homelessness. However, it has been private non-profit organisations, operating primarily in the main cities of Lisbon and Oporto, that have launched such projects (with some public funding). Given this origin, supported housing has tended to take the form of transitional accommodation between traditional homelessness hostels and more permanent accommodation. Access to the accommodation is linked to a reintegration philosophy and hence employment is a requirement of occupancy and the period of occupancy is restricted (normally four months to one year). Bruto da Costa (1999) suggests that the shift from general institutional provision to individualised support and assistance has been relatively unstable and not particularly persistent. He further suggests that innovative projects, linking support and housing, have been circumscribed to specific groups and have been experimental in nature.

Spain

While the spirit of the objectives of supported housing is well understood in Spain by individual professionals, the lack of an agreed terminology reflects the lack of general debate or exchange of ideas among these professionals and the absence of an articulated strategy – national, regional or local – to tackle the issue. A variety of expressions exist in Spanish terminology, such as *viviendas tuteladas*, *viviendas protegidas* or *viviendas sociales*, referring to different types of housing support, but none of these exactly matches the concept of 'supported housing'. However, the essence of 'supported housing' is revealed by the idea of housing as a fundamental element for the social integration of the individual and as one of the basic work tools in the fight against social exclusion. This is exemplified in the following quotations taken from interviews with professionals working in different homelessness NGOs: "We observed that housing, in some manner, is an important integration factor and that the loss of the home implies the beginning of the family's involvement in an extremely dangerous set of circumstances"; and "The subject of housing is one of the main issues in the fight against social exclusion" (Leal Maldonaldo and Laínez, 1999).

Conclusion

The provision of supported accommodation and supported housing is a relatively recent phenomenon throughout Europe; in most cases, it is a development which has occurred since the early to mid-1980s. Our theoretical model, using the three dimensions and the levels of support, suggests the possibility of a complexity of provision. Indeed, this is reflected in the diversity of forms of provision in evidence throughout Europe; a diversity which is apparent in the terminology employed to describe such forms of provision: community lodgings, group homes, protected apartments, sheltered housing, transitional accommodation, and supported housing. The model also suggests that the form of provision is likely to evolve and, it is our impression, that this too is occurring. The evolution is likely to be from more institutional or residential (and larger) forms of provision to more normal (and smaller) forms of housing.

An important distinction, which is apparent in most countries, is reflected in the twin terms – supported housing and support in housing. The former describes an approach where a planned programme of support is provided in a particular physical space (which may even have been purpose-built); the support is centred on the accommodation which people move through. The latter term indicates a situation where people live in ordinary housing (self-contained or shared) in the community and support is provided (either permanently or temporarily) as required by tenants. Although the preferred approach is perceived by most to be in the form of support in housing, the reality of current provision in the majority of countries is characterised by supported housing.

Different approaches to the provision of supported housing can be discerned from the evidence. At one level the objectives for supported housing are described as rehabilitative, preventative and reintegrative objectives. The objectives reflect the different roles of supported housing for the client groups for whom it is intended – the rehabilitation of people with a drug addiction, prevention of homelessness among people released from institutional environments, the reintegration of the long-term homeless. At another level it is possible to identify a distinction in approach depending on the context in which supported housing has developed. In those countries where supported housing has emerged as part of a process of de-institutionalisation and the associated community provision of care services, the concept of supported accommodation has developed in more distinctive forms underlain with a legislative framework. In those countries where it has emerged in response to policies of social inclusion and from a reintegration philosophy, the forms of provision are structured more around the interlinking of support and housing. In those countries where the provision of supported accommodation is most weakly developed, it is more likely to be characterised by transitional accommodation linked to low threshold, traditional homelessness hostels.

In all countries the form and the range of types of provision of support in housing or supported accommodation reflects both the form of the accommodation itself and the funding and management arrangements which link the housing with the support. The next chapter discusses the relationship between these three dimensions of housing, support and management.

FIVE

The practice of housing and support

If supported housing is to successfully address the social exclusion of homeless people, it requires the careful assessment of client needs and the matching of these needs with appropriate housing and personal care and support packages. It has to deliver housing which is not only well-maintained, secure and affordable, but also of an appropriate size and adapted, as required, to the needs of individual clients. It has further to deliver support which is individually tailored and targeted and sufficiently flexible to meet independent living criteria. The delivery of supported housing that successfully combines all these features needs careful management and coordination, requiring a constructive partnership between housing provider and support provider. If we add to these basic service requirements the desirable characteristic of empowerment – the freedom of users to give expression to their preferences and the exercise of control and direction over their life courses – the tasks of coordination and management involved in the delivery of supported housing grows exponentially in complexity and difficulty. With possibly three agencies involved – housing provider, support provider and funding agency – as well as the service user, the likelihood of slippage and the potential for conflict is always present even in the best coordinated of schemes. In this and the following chapters we address these topics. In this chapter we deal with governance issues in the provision and delivery of supported housing and the form this takes in various national contexts. In Chapter 6 we extend the analysis to consider the detail of the variety of practices in the provision of supported housing within EU member states through an examination of the experience of a range of user groups. In Chapter 7 the emphasis shifts to a consideration of the issues of empowerment.

Imposing a somewhat artificial division on what in the most successful instances should be an integrated package, we look separately in the following account at the housing and the support dimensions of supported housing provision and then move on to consider issues of coordination and management. Our examination of these three dimensions suggests a pattern of delivery which varies from those countries in which, through the enactment of national legislation often associated with the development of care in the community programmes (see Chapter 3), national frameworks of supported housing provision have been introduced, to countries in which the formal provision of supported housing is largely absent and such supported housing that exists is provided in an *ad hoc* manner largely through the auspices of voluntary organisations. As we have suggested in earlier chapters, countries such as the UK, Sweden, Finland, Denmark, Netherlands and Germany illustrate the former situation, while Greece, Portugal, Ireland and Spain illustrate the latter. Belgium, Luxembourg, France, Austria and Italy are probably best seen as representing an intermediate stage between these two positions. The development of supported accommodation in some of the countries which make up the latter two groups has most commonly, but not exclusively, been associated with reintegration objectives rather than with the development of care in the community programmes designed to deal with issues of de-institutionalisation.

Evaluation and critical assessment of the provision and delivery of supported housing, even in those countries such as Sweden, the UK and Germany, where supported housing has been relatively well developed, is patchy and piecemeal. While there are assessments of the effectiveness of individual projects, there are few overall evaluations of, for example, the extent to which supply meets demand and need. The following is therefore largely descriptive, presenting a picture, as far as it can be established, of the extent and type of supported housing in each EU member state as of 1999. Evaluation and critical comment is included where available, but much of our assessment of the effectiveness or otherwise of supported housing delivery and provision is recounted in Chapters 6 and 7.

The accommodation dimension

In Chapter 4 we argued that the nature of accommodation associated with supported housing will vary depending on the intensity of the support provided. Thus institutional level support would normally be provided in hostel-type accommodation as well as in an institutional setting, while intermediate levels of support would, typically, be provided in residential accommodation or group homes and community-based support would, most commonly, be associated with shared housing and self-contained housing. The diversity in the forms of provision of supported housing across EU member states identified in the following account illustrates some of these relationships. However, as we have shown in previous chapters, the mix of accommodation types varies from country to country reflecting not only different service objectives and different client group needs, but also differences between countries in legislative and funding frameworks. The forms of provision range from 'mini-institutions' through group housing and shared dwellings to ordinary, mainstream housing and, as supported housing expands and develops, this range of provision, at least in the medium term, is likely to persist.

In the longer term, if the objectives of independent living for homeless people and for people previously resident in long-stay hospitals and institutions are to be attained and if the principles of normalisation embedded in the concept of supported housing are to apply (see Chapter 3), we might anticipate that supported housing will, ideally, move away from any resemblance to institutional provision and become increasingly indistinguishable from ordinary housing in both its physical form and location. Indeed, the following account suggests that there is already some evidence of such a trend, at least in the expressed intentions of governments and other supported housing providers, if not always in practice. Thus, while a distinction can still be drawn between policy contexts where a place-centred perspective (support is linked to the place of abode) is dominant and policy environments where a person-centred perspective prevails (support is directed at the client, regardless of place of abode), there is also a general, but not universal, evolution from place-centred to the person-centred perspectives as support becomes increasingly independent of the type and form of dwelling. As Table 5 suggests, person-centred provision is, however, not divorced entirely from accommodation type, for it is likely to be more achievable in self-contained housing where support can be more directly targeted to explicitly meet individual needs and where the possibility exists of involving several different specialist support providers. At the other end of the spectrum, larger-scale accommodation, by its very nature, militates against a person-centred approach. Further, since a key role of supported housing is to provide a transitional stage in the move to fully independent living then, even in the context of person-centred provision, we may expect the accommodation characteristics of supported housing to continue to demonstrate some diversity in both form and location, some of which will fall short of the ideal.

Table 5: Person-centred and place-centred support provision

	Self-contained	Small-scale shared	Large-scale shared
Person-centred	No set rules Support not attached to housing Support designed to meet individual need Can stay if support no longer required Full tenancy rights	Collective setting of rules Support attached to housing Support to meet individual needs Move if support no longer required Possible full tenancy/ probable non-tenancy contract	
Place-centred	Some rules may apply Support attached to housing Support designed to meet individual need Move if support no longer required Possible full tenancy or sub-lease	Imposed or collectively decided rules Support attached to housing Support to meet individual need within capacity of service Move if support no longer required Non-tenancy contract or no agreement	Rules set by service Support attached to housing Support determined by service provider Time-limited duration Non-tenancy contract or no agreement

In the following section, we consider the extent to which supported housing in each of the member states either currently reflects or is evolving towards a person–centred rather than a place–centred perspective. We examine the practice with particular reference to provision for homeless people and ask whether or not general trends towards person–centred approaches, where these exist, can equally be seen for this client group. Finally, drawing on what evidence is available, we attempt to identify the factors which may be promoting such a development and those which may be hindering it.

De-institutionalisation countries

We begin our consideration of the accommodation dimension of supported housing with an examination of those countries where a national framework of provision has been established through the enactment of national legislation, often linked to the pursuit of community care objectives.

The provision of supported housing in the *UK* provides a clear demonstration of the range and variety of accommodation available in a country which has legislated for the provision of supported accommodation as part of a national framework of community care (Chapter 3). Over at least two decades a diversity of housing options have been encompassed within the definition of supported housing as employed in the UK, ranging from purpose-built hostels to ordinary housing (Table 6).

A recent emphasis on the provision of smaller-scale supported housing aimed at increasing the provision of self-contained, rather than shared, accommodation integrated into mainstream housing environments, reflects a trend in the UK towards diminishing the differences between supported housing and 'ordinary' housing. That is to say, policy has been moving, albeit slowly, to an approach which creates person-centred, supported tenancies rather than place-centred, purpose-built supported accommodation.

Desirable as these trends are, this is not to argue that the UK – or indeed any other EU country – can be held up as a 'model' of provision. Shared accommodation, for example, remains the dominant form of supported housing in the UK, reflecting historic stock and the imperatives of funding efficiencies. Further, there are persistent and continuing problems with the provision of supported housing in the UK associated not least with under-resourcing, creating a shortfall between demand and supply. There are also problems of poor organisation and cooperation between administrative, support and housing agencies, creating problems with the maintenance of long-term provision of care to those in need. Many people in need of care, particularly those who were formerly institutionalised, are falling through the safety net as a consequence of inadequate monitoring and for the want of clear lines of responsibility for such monitoring. As the process of de-institutionalisation progresses with the discharge of people with greater care needs, it is possible to envisage a reversal of trends towards larger shared accommodation, at least for certain client groups.

Table 6: Supported housing in the United Kingdom

Purpose-built hostels	Housing designed to house six or more people in single or shared rooms or shared rooms with support provided from staff in the building
Very sheltered housing	Housing designed to cater for frail older people
Core and cluster	Housing provided within a defined area supported by a team of individual workers. It is composed of a 'core' property and associated 'cluster' accommodation; the core property provides housing with a higher level of support and acts as an administrative base from which support is provided
Dispersed housing	Consists of two or more properties (houses or flats) dispersed in an area
Staffed group homes	Small communal dwellings with shared living space, kitchen and bathroom in which all residents have their own room or beds. There are normally no more than four residents and homes are staffed up to 24 hours a day
Shared house/flat	A small communal dwelling with shared living space, where each resident has their own room or bedsit. It differs from a staffed group home in that support staff are independent
Non-shared house/flat	A property occupied solely by the client or by the client and his/her partner/family members. Self-contained housing is either purpose-built or provided in existing general needs housing with planned regular support

Source: Aldridge (1999)

Sweden demonstrates a similar range of supported housing accommodation to that available in the UK. Sahlin (1999), reflecting on the two dimensions of normalisation of lifestyles and living conditions, identifies four main types of accommodation (Figure 4). While the most common form of supported housing to emerge from this categorisation is group housing, several other types are also apparent.

The housing situation is least 'normal' in group housing, where rooms or small apartments are clustered together and attached to common spaces in which support personnel are often located. The aim of group housing is to normalise residents' behaviour through training, supervision and activities, or, as in the case for frail older people, to provide continuous care. The reason for co-locating the homes is sometimes said to be that the residents want each other's company, but it is also, and probably more so, based on the desire to rationalise the provision of support in

Figure 4: Typology of supported accommodation in Sweden

		Normalising lifestyles	
		Yes	No
Normalising housing conditions	Yes	1 **Special contracts** Support in own homes Service flats for mentally retarded	2 **Service flats** Physically adjusted flats
	No	3 **Group housing** with shared kitchen Collective housing	4 **Night shelters**

Source: Sahlin (1999)

order to make it cost-effective. 'Collective housing', where several individuals have to share a home, is another instance of 'non-normal housing' as are 'night shelters' which provide, as the name suggests, temporary, transient accommodation responding to an immediate need; they do not have explicit normalising objectives.

Sahlin (1999) also categorises the diversity of housing solutions which have emerged for each major client group (Table 7). Five different types of housing for people with a learning disability are identified and similar options have been provided for people with mental health problems. Three main forms of supported accommodation are available for older people – group housing, service flats and ordinary homes. Supported accommodation for homeless people is provided along similar lines, but with a greater emphasis on transitional accommodation and training. In addition to the provision of supported housing for these client groups, there is the provision of refuges for women fleeing domestic violence.

With specific reference to the homeless, Sahlin (1999) identifies several distinct forms of accommodation provision (Table 7):

Table 7: Supported housing in Sweden

People with learning disabilities	People with mental health problems	Older people	Homeless people
Boarding homes – where four to five people share a house or flat	Boarding homes – where four to five people share a house or flat		Category housing – targeted at people with drug/alcohol problems
Traditional group housing – where five self-contained flats are located together and connected to common rooms and rooms for staff	Traditional group housing – where five self-contained flats are located together and connected to common rooms and rooms for staff	Group housing – from refurbished nursing homes to newly built properties housing six to eight people each with private rooms and shared living areas	Group housing – converted clinics or institutions, intended as transitional accommodation
The stairs model – where a few flats for residents and one for staff are located on the same staircase but where there are no common living areas	The stairs model – where a few flats for residents and one for staff are located on the same staircase but where there are no common living areas		Collective housing – housing several people in one flat with private rooms and shared living space
Service flats – which are separate ordinary dwellings dispersed in a residential area and serviced by visiting staff located in the area		Service flats – self-contained apartments grouped together with access to support in the home and outside services	Training flats – transitional accommodation with visiting support from social workers
Own housing – where the tenants receive support in their own homes through home service or personal assistants.	Own housing – where the tenants receive support in their own homes through home service or personal assistants.	Ordinary housing – where practical and social support and medical care is provided by the municipalities through home services	Special contract flats – dispersed flats in the community, with a specified contract for support; flat intended as a permanent home

Source: Sahlin (1999)

- *category houses:* which may or may not be targeted at alcohol or, less frequently, drug abusers, and may or may not be associated with social support and control;
- *welfare hotels:* which are characterised by very low standards, run by private owners or sometimes by the municipality; in general, no organised social support is provided;
- *group housing:* which may be converted clinics or institutions, intended for temporary residency, or category houses which are supplemented with common facilities;
- *collective housing:* where a few homeless clients live together in one flat, each having private rooms, but sharing the bath, kitchen and living room;
- *shelters:* open day and night, intended for temporary stay, where the staff sometimes provides social support;
- *training flats:* also intended for temporary occupancy, generally with regular follow-up visits by social workers;
- *separate flats:* subleased with special contracts and dispersed in established residential areas; these generally include regular follow up visits by social workers, and the flats are sometimes intended to become permanent homes for the residents.

'Special contracts' for dispersed flats, subleased by the local social authorities to homeless clients and families, are used as tools for normalising both lifestyles and housing conditions (or for preventing the loss of normal housing conditions). In principle, the flat is indistinguishable from ordinary housing. However, the tenancy agreements often include special rules of behaviour, for instance that residents must not use drugs or alcohol or have overnight guests. Special contracts also exist for 'group housing', of the kind frequently provided for those who are mentally ill, and for people receiving organised support in their own homes; for instance, outpatient support to mentally disordered people who control their own dwellings. No explicit endeavour to normalise people's lifestyles is involved in 'service flats' for older people. Here residents have full tenancy rights and choose for themselves the level of support and services, and whether these should be provided within their flats or in common localities. The same concept applies to 'adapted flats' leased to physically disabled people. Through physical adaptations (for example the installation of elevators) or the location of the home (for example close to services), the housing situation, with due consideration for the frailty or handicap of the tenant, is made as normal as possible. We can perhaps conclude that in Sweden, supported housing for homeless people tends to be more place-centred within a staircase of transition, whereas supported housing for other groups such as elderly people and people with physical disabilities may be more person-centred.

In *Finland*, from the time of its first introduction, the overriding objective of supported housing has been the provision of support for families living in ordinary housing located in community neighbourhoods and for single households living in self-contained, supported apartments (Kärkkäinen, 1999). While these objectives, which embody the principles of person-centred support, still dominate, over the years there has been some departure from the ideal in the types of accommodation provided. Responding to cost considerations and the transitional needs of some client groups, shared apartments providing rooms for several people, with a communal kitchen and bathroom, have been built. Supported housing in Finland today involves a variety of forms of provision directed at a wide range of client groups. Several types of provision can be identified (Heinonen, 1997). Supported dwellings situated among ordinary blocks of flats or terraced houses are regarded as suitable for people whose need for support is minor. Grouped apartments, either situated in ordinary housing stock or in specifically designated buildings (for example a terraced house) are designed to accommodate people with alcohol or drug problems. Grouped apartments with a common day centre, located close to a support provider or to a client's family, are designed to enable intensive support and are regarded as suitable for temporary housing following institutional residence, when independent living is not yet possible. Supported housing for young people adjusting to independent living is most typically located near, or even incorporated in, the dwelling which houses the support providers. Finally, supported dwellings, intended to cater for those who are able to manage everyday activities independently, are located near to a day centre or some other service unit which offers various daily activities and recreation facilities.

Under new legislation introduced in the mid and late 1990s, the provision of supported housing in *Denmark* has moved from a focus on 'institutional' settings (Section 105 of the 1976 Social Assistance Act) to embrace shared housing and ordinary homes. Increasingly, a person-centred perspective in the provision of support and care has been adopted under which support is tailored to the needs of individuals and families, regardless of their housing circumstances; that is, the type and level of support is provided without reference, necessarily, to the type of dwelling. A variety of accommodation settings can be identified. These include

(i) places in '105 institutions', redefined in the 1995 Social Assistance Act as "places intended for temporary occupancy for persons who do not have access to a dwelling or are for some reason unable to remain in their own home and who have special difficulties" (Børner Stax et al, 1999); (ii) shared dwellings, designed as transitional accommodation between 105 institutional places and ordinary housing (this provision explicitly links support and housing); (iii) core and cluster housing; and (iv) single apartments in ordinary housing.

From interviews conducted in four municipalities it appears that the most prominent form of supported housing is shared dwellings, many previously rooms in 105 institutions. These can accommodate between five and eight residents, each with a room of their own and in most cases sharing a living room and a kitchen. The difference between shared dwellings and the core and cluster housing arrangements is mainly that the residents in the latter each have their own apartment, but live in the same block of apartments or group of small houses. Denmark's recent legislative changes (1995 and 1998), in de-coupling support from accommodation provision, provide one of the most explicit examples in the EU of a shift towards person-centred approaches. It will take some time, however, to evaluate the extent to which legislation leads to changing practice.

In the *Netherlands* a distinction has been made between 'supported accommodation' projects and 'floating support' projects (de Feijter and Blok, 1999). In the former, the support and the accommodation are integrated and may involve a single provider. In the latter, support is independent of the housing situation. 'Floating support' projects involve people living in ordinary housing which can be either shared or self-contained. Support is provided for a variety of client groups and is designed to create the conditions for independent living. 'Supported accommodation', on the other hand, includes a variety of forms of housing, including 'social boarding houses', short-stay facility and 'single-room occupancy hotels'. To the extent that they provide only temporary accommodation and transitional support arrangements and are not directly targeted at facilitating permanent independent living, some of these types of accommodation can be regarded as marginal in terms of the definition of supported housing used in this study.

In *Germany*, while many large-scale institutions set up 'external residential groups' (*Außenwohngruppen*) for people with mental health problems, vulnerable young people and people with drug or alcohol dependencies, support in housing is provided mainly in ordinary self-contained or shared apartments. The majority of places in supported housing are provided in shared accommodation, normally of between two to six people with shared kitchen, bathroom and a communal living area. With the largest privately rented housing sector in Europe (36% of the housing stock), the majority of such accommodation in Germany is in private housing or is provided by welfare and church organisations.

Supported accommodation in a reintegration context

We now move on to consider accommodation provision in the context of a cluster of countries that manifest some forms of national provision, but are also characterised by inconsistency and frequently driven by reintegration imperatives, rather than community care objectives.

De Decker and Hardouin (1999) report that there are 1,178 designated supported housing 'reception places' in *Belgium* (651 in Dutch-speaking Belgium and 527 in French-speaking Belgium). The provision varies considerably in type and location, from row housing and apartments to farms and vacation houses in the countryside. In Dutch-speaking Belgium, 'general reception houses' form the largest group (44%). They vary considerably in size and while they are not designated for specific client groups, some specialise in provision for former prisoners or refugees and over 80% provide accommodation for men, while the remainder accommodate a mixed population of single men and women as well as families. Many reception houses are designed to facilitate a rapid 'move-on' of residents; others adopt a slower approach; most provide support on an individual basis and some mix this with group support provision.

Other types of supported accommodation in Dutch-speaking Belgium include residential care provision for women with children and for young adults as well as crisis reception centres and Social Rental Agencies (SRA) supported housing for young adults and homeless people. SRAs act as mediators between private sector landlords and support providers to offer homeless households supported housing (usually in self-contained dwellings) under a subleasing arrangement. In some cases, the sublease can be upgraded to a full tenancy enabling the occupants to remain in the dwelling even if support is no longer required. In contrast to this individualised and person-centred approach, 'pension housing' provides accommodation for up to 40 people who have lived in reception centres for over a year and are experiencing difficulties in moving on, either because they cannot adapt to independent living or because no suitable accommodation is available.

Pension houses are institutional in character with each client having his/her own room but sharing bathrooms and kitchens.

In contrast to Dutch-speaking Belgium, there is no official recognition of supported housing (*logements supervisés*) in French-speaking Belgium. However, there are reception centres comparable to the Dutch-speaking counterparts and supported housing is provided by SRAs through the 'social management of private rented accommodation'. These types of accommodation are designed to enlarge the number of available houses for vulnerable people. To the extent that tenants here experience an improved quality of housing with affordable rents and are provided with support, a person-centred approach similar in some respects to that in Dutch speaking Belgium, is in evidence.

Throughout Belgium, the providers of supported housing have to rent on the private market, buy houses or receive them through donation. Overall, supported housing in Belgium aims to conform to a set of specified criteria: centrally located and accessible, situated in a neighbourhood with a minimum of a separate room for each inhabitant and a communal area/meeting room. The emphasis is on ensuring that the infrastructure provides a safe place for people to live as autonomously as possible without stigma.

Perhaps France and Luxembourg provide the clearest examples of countries where the understanding of supported housing has developed in a reintegration (reinsertion) framework rather than a community care framework. The notion of supported housing is relatively recent in *France*, but the association between housing and social action has a long history and many precedents. Growth in supported housing grew out of the establishment of the right to housing in the early 1980s, and especially following the *Loi Besson* of 1990. Supported housing in France has a clear objective of reinsertion into the labour market and into wider society; it has developed alongside the adoption of the concept of social exclusion. Two types of support can be identified: *pacours residentiel*, whose aim is to provide the support necessary to enable people to move on from temporary to permanent accommodation in ordinary housing, and *accompagnement sociale*, which provides individualised support in stages, to enable a family or individual to move to more permanent accommodation. Several types of accommodation are provided ranging from general reception centres to centres designed to cater for specific target groups, such as young workers or immigrants.

Pels (1999) argues that supported housing in *Luxembourg* grew out of the perceived need to provide affordable housing with support, rather than from institutional decommissioning. Three types of supported housing can be identified in Luxembourg. First, group housing, which shares many of the characteristics of 'mini-institutions' providing high levels of support and community living in foyers and residential reception centres for vulnerable and disabled people. Second, shared small housing units, typically housing four to six people providing socioeducational support to people with lesser support needs. Third, *Wunnengshellef*, a group of associations works with private sector landlords and support agencies to provide individual houses or flats at moderate rents for a single person or a family to enable them to live independently with a modicum of support; the aim is to prepare people for fully autonomous living. As with SRAs in Belgium, the possibility of upgrading the subleasing arrangement to a full tenancy exists although, in practice, the likelihood of such a change is remote.

In *Austria* the term 'supported housing' is used to refer to a range of provision with different approaches, methods and standards (Schoibl, 1999). There is little commonality between these forms of provision other than that they simultaneously offer accommodation and support. Social care for specific target groups – such as older people, people with mental illness, people with disabilities, vulnerable young people and women fleeing domestic violence – is provided in either therapeutic communities, shared flats or self-contained dwellings. Shared accommodation is most common, self-contained dwellings are a fairly recent development. Homeless people *per se* are not an identified target group and what provision there is is mostly linked to reception centres, is fragmented and lacks coordination, although as indicated earlier (Chapter 4), some attempts are being made to bring a greater coherence and standardisation to the quality of support and accommodation provision.

In *Italy*, the nature of the accommodation varies depending on the type of programme under which it is provided. Where the objective of the reintegration plan is concerned with housing insertion then the accommodation is most likely to be in ordinary apartments. Where the aim of intervention is focused on other forms of support then transitional accommodation is provided in 'community lodgings' or protected housing. Ordinary housing with ordinary legal conditions of occupation makes up only a small part of the provision. The most common facilities are small shared apartments (maximum size of 12 people) organised on the model of 'community lodgings', the precise nature of which varies according to the type of provider agency and the focus of the service. Community lodgings range from larger apartments (12 beds) with shared bedrooms, to smaller two-bedroom apartments with individual bedrooms. The objective of community lodgings is to enable people to move on from dormitory and emergency accommodation, while the objective of protected apartments is to enable people to move on to independent living. The intended period of this transitional living is up to 18 months – although it often lasts longer due to the length of time required to find suitable alternative accommodation.

When considering accommodation provision for homeless people in Italy, Tosi and Ranci (1999) make the point that the distinction between emergency and transitional accommodation is becoming blurred. Dormitories, traditionally emergency accommodation, now also provide social support and are often linked with or associated with transitional accommodation. Thus, for example, the San Marcellino project in Genoa, in addition to having two dormitories, has organised a community lodging, a protected facility and sheltered housing. The Cena dell' Amicizia has also organised a transitional centre and 20 protected apartments. Such a linkage between emergency and transitional accommodation with support is common in all countries in this group (Austria, Belgium, France and Luxembourg) and may reflect the fact that, in the absence of comprehensive legislation on community care, supported housing has grown out of and alongside more traditional forms of provision for homeless people. The close physical and professional ties between emergency shelter provision and these transitional forms of provision may constrain the development of person-centred approaches as traditional working methods are transferred from more institutional to more individualised services.

Civil societies and supported accommodation

This section covers those countries with no formal provision of supported housing; that which exists is *ad hoc* and piecemeal. Indeed, in several EU countries the concept and practice of supported housing is not well established and there is little formal provision. O'Sullivan (1999), for example, suggests that "supported housing is a strange concept" in Ireland, and in Greece, Portugal, and to a lesser extent Spain, supported housing is notable by its virtual absence.

Spanish professionals and researchers increasingly subscribe to the idea that housing in itself does not constitute a mechanism of social integration, but that a series of risk factors or processes of exclusion exist, both individual and structural in nature. With this understanding, the home is seen as the family 'headquarters' and as the starting point for attempts to mitigate the processes that could result in the disintegration of the family and in the forfeiture of the home. In this context Leal Maldonado and Laínez (1999) identify the following types of supported housing. First, one of the more widely used formulas is the provision of *support within the home* itself, designed as an instrument for the prevention of disintegration. Second, *B&B accommodation* constitutes another common housing alternative. Third, *integrated housing in condominium flats* is used as an intermediate step for reintegration projects catering for homeless people moving from refuges and shelters. Fourth, *viviendas en propriedad* (homes in ownership) are used by institutions such as Fundació Privada Foment de l'Habitage Social to provide assistance to single-parent families coming from Caritás shelters or families facing eviction. Fifth, *transfers of public or private housing* to institutions of a social nature constitutes one of the most efficient ways of obtaining houses and assigning them to programmes for social integration. Occupancy agreements define compliance conditions and are linked to 'loan contracts' which lay down the criteria for rescinding occupancy if the agreement is violated. Sixth, *shared flats* offer a true housing option, providing a margin of privacy and greater independence than that provided by the shelters or refuges, while at the same time offering a space supervised by flatmates. Last, there are examples of pilot or innovative projects of housing in buildings with common areas that serve as a meeting point for neighbours, designed to support people or groups experiencing social difficulties. The *Mini-Residencia Cechanca* of the Fundación San Martín de Porres is an example of supported housing geared towards completing the normalisation or social process of reinsertion of the homeless, and there are plans to create a similar housing complex in Madrid directed mainly at families facing eviction.

In some countries, such as *Portugal*, *Greece* and *Ireland*, there are no nationally organised systems for the provision of supported accommodation. However, even here there are a number of fragmented programmes which provide support in relation to reintegration or homelessness projects and are often targeted at specific groups requiring particular types of support. In *Greece*, for example, transitory accommodation is provided to assist in the repatriation of Greeks from Pontos; equally hospital patients and people in prisons, asylums or other institutions are often able to access the special annexes of hospitals or rehabilitation centres or are provided with transitory housing as well as social and psychological support. The absence of a statutory framework for supported housing in *Ireland* is paralleled by the absence of dedicated funding for those voluntary groups who wish to provide elements of social support as well as physical dwellings. Supported housing, such as exists in Ireland, is provided by the voluntary sector who rely almost exclusively on their own resources. In *Portugal*, provision is characterised typically by transitional accommodation linked to traditional, low-threshold homeless hostels. The accommodation remains mostly institutional in form, although residents have their own bedrooms. There is a communal living area, day centre activities and meals are provided. Residents must have progressed to the point of having (or being able to undertake) paid employment and residence is time-limited to a period, normally, of four months.

The support dimension

In this section we examine the nature of support and the method of delivery in different welfare and housing situations in the EU member states. For the purposes of presentation, we adopt the same three-part grouping of countries employed previously. In Chapter 4 we suggested a three-part classification of support provision: housing support, counselling/skills support, and personal/healthcare support, each of which can be provided on a temporary or permanent basis, either as visiting, floating or as 24-hour, on-premises support (see Table 1). As we move through the three groups of countries which frame the following account, the range and scope of support narrows in terms of the variety on offer and in terms of its availability both geographically and socially. Those countries with an established national framework demonstrate the full range of support types, available, at least theoretically, to all needy segments of society. In those countries which have only a partial or no national framework, the range and scope of support diminishes to the extent that, in some instances, only specified target groups in particular, usually urban, areas have access to supported housing and then to a limited range.

Support provision in a deinstitutionalisation context

In the *UK*, while supported accommodation has experienced considerable development over the past 15 years, the concepts of support are not static; they continue to evolve, partly in response to changes in the funding regimes, and partly in response to changing ideas of best practice. Among the most topical issues currently being debated is the distinction between housing support and social care, and between social and healthcare. In the initial consultation to a major government review, the Department of Social Security (1998) produced a list of the different elements of support which conform to the three types identified in earlier chapters: housing, social and personal support (Table 8). These range from assistance with repairs and maintenance, through assistance with budgets, benefit claims and food preparation, to assistance with personal hygiene and medication.

While this identifies a fairly comprehensive list, the actual provision and delivery of support in the UK tends to reflect the dictates of the financing system rather than the needs or preferences of service users (Clapham and Munro, 1994). Different types of support services are funded in different ways – by subsidy to the housing provider for enhanced management, in the form of support services commissioned by social work, as health service payments or in the form of benefits to tenants – and as a consequence are often managed and delivered in different ways. A recent analysis of supported accommodation in Britain (DSS, 1998) found that such current funding streams are complicated, uncoordinated and overlapping and that no one has overall responsibility for ensuring quality or adequacy of support. As a result there is a tendency in supported accommodation to concentrate on high cost and highly intensive support packages. The lack of provision of low intensity, preventative support can sometimes result in some individuals receiving higher levels of support than they require but, perhaps more commonly, it results in vulnerable people missing out altogether on support provision, leading, almost invariably, to a failure of the tenancy followed by homelessness or transfer of residency to a high cost institutional setting.

In *Germany*, the definition of the kinds of support provided in supported housing is given in the guidelines for social welfare agents operating at the level of the *Länder*. The following agreement for Hesse can be cited as typical of the nature of support provision (Busch-Geertsema, 1999):

- for settling into a dwelling and managing everyday life which includes, among other things, the handling of financial matters, housekeeping, self-catering, organisation of leisure time, settlement of debts and arrangement of medical treatment;
- for securing the resources for housing costs;
- for crisis intervention;
- for establishing contacts in the community;
- for providing information on local support and advice services;
- for gaining access to education and work.

Table 8: Classification of support

Category A	Category B	Category C
Housing support	**Social support**	**Personal/nursing care**
• Assistance for tenants in arranging for plumbers, builders etc	• Assistance with budgeting/debt counselling	• Assistance at meal times
		• Assistance with personal hygiene/bathing/dressing/getting into bed
• Assistance for tenants in ensuring security of dwelling (eg reminding them to lock up)	• Help tenants feel they are individuals	
	• Assistance in claiming benefits	• Counselling to deal with alcohol/drug addiction, overcoming mental problems – including running group therapy sessions
• Arranging adaptations to cope with disability	• Dealing with disputes with neighbours	
• Controlling access	• Resettlement activities	
		• Administering/supervising taking of medication
• Minor repairs eg changing light bulbs, unblocking sinks	• Teaching life skills	
	• Advice on diet or food preparation	
	• After care support organising access to professional help/social services departments etc	
	• Liaison with relatives	
	• Arranging move on accommodation	
	• Reminding tenants to take medication	
	• Shopping	
	• Supervision of cooking food, storage, ironing etc	
	• 'Good neighbour' tasks (eg welfare checks)	
	• Arranging social events	
	• Arranging services of tenants' appliances	

Source: DSS (1998)

Busch-Geertsema (1999) indicates that, since most supported housing involves shared housing with time-limited tenancies, support also extends to dealing with housing arrangements after the termination of formal support provision. In contrast to the provision of support in the UK, this latter form of support is more orientated towards a philosophy of reintegration, an orientation which is emphasised by the time-limited nature of the provision. The national guidelines for social welfare agents at the *Länder* level suggests that the normal duration of support should not exceed 12 to 15 months.

The procedures for financing of support in Germany are laid down by the Federal Welfare Act, which deals with 'people with particular social difficulties'. These procedures establish the intensity of support offered based on ratios of personnel to clients which should "usually not be lower than 1:16" (BAG ueoe Tr, 1995, p 163). The Act also provides for higher staff-to-client ratios for so-called integrative support provided for people with special needs, such as drug addicts and people with a mental or physical disability. Typically, finance for support is individually tailored following an assessment of needs. In several *Bundesländer* a monthly lump sum is paid to support providers for each supported homeless person (based on this fixed ratio of staff to client).

In *Sweden* the 1994 Act of Support and Services (LSS) for people with disabilities identifies support and special services as embracing advice and other personal support which requires trained personnel, help through 'personal assistants' or key workers, foster care for young people and daily activities for adults who have no work and are not involved in education and special services. In 1998 more than 44,000 people received support under these provisions, the majority of whom were people with a learning disability for whom the most common form of support was personal counselling.

The precise forms of support provided reflect the purpose and objective of the different forms of housing (identified in the preceding section of this chapter) provided for specific client groups. In relation to regulated special housing and group homes, primarily aimed at people with learning disabilities, Sahlin (1999) describes a distinction between support aimed at cultivating individual skills linked to everyday living and independence, and social skills related to developing networks and social contacts. Support for homeless people is often defined in relation to a 'chain' or 'staircase' of supported accommodation where the nature and level of support is structured to the position on the staircase (see Sahlin, 1998). On this staircase housing conditions are gradually normalised and behaviour regulation loosened as a reward for good behaviour at each 'step'. Such a staircase starts in shelters with intense surveillance and strict rules, advances to flats in category houses without contracts or letting agreements and ends with a special contract in a normal, integrated flat, the contract for which is finally transferred to the tenant. This staircase of transition employs a place-centred form of support provision in that it explicitly links support to accommodation.

Twenty years ago, the normal routine for people with drug or alcohol dependencies in Sweden was an initial medical treatment and an observation period in a psychiatric clinic or mental hospital, after which the patients often (but not always) were transferred to institutions. This first stage has now been abolished. People with substance abuse problems generally must stop abusing substances first, and then prove their sobriety as an expression of their genuine ambition to be rehabilitated, before they are allowed any treatment resources. In 1994, the Commission for Alcohol Policy recommended that municipalities develop – instead of institutional care – more outpatient support and 'protected housing' for chronic addicts which include various degrees of social control. Results from a 1993 survey showed that 86% of the municipalities gave priority to 'outpatient care' and that 60% had implemented changes in this direction since 1991. According to a 1996 study, half of the municipalities had changed their policy for substance and alcohol abusers since 1992. It is difficult, however, to verify the extent to which these policies have actually changed practice. The support connected with these units often involves control and regulation more than personal assistance (Sahlin, 1999). Moreover, the requirement to prove sobriety prior to admission is likely to increase the risk of homelessness and particularly rooflessness for people who need support in order to abstain.

In *Finland*, four key types of support are identified, related to the purpose for which the supported accommodation is provided. These types of support are best understood in the context of a chain of care leading from institutional to community living. Thus the underlying philosophy of support relates to a de-institutionalisation rather than a reintegration philosophy. The first type of support we can identify in Finland is rehabilitative in nature, focused on assisting people to adjust to life outside an institution. Support in this context is also described as being therapeutic and is often delivered in a setting where the care is of an institutional nature (there is still a high level of control involved). The second type of support is equally controlling, but takes place in more ordinary settings, and is rehabilitative in nature. This form of support is aimed at people who are thought to need supervision and guidance because of their way of life linked to drug/alcohol abuse. The support is designed to guarantee that people will be capable of living in a normal housing environment without disturbing others. A third type of support provision is aimed at providing help in everyday situations, in household work and in financial matters. The fourth, and final, type of support focuses on the client's social activities and social relationships, with an explicit goal of finding meaningful activities for the client.

To understand the nature of support provision in Finland, it is necessary to posit supported housing as an intermediate service in a chain of care services. The nature of and approach to support is varied so that there are about 30 different professional titles in the field for permanent, part-time and voluntary jobs. The continuum of support occupations ranges from professional social workers, social counsellors and therapists to youth advisors, deacons, housing support workers and substance abuse counsellors. The use of voluntary support workers is increasingly important (Heinonen, 1997). The boundaries between professional and voluntary work are somewhat vague (Poteri, 1997), but voluntary work usually involves those aspects related to the issues that Wolfsenberger and Thomas (1983) describe as improving social relations and quality of life. It often involves recreation and conversation and activities based on relationships. Professional support, on the other hand, concentrates on counselling, skills attainment and related personal care which often involves an element of control. This may be mediated by the contractual nature of the special housing situation in which the support is provided and on which occupancy is conditional. Thus the need for control, to enable a person to adapt to independent living, and of development or emancipation, in which a person's social relationships are rebuilt, is moderated by the joint use of professional and voluntary support workers.

In the *Netherlands*, as in many other countries, the form of support differs according to the type of support project involved. In supported housing projects the form of support is similar to that described as enhanced housing management in the UK context. It does not include any element of personal care, although skills training and counselling are involved. In 'ambulatory' support projects 'coaching' is aimed at tenants who live independently but have difficulty sustaining a tenancy as a result of rent arrears or anti-social behaviour and tends to be focused on housing management support (de Feijter and Blok, 1999). Three forms of support are offered in social boarding houses:

- *care:* including meals, personal care and assistance with medication;
- *support:* dealing with [family] relationships, daily activities, assistance with institutions and form filling;
- *control:* dealing with behaviour, living conditions and conformity to house rules.

Supported housing in the Netherlands is characterised by a variety of different types of contract between the client, the service provider and the housing provider. These contracts link directly the type of support provided to the ability to sustain a tenancy or independent living. Four types of contracts are defined:

- *pension agreements* in which the emphasis lies more on care than on housing and the client pays an all-in price which includes food, care and housing;
- *rent and coaching contracts:* the rent contract terminates when the 'coaching' ends; in supported housing the client makes both contracts with the service provider, whereas in ambulatory coaching projects clients agree a rent-contract with a housing association and a support contract with a service provider;
- *standard rent-contracts:* clients have a normal rent contract with a housing association and separately agree an ambulatory support contract with a service provider;
- *rent contracts with a service provider:* the client agrees a standard rent contract with a service provider, with additional support clauses included (FO, 1998, p 18).

Support provision in *Denmark* is increasingly characterised by the decentralisation of responsibility from central to local government, by a concerted move to de-institutionalisation and by the recognition that social assistance is a civil and universal right. Current legislation clearly indicates that responsibility for support provision lies with municipalities who are entrusted with the duty of ensuring that there exist appropriate mechanisms for the provision of assistance, care, and general support as well as facilities for the rehabilitation of people with physical or mental disabilities or special social problems. While formulated in a very general way, the Social Assistance legislation of 1995 and 1998 clearly indicates that the support can now be provided independently, that is, separately from housing. The level and intensity of support provided is variable. In one municipality it averages 10 hours of support per person a week. In the core and clusters schemes the amount of support varies from two full-time employees for every 16 residents, to two full-time employees for six residents. The support is given according to an estimate of the resident's needs, and it appears to be more intensive than in the 105 institutions.

Support provision in reintegration countries

In *Austria*, social care is provided for defined target groups – mentally ill people, older people, people with disabilities and, to a lesser extent, young people and women fleeing domestic violence. Support for homeless people *per se* is less well developed or targeted and tends to be unregulated and characterised by insecure funding. Some of these latter problems are recognised and presently being addressed. As in Denmark and elsewhere, there is a purposeful decentralisation of responsibility which has led to an uneven development of services between provinces, with smaller provinces, such as Vorarlberg and Salzburg, better serviced than larger provinces such as Nether-Austria and Styria (Schoibl, 1999). Support provision overall has a strong emphasis on counselling and is closely linked with obtaining access to a job, that is, reintegration objectives. Supported housing in Austria developed from the 'bottom up'; it has not been introduced as a result of systematic planning.

Support and care in Austria are provided by non-governmental bodies, and are characterised by high levels of part-time and non-contract employment. Few staff are professionally qualified, and security and administrative staff tend to be over-represented. This imbalance is sometimes reflected in low standards of service provision. Over half of all qualified support staff are female.

Supported housing is more or less well established in all areas of social work in Austria, but until recently there was no standardisation of provision. Supported housing, in the sense of mobile and individual support in single or family accommodation, was introduced in areas which are not connected directly with services for the homeless. Recent developments include the provision of high standard support for senior citizens, designed to enable them to maintain autonomous living. These services – nursing, medical care and support in the household – have been established in addition to and as an alternative to the traditional provisions of residential housing. Other recent developments include the provision of mobile support for vulnerable young people in dispersed, individual flats. This service, while still not available in all provinces, is designed with the objective of moving young people on from the intensively supported context of youth welfare (in their families or in pedagogic, partly therapeutic communities) to autonomous living. Direct access to supported, individual housing is still exceptional and restricted to the target group of youths of 18+ years. The anticipated adoption of provincial legislation for individual support in communities – as currently exists in some provinces – will provide appropriate regulation for these types of support and furthermore ensure appropriate standards and secure financial foundations.

With regard to psychological and social support for individuals with chronic psychiatric illnesses outside the hospitals there is a longer tradition in ambulant and mobile support provision in a family context. Recently this approach has been complemented by the provision of supported housing in single and dispersed flats. Innovative developments are being experimented with in some areas. In Upper-Austria, for example, non-governmental service providers have started to build up small informal neighbourhood networks of clients so that they can easily come into contact with and obtain informal support for everyday activities.

The link between these support services and those provided to other target groups, such as homeless people and women fleeing from domestic violence, are limited. There is a lack of professional communication, and although the same support services are available to homeless people, their access to these services can be inhibited by the lack of systematic contacts. In relation to services for the homeless there is an evident trend in the direction of the provision of more mobile support in individual homes as well as in the direction of diversification according to specific target groups (Schoibl, 1999). As a result of an insufficient legislative foundation and inappropriate means of financing, these developments have not been established throughout the country; there are also differences in the standards of accommodation and individual support between the services in the same county and/or town.

The objectives of support provision in *Belgium* are explicitly geared to concepts of normalisation, independent living (according to individual capacity) and integration. The role of welfare workers in the support provision can be seen in terms of mediation, facilitation and stimulation. De Decker and Hardouin (1999) describe this as "walking alongside" rather than "leading" the client. Support is offered through an integrated approach which seeks to identify individual needs and match those needs to specific support programmes. Thus, the range of support offered is wide and includes: material support, psychosocial support, personal care and counselling.

The principal target group of supported housing is homeless people, particularly those threatened by institutionalisation and those unable to access social housing or private rental due to support needs. Clients are usually people who need support in order to live as independently as possible within the community. Some clients may eventually be able to live independently without support but many will continue to require some level of support for a period of time.

In both France and Luxembourg support is explicitly directed by reintegration goals, designed to rehabilitate clients into society and into the workplace as far as possible. In *France*, support is available for budgeting, for the maintenance and improvement of housing and common areas, as well as for information and for improvement in neighbour relations. Under the *Loi Besson* of 1990, the dominant and explicit aims of social care were identified as: assistance in identifying housing needs and options; practical support to maintain tenancies (housing management support); and social support for integration into the labour market and for social reinsertion.

Support has evolved from its foundations in socioeducational interventions delivered by specialist professionals, into a more generalised notion of support delivered by professionals from a wide range of backgrounds. Accompanying this there has been a shift from a focus on education to 'mediation' – similar to the change identified in Belgium from 'top-down' to 'alongside' clients. The objective is to allow disadvantaged households to maintain a house in their own right. Two broad categories of support can be identified. First, general social support delivered by social workers who diagnose problems, search for practical solutions and seek agreement from the user. In these circumstances social workers act as assessors of need and as mediators to facilitate access to other professionals; support is time-limited. Second, individualised support – *accompagnement sociale lié au logement* – which may be delivered by a qualified social worker or by other specialists. This type of support is directed at problem clients and is designed to provide housing, health, employment and training. Specialised support can include all the support types provided under general social support, but in a more intensive form; it also includes budget management and access to public services.

Examples of support provision in France include younger worker foyers providing socioeducational support in groups rather than individually, support for immigrants, which is primarily social support combined with information and advice, and support for homeless people, often attached to existing reception centres and involving individualised and short-term programmes to help access to housing. In all these examples, support is focused primarily on reinsertion into the housing market and less on changing behaviour.

Luxembourg, in pursuing social and labour market integration, has targeted seven groups for supported housing: homeless people, people at risk from homelessness, immigrants and refugees, women, young people, disabled people and people with substance dependence and/or mental illness. Support services are equally divided among these with a slight favouring of services for women. There are no services provided exclusively for homeless people; indeed mixed targeting (seen as something positive in rehabilitation work) is encouraged. A wide range of support services is offered with the primary goal of encouraging independent living. The most comprehensive of these is the *prise en charge totale*, which provides for all basic needs – food day and night, physical care, mental care, personal support and counselling, as well as laundry, budgeting and administration.

In *Italy*, Tosi and Ranci (1999) distinguish between the forms of support provided to people who are at risk of social exclusion and those forms aimed at people who are already homeless. In the first situation, support is aimed at prevention, protection or cushioning of the crisis situation. Support consists of special services, provided by voluntary associations or local authorities. Called 'services for adults in difficulty', they cover a wide range of issues – help with benefit payments, work and housing advice. The second support situation is aimed at people experiencing 'serious *marginalisation*', including the *senza dimora* (those of no abode), and is aimed at social reintegration. The integration measures combine a range of support action which can include:

- economic support, including a discretionary municipal 'minimal survival' benefit and 'shopping vouchers';
- social support, which can include counselling and therapy, but is essentially aimed at social relations and structuring daily life;
- work support, including job training and related skills to facilitate entry to the job market.

Within Italy a target group of particular interest in the context of supported housing are foreign immigrants. Supported accommodation aimed at foreign immigrants have three functions: facilitating housing and social insertion at the arrival stage, assistance with housing integration to deal with specific or additional difficulties that immigrants meet in the job market, and assisting/reintegrating immigrants suffering severe hardship or marginalisation. The latter case may be assimilated with those identified above, but accommodation specifically designed for immigrants is often used. A two-stage approach to the provision of support for immigrants can be identified. First, the provision of temporary accommodation on arrival in special purpose structures with support for housing and social insertion. Second, transitional arrangements, in more permanent special-purpose structures or in ordinary housing, with support for housing integration and for dealing with specific difficulties that immigrants may encounter in the employment market. In both cases housing is the primary element of the intervention. The social support consists of advice and orientation and social work support during the first stage and of social work support and/or intervention in the housing market during the second stage.

Support provision in a civil society context

In those countries where there is little formal recognition of supported housing, at least at a national level, trends in the provision of support suggest that the philosophy and objectives that drive supported housing in other countries, where formal provision is more apparent, are also present. In *Spain*, for example, while the concept of community care is not well advanced and reinsertion is the declared primary objective, the concepts of normalisation and independent living are very much to the fore. In Spain supported housing is largely the province of charitable and church-based NGOs, with the backing of at least some of the autonomous regions and municipalities. The role of a national state is limited to the provision of some finance and to the formulation of general policy issues (Leal Maldonado and Laínez, 1999). The major increases which have taken place in the past few years in the provision of support in people's own homes rather than in communal houses or transitory residential centres, provides tangible evidence of a move in the direction of the adoption of the 'ideal' model of support in housing.

Despite the sparse and uneven provision of supported housing in Spain, the relative sophistication of its provision, albeit within an exclusively reinsertion framework, is demonstrated in that it is recognised and accepted that full autonomous living is not an objective that is in everyone's reach. Supported housing provision in Spain also embraces the view that the specific needs of different target groups need to be responded to in a differentiated way. There is further recognition of the variability of clients within specific category needs. For example, people with drug/alcohol problems are typically divided into two groups: those who wish to give up, and those who cannot give up. The latter are directed to damage reduction and risk limitation programmes. This provision falls short of individually tailored support, but suggests a recognition of the issue and a move in that direction.

With reinsertion objectives in mind, the focus of support in Spain tends to emphasise income and the acquisition of life skills designed to assist in the move to independent living. Financial aid, in particular, is seen as a key component in that it provides for rent and other aspects of housing finance. But support also embraces access to information on housing and work, advice on other issues of housing management such as rental agreements and training in interpersonal skills and workplace skills. The support provided reflects the type of housing: shelters and refuges focus on personal recovery, training and work capability; so-called insertion flats and shared flats focus on home economics, the administration of resources, relationships with neighbours and cohabitation skills. Throughout there is an increasing emphasis on the flexibility of provision with a decisive movement away from regimented and formulaic provision (Leal Maldonado and Laínez, 1999).

In Greece, Portugal and Ireland the level of supported housing provision, as noted earlier in this chapter, is very restricted. Indeed in *Portugal* and *Ireland* currently available information (O'Sullivan, 1999; Bruto da Costa, 1999) suggests that, while there is apparently some awareness of the potential of supported housing in addressing problems of homeless and other vulnerable people, the practice of supported housing is effectively encompassed in a few projects run by charitable and/or church-based NGOs (the Emaus project in Lisbon being one such example). Vulnerable groups in society are accommodated in an institutional setting or in short-term emergency accommodation, where support and care are more about containment than directed at independent living objectives.

In *Greece*, supported housing is, likewise, not widespread and where present is directed at rather specific groups whose support needs are largely predetermined by the providers. However, despite its relative underdevelopment, Sapounakis (1999) is able to identify six groups who benefit from supported housing provision, each with specific support needs. The first and second of these groups – workers and employees and people at risk from homelessness – stretches the definition of supported housing in that support is confined to financial aid in the form of benefits and loans designed to allow the acquisition of secure and affordable housing. The third group comprises 'Greeks from Pontos', whose support requirements are identified as assistance with 'social integration', and this is provided in a planned four-stage programme. The fourth of Sapounakis' groups includes 'people in the process of de-institutionalisation'. In explicitly recognising the needs of this group for supported housing, Greece, at least tentatively, would seem to be moving beyond an exclusive focus on reintegration to embrace care in the community concepts. Support for this group is also identified as designed to achieve social integration. However, reinforcing the tentative nature of its adoption, support involves only the provision of temporary accommodation; there is no systematic programme of social, personal or work-related support provision. The fifth group is the 'Romany population'. Again, although the objective is social integration, support goes little beyond the provision of accommodation. Homeless people make up the final group. Yet again support concentrates on the provision of shelter, in this case, on time-limited residence in temporary accommodation. The Ministry of Health and Welfare has set up a programme called 'Popular Housing', targeted in part on homeless people; this allows for the provision of support in the form of economic benefits (social support is not included). The impact of the programme has so far remained minimal due to shortage in funds.

In Sapounakis' (1999) judgement, "there is not one, but many supported accommodation policies, the number of policies being equal to the number of existing programmes in the field" (p 15). Such national policies that exist for social cohesion and reintegration of the particular target groups stemming from European Union initiatives, have only been elaborated quite recently, and have not been widely applied. Social service provision for vulnerable groups in Greece operates separately and independently from the provision of accommodation and housing.

The management dimension: integrating housing and support

In this section we discuss two aspects of the management of supported housing. Both are central to the effective delivery of supported housing. Under *resourcing* we examine three interrelated issues: the problems arising from a lack of resources devoted to the collection of data and statistical evidence on the supply of and demand for supported housing; the problems of securing proper funding, especially revenue funding and problems associated with the shortfall in the availability of trained housing and support staff. Under *coordination and delivery* we examine the problems associated with the difficulties of securing efficient collaboration between the various agencies – especially housing and social services – involved in the provision of supported housing.

Resourcing

For supported housing to be effective it is necessary to match supply to identified needs and to be able to establish priorities for investment in the face of restricted budgets. This requires the availability of appropriate information at a detailed, local, level of aggregation. Evidence from all countries, even those with the most developed provision of supported accommodation, indicates that data collection is not a strong feature of service planning and provision. In the UK, partial information is available for housing association provision (in England) and the stock of supported housing (in Scotland). A survey of supported housing was undertaken in 1998 in Finland in connection with this research. Elsewhere, homelessness NGOs have been developing databases of service users (for example in the Netherlands, Luxembourg, Austria and Germany), which includes support provision where this is a feature of service provision. Despite these examples of national, local and organisational information systems, it is apparent that there is generally a dearth of information which militates against a rational system of planning and management. This lacuna also means that an evaluation of the effectiveness of supported housing in achieving desired outcomes is difficult to undertake. Where target figures for planned expansion of supported housing are in evidence (for example in the *Bundesländ* Hesse in Germany) the suspicion is that these are influenced more by financial considerations than by an understanding of need (Busch–Geertsema, 1999, p 24).

This information inadequacy is even more starkly highlighted when the lack of funding for capital construction and support provision is considered. The major funding issues surround the financing of the ongoing revenue costs of support provision, rather than the 'bricks and mortar' costs of accommodation, which determines the nature of management and provision of supported housing in a number of ways. In many countries social services authorities have legally defined obligations towards particular groups (elderly people and young people for example). In a cash-limited scenario other groups, such as the homeless, which are not a priority group for social services support, can lose out, unless specific initiatives are developed (for example, the rough sleepers initiative in the UK, or the national homelessness strategy in Finland).

There is often a confusion of departmental responsibilities and, in the context of decentralisation of responsibility from central government, concern that the devolution of budgets will lead to greater fragmentation of services. In the UK, for example, the major debate surrounds the issue of 'who pays' and whether housing, care and health costs can be distinguished in departmentalised funding systems (see Chapter 3). In other countries (Germany, Austria, Denmark) this split of responsibilities for housing and support costs occurs between tiers of government (regions or *Länder* and municipalities). This difficulty of distinguishing between housing costs and support costs which are eligible for subsidy is identified in most countries, despite the diversity of tenure structure and welfare systems. Thus the resource issue is not simply about the level of funding; it also involves the need to ensure the coordination and cooperation between departments and agencies involved in funding, management and provision.

It has been identified earlier that the provision of supported housing generally involves local authorities as purchasers and voluntary organisations as providers of services. Competition for funding and the need for authorities to ensure 'best value' is likely to become a determining and controlling factor in which the systemisation and reduction of costs lead to rationalisation (and rationing) of support providers in the future. In this context it may also be easier to justify the provision of high intensity support services based on crisis intervention rather than preventive measures (Aldridge, 1999; Tosi and Ranci, 1999). Indeed, concern is already evident in many countries that support provision tends to be reactive rather than proactive (preventive), resulting in imbalances in support relative to needs (see, for example, the UK, Italy, Germany, Belgium and Austria).

Schoibl (1999) suggests that, in Austria, with the exception of a few umbrella organisations (*Arbeitsgemeinschaften*), which are able to negotiate a single long-term contract for common services such as supported housing, the majority of service providers depend on annual renewable contracts which are negotiated with different partners at the federal, regional and local levels. This uncertainty in funding for supported housing is also repeated in many other countries and must be a factor, we assume, in explaining the relatively low levels of provision and the slow pace of dissemination. There is also evidence from diverse social welfare systems (Greece, Portugal and Spain on the one hand and Sweden, Finland and Germany on the other) of a continuing reliance on funding by philanthropy which is also likely to militate against rational and long-term planning and management. A related aspect of this uncertainty in funding structures is the frequently reported time limits set for support provision where this is associated with reintegration of homeless people. The *Landschaftsverband Rheinland* assesses the maximum period for the resettlement of 'people without a settled way of living' at 12 months, while elsewhere in Germany (Stuttgart) it can be 18 months to a maximum of three years. Time limits from four months to 15 months are mentioned in countries as diverse as Austria, the Netherlands and Portugal. Whether or not such time limits are realistic in the process of resettlement of homeless people, their impact is to act as an effective rationing device.

If transitional supported accommodation is to be successful in moving people from street living to permanent housing, there will be a need for both outreach work with people living on the streets and for follow-on support for people who leave supported accommodation for permanent normal housing. Experience in this respect is mixed. In some countries there is a developed approach to the provision of 'ambulatory support or coaching' (the Netherlands, Germany); in other countries practice has developed in a philosophy of reintegration to provide supported housing (Italy, France). However, where transitional supported accommodation is provided, it is often reported that the funding of outreach and follow-on support is the most precarious.

The availability of finance, together with the conditions under which it is regulated, have a direct impact on the staffing of support provision. This is most clearly evident where there are regulations governing the ratio of staff to users laid down by funding providers (Germany and the UK, for example). Funding procedures or criteria can also affect the quality or type of staff employed. In both the UK and Germany, for example, rules which require suitably qualified staff have a direct effect on costs of projects. A reliance on voluntary work is also evident, in contexts from the Nordic countries to the Mediterranean countries. In Finland, for example, supported housing for people with mental health problems is based on voluntary work to the extent that the volunteers are involved in drawing up the individual service plans. In Spain, for example, according to their 1997 annual report, *Caritás* mobilised 47,933 volunteers.

Coordination and delivery of supported housing services

The effective management of supported housing involves issues of coordination and collaboration, both in relation to the partnership between housing, social services and health, and between public authorities and NGOs in the organisation and provision of services, and in relation to the integration of housing and support.

The partnership between agencies can best be understood in relation to our threefold typology of countries described earlier. In those countries where supported housing has emerged from a de-institutionalisation/care in the community framework, there is a tendency for structures of coordination to be driven more by the 'enabling' authorities and for the agenda to be determined more by the requirement to plan for the needs of particular client groups (for which agencies have statutory responsibility). In Finland, for example, coordination operates through the direct purchaser–provider split between public and voluntary agencies. In the 1980s supported housing became almost entirely the responsibility of the municipal authorities following which the dominant trend has been for municipalities to purchase services from voluntary organisations. In this system, the service provider and the municipality enter into a contract where the client is housed by the municipal authority in mainstream housing, while the voluntary organisation provides the necessary support. In the UK, legislation in 1990 required social services authorities to prepare community care plans which are required to make an assessment of needs for support and encouraged the use of a variety of providers from all sectors.

In countries where reintegration philosophies prevail, partnership arrangements have emerged both from top-down and from bottom-up initiatives. Austria exemplifies the emergence of bottom-up structures of local agencies, France describes a coordination which has a framework of public sector direction. The Italian example, as described by Tosi and Ranci (1999), provides evidence of the range of approaches which have been evident in such countries. They describe three forms of interaction between public and private sector actors and the role played by the public sector in coordinating services, and the nature of the networks on which third sector agencies depend. First, the coordination of policy is exemplified in the city of Bologna, where the Technical Committee for problems of marginalisation, established by the Municipality in 1991, comprises agencies working with the *senza dimara* (roofless) which meets monthly to consider operational issues. This has recently led to the establishment of a Permanent Committee on Social Exclusion as a standing conference to consider problems of marginalisation involving housing, work and social problems at a more strategic level. Secondly, Tosi and Ranci describe cooperation in relation to individual reintegration plans for users which are agreed jointly between *Caritás*, areas' social services and the adult social services office. Finally, they describe public-voluntary sector purchaser–provider contractual agreements.

Housing and support can be linked in different ways, each of which have implications for the methods of support delivery, funding and the housing rights of the service user. If we consider the possible combinations of housing and support provision independently of the particular housing or welfare system in operation, then it is possible to identify the following three broad set of arrangements. First, the single agency model where the same agency is responsible for the provision of both the accommodation and the support. Second, the two agency model where different agencies are responsible for housing and support provision; this can occur either where the housing provider buys support for its tenants, or where the support or welfare agency buys housing for its clients. Third, the partnership model, where a managing agency establishes partnership arrangements with a number of different housing providers and support providers. The types of arrangements that emerge reflect a number of factors including housing tenure, the importance of the voluntary sector in provision, the nature of contracting arrangements (in a purchaser–provider model), as well as legislative structures. The importance of separating the landlord functions from the support role is understood to be a model of best practice, but is not always achieved.

The UK and the Netherlands are examples of countries where housing associations play an important role in the provision of supported housing. Practice is different in the two countries since the role of associations in the Netherlands is restricted to supplying housing, while in the UK associations are often support providers as well as housing providers. In the Netherlands, the housing association leases accommodation to a service provider who allocates the dwelling and it is the service provider who guarantees the rent and absorbs the risk of vacancies. Although government policy in the UK places an emphasis on interagency and partnership working in the planning and delivery of support services, in practice a range of models of provision as indicated above have emerged.

In *Germany*, the dominance of the private rented housing sector, and of the primary role given to voluntary organisations in the provision of social welfare and support services by the Federal Welfare Act, could lead to a potentially complex situation in the management and provision of supported living. A typology of organisational arrangements for support and housing is given in the Bundesarbeitsgemeinschaft Wohnungslosenhilfe (1998), which is adapted by Busch-Geertsema (1999; see Table 9). This typology illustrates that only in type a is housing and support clearly separated. In type b the risks implied in the tenancy or housing administration lie with the agency responsible for providing the support. This confusion of support and landlord roles can lead to a more precarious situation for residents. In types c and d the resident has no tenancy rights. Although the separation of housing and support is understood to be an essential requirement of good practice, the provision of supported housing has been predominated by those types which closely link housing and support and are organised by one agency.

In countries such as Italy, where "integration and multi-dimensional approaches are the key words of the new social services culture and policies" (Tosi and Ranci, 1999, p 22), organisational arrangements reflect the objectives of reintegration. It is also probable that the diversity of practice reflects the local authority approach, the importance of the voluntary sector and the significance of owner-occupation as a tenure. The case studies in evidence in Italy describe:

- agencies which provide both accommodation and support directly, usually employing individual reintegration plans (Farsi Prossimo in Milan, and the Adult Social Services office in Bologna are voluntary sector and municipal examples);
- services that offer integrated support and which use the network of services to find accommodation for people (the Siloe of Milan, the advice centre of the *Caritás* in Bologna);
- associations which make apartments they own available and take referrals from parishes and social services offices, delegating social support to the referring agency (the Riparo of Turin is one example).

In the Nordic countries, the legislative framework identifies municipal responsibilities for the provision of support. Thus while different arrangements of accommodation and support provision exist (see earlier sections), the common features are the provision of special housing and ordinary apartments by municipal authorities and the purchasing of services from support providers. Following the enactment of social services legislation in 1982 in Finland it was intended that supported housing become almost entirely municipal, but at present supported housing is provided by municipalities and voluntary organisations alike. The Finnish municipalities have considerable autonomy for providing social and health services in their region, but it is a dominant trend that

Table 9: Types of combination of support and housing in Germany

Type of combination of support and housing	Agency in charge of provision with housing	Agency in charge of provision with social support
a Tenancy and support are strictly separate and are managed by different organisations	Private landlord, housing enterprise or welfare organisation in the voluntary sector not acting as support agency	Usually welfare organisation in the voluntary sector
b Tenancy or housing administration are managed by the same organisation	Same agency as the one responsible for social support (voluntary welfare organisation)	Usually welfare organisation in the voluntary sector
c Supported housing in a dwelling which is (part of) an institution and let to homeless persons for use (no tenancy contract)	Same agency as the one responsible for social support (voluntary welfare organisation)	Usually welfare organisation in the voluntary sector
d To avoid danger to public order and security a dwelling is assigned to homeless person by municipality without any legal tenants' rights where the homeless person receives personal support	Municipality	Usually welfare organisation in the voluntary sector

Source: Busch-Geertsema (1999), adapted from Bundesarbeitsgemeinschaft Wohnungslosenhilfe (1998)

municipalities purchase services from organisations. In Denmark legislation in 1995 and 1998 has formalised the separation of housing and support provision making it possible for the municipalities and the regional counties to organise the provision of measures with respect to the individual, independent of the type of dwelling in which she or he is living (Børner Stax et al, 1999).

In countries such as Portugal, Spain and Greece, where supported housing is often provided in the form of transitional accommodation linked to traditional homelessness shelters, the same agency coordinates the integration of support services in their own accommodation. However, the Spanish evidence reminds us that the level of home ownership means that "the excessive commercialism of housing has been an obstacle regarding many projects for independence" (Leal Maldonado and Laínez, 1999, p 29). Thus financial support and assistance is an important component of reintegration strategies for people who can not access appropriate housing.

Conclusion

Supported housing is a relatively new concept in most EU countries. Its current popularity is in part explained by the adoption of a social exclusion perspective on social welfare (see Chapter 2), which provides a vehicle for the combination of reinsertion policies with those of community care. Where supported housing has been introduced, its advantages and potential have been widely recognised, although this is not an uncontested conclusion (see Chapter 8). However, the effectiveness and contribution of supported housing, even in those countries where it has been widely adopted, has been limited by resourcing problems and by problems of administration and coordination. In those countries where supported housing has, so far, made only a minimal impact, its adoption is curtailed by similar problems of resourcing.

SIX

The contribution of supported housing to the prevention of homelessness

This chapter uses the understanding, developed in Chapter 5, of the main dimensions of accommodation, support and management in order to consider the contribution which supported accommodation, or supported housing, may make in the prevention of homelessness and in the reintegration of homeless people in Europe. In this respect we accept the argument that:

> ... strategies for a permanent solution of the problem (of homelessness) may not be restricted to housing provision, but their conception has to include services in support of housing from the start: aids and support to secure the standard of living, to organise everyday life, to restore and maintain health and to establish social contacts. (Deutsches Bundestag, 1998, p 2)

Our assessment aims to identify common themes and trends where these exist and to reflect diversity of practice. Differences in practice between countries may, in part, be the result of different systems of social welfare and social protection. However, they may also be the result of different approaches to the resettlement or reintegration of homeless people into the community. Practice may also differ as a consequence of the development of particular systems of service delivery and implementation – in other words, the result of good or innovatory practice. Consideration of both the commonality and divergence of practice should assist in understanding the factors which may contribute to the successful use of support in the prevention of homelessness or in the reintegration and resettlement of homeless people.

The empirical evidence from the national reports of the correspondents of the European Observatory on Homelessness is used to assess the role of supported housing in meeting the needs of different groups of homeless people. This discussion is developed within the context of a generally low level of provision of supported accommodation (or supported housing) throughout Europe, and a particular lack of provision in some countries (such as Greece, Ireland, Portugal and Spain). We conclude by making the case for the development of more accommodation with support to meet the objective of reintegration of homeless people into society, and raise policy and practice questions regarding such development.

Access and availability

Supported housing will only be effective in meeting the needs of homeless people if they are able to gain access to it, and there are several reasons why homeless people may have difficulty in gaining such access. First, there is a lack of provision relative to need, either of supported housing, of suitable accommodation within which support can be delivered, or of support services. Second, the lack of provision may be manifest in a spatial concentration of supported housing, resulting, for example, in a paucity of provision in rural areas or, in countries with a federal structure or highly decentralised system of governance, in particular parts of the country. Third, 'gatekeepers' filter the allocation of this scarce resource. This may result in systems of assessment and allocation which favour only those homeless people who, in the judgement of the gatekeepers, are most likely to benefit (ie be able to live independently), or who can demonstrate a motivation to change their behaviour to conform to norms of the provider organisation. Finally, the process or trajectory of homelessness may itself exclude homeless people from this housing option; for example, if available supported housing has been developed as part of a process of institutional closure, then people coming from an institution will have easier access than people coming from within the community. Additionally, it is frequently the case that existing supported housing is targeted at particular client groups (for example substance abusers or people with learning disabilities); this will restrict its availability to other categories of homeless people.

There is a low level of provision of supported housing in all countries of the EU, even in those countries where institutional closure has progressed furthest. It is difficult to estimate the precise scale of provision, due in part to the differences in definition (which are described in Chapter 4), and also to the fact that, with some notable exceptions such as the UK, there is a lack of consistent national data available. In order to confirm that this low level of provision also represents a 'lack' of provision, it would be necessary to have a measure of need as well as of supply. Nowhere is the data robust enough to allow such comparisons to be made. Yet we can, with some certainty, conclude, since the level of provision is so low in most countries, that, even using the most modest estimates of need (for a range of client groups), the prevailing levels of provision also represent an underprovision.

There is evidence in most countries, where supported accommodation exists, that the provision is very highly concentrated geographically. In the UK, for example, supported accommodation is concentrated in the major metropolitan areas (especially in London and in Glasgow). Even in countries with a more rural or dispersed population, such as Finland and Sweden, the evidence indicates that supported accommodation is concentrated in the urban areas. Such concentration reflects, in part, population distribution, even though the degree of concentration is more exaggerated, and hence also reflects the focus of activities of provider organisations. However, such spatial concentration may also reflect the municipal origins of innovations which have not yet disseminated to other non-metropolitan regions. In Germany the 'Experimental Housing Construction and Urban Development' scheme led to the development of supported housing projects in particular urban areas (Busch-Geertsema, 1998). In Belgium, there is a clear difference in the legal framework, and therefore the nature of supported housing, between the Dutch-speaking and the French-speaking communities, which has a clear impact on the spatial distribution of supported housing in that country. In Italy, differences in regional or provincial legislation lead to a spatial variation in provision which is reflected, overall, in a concentration in the northern regions.

Access to the available stock of supported accommodation is constrained by procedures of assessment and allocation as well as by the nature of the accommodation itself (for example a large proportion of supported accommodation is shared accommodation and, in some countries, is located in the private rented sector). While the ideal model is often seen to be the provision of support to people living in 'ordinary', self-contained housing, in reality designated shared supported housing or group homes constitute the main form of provision. It is often the case that such accommodation is intended for (or restricted to) people who are determined (on the basis of social work assessment) to possess sufficient capacity or motivation to progress to independent living. For example, in Finland,

A person who is considered incapable of independent living may not be eligible, and the same applies to uncooperative clients or persons who probably will not benefit from supported housing. (Kärkkäinen, 1999, p 17)

[In Italy] ... facilities are designed for persons in the pre-independence stage, people who have already followed a reintegration plan: ... are not yet ready for their own completely independent accommodation. (see Tosi and Ranci, 1999, p 25)

It is also evident that the nature of the shared living arrangements in the majority of supported accommodation can, of itself, exclude some people. Because of the need to exercise a 'duty of care' to all clients in a shared house or group home, people with a chaotic lifestyle or 'challenging behaviour' may not be admitted to such supported housing (Edgar and Mina-Coull, 1999).

In Chapter 1 (Figure 1) we defined three trajectories of homelessness which can characterise the route to supported accommodation for people living in institutions, living in the community or for people sleeping rough. A cursory consideration of this model suggests that the process of access and allocation will differ in each of the three trajectories. For people living in institutions, access to supported accommodation will often be facilitated by a reprovisioning process involving formal assessment and funding procedures. For people sleeping rough, access to supported accommodation will often be part of a resettlement process commencing in (traditional) homeless hostels. For people living within the community, access to supported housing will often arise as a result of a life crisis. In Britain, for example, the main reason cited for rehousing people in supported accommodation related to people who were required or asked to leave home. This was the main reason given for women fleeing domestic violence, vulnerable young women with children, young people and single adult homeless people.

What is the contribution of supported housing?

Before we consider the contribution of support provision, it is important to recall that some homeless people may not want, or need, to receive support in order to be resettled into permanent housing. Equally some people will find their network of social relationships (and social support) on the street or in hostel accommodation and thus challenge the professional view that the end point of reintegration is settled housing (see Aldridge, 1998). There are, however, a proportion of homeless (roofless) people who do require support if they are to live independently in the community. In the UK, for example, it has been estimated that as many as three quarters of rough sleepers would require support in order to be rehoused successfully (Randall and Brown, 1993). In this context it is possible to distinguish between those who have support (or care) needs which they are not able to access because of their homeless circumstances, and those who need support during the rehousing process. The former situation perhaps reflects the need for improved integration of services; the latter reflects the need for new forms of service delivery.

To understand the contribution of supported housing to the prevention of homelessness it is necessary first to consider the relationship it has to the provision of services for homeless people, and to understand the objectives which it may fulfil. Edgar et al (1999) identified the nature of services for homeless people in relation to the three categories of emergency needs, transitional support needs and reintegration needs. In this simple typology supported housing is perceived to provide the link between traditional direct access shelters and permanent accommodation. However, our discussion in the previous chapters identifies a range of different forms of provision of supported housing and types of supported accommodation. Hence the role of supported housing is more than a mere stepping stone between emergency accommodation, on the one hand, and permanent secure housing on the other. Given the range of forms of provision, we need to consider the role, or roles, supported housing could play in the solution to the problems of homelessness (as distinct from the objectives it may fulfil in relation to social welfare or health policies).

The national reports of the researchers of the European Observatory on Homelessness make reference to three distinct functions or objectives underpinning the provision of supported housing. For example, de Feijter and Blok (1999), Børner Stax et al (1999) and de Decker and Hardouin (1999) describe a preventative role, in relation to the Netherlands, Denmark and Belgium respectively. De Feijter and Blok describe the situation of people who have serious rent arrears or who cause trouble in their immediate living environment, for whom 'ambulatory coaching' is a means of preventing homelessness. Børner Stax et al, on the other hand, refer to recent legislation in Denmark which broadens the statutory responsibility of regional councils to provide temporary accommodation and/or support to people with 'special social difficulties' who cannot remain in their own home. De

Decker describes the role of Social Rental Agencies (SRAs) in providing rent and tenancy guarantees to enable people to remain, or be rehoused, in private rental tenancies.

Kärkkäinen (1999) and Busch-Geertsema (1999) make reference to the role of supported accommodation in the rehabilitation of people with support needs. The rehabilitation objective, which is also referred to as 'therapeutic' support, is mostly associated with the move from institutional living to life in the community. While the term has negative overtones, which reflect the medical model rather than the social model of disability, it suggests that the intention of the support is to provide people with the personal, social and life skills they require to live in the community. It is thus perhaps best understood within the framework of a continuum of care moving from institutional support to residential living, to care in the community.

Other researchers in the Observatory (Tosi and Ranci, 1999; de Decker and Hardouin, 1999; Schoibl, 1999; Leal Maldonado and Laínez, 1999) describe supported housing within the framework of approaches to reintegration or reinsertion (de Gouy and Damon, 1999). Reintegration can be viewed in terms of the reintegration of people who are already homeless (roofless, no abode) or those who are at risk of homelessness (for example in an insecure tenancy situation, facing threat of eviction, young people leaving foster or childcare). In this scenario, support is described to be of a 'pedagogic' nature, and aims to address the specific requirements of the individual (for example, young people leaving care, people at threat of eviction, vulnerable young women with children, women fleeing domestic violence).

While it is helpful to distinguish these distinct objectives, in practice it is likely that the provision of supported housing will fulfil more than one objective. Thus, in the rehabilitation and reintegration situations, intervention will have an ameliorative role in dealing with the present circumstances, as well as a preventative role in combating the risk of homelessness.

This broad level description of the objectives of supported housing does not, however, enable us to understand whether, or in what ways, support provision may be appropriate to the needs of homeless people. It would be more helpful to consider the specific needs of different groups in assessing the contribution that support provision may make to the prevention of homelessness or the reintegration of homeless people. An understanding of the underlying factors and triggers of homelessness for different groups of homeless people should enable us to identify the distinctive contribution which support provision may make to enable people to move into permanent and stable housing.

Different approaches are evident in the literature to conceptualise the underlying factors causing homelessness and the immediate events which may act as a trigger to the event (Avramov, 1996; see also Fitzpatrick et al, 2000, for a review), and these describe distinct categories of the homeless population. Adapting these approaches for our purposes, we define (in Table 10) the underlying causes of homelessness to be structural, institutional, and personal in nature (adapting from Avramov's structural, intermediate and proximate causes of homelessness). Structural causes of homelessness can be linked to socioeconomic factors flowing from an individual's relationship to the labour or housing markets; generally these factors are related to issues of poverty resulting from low income or unemployment. The institutional causes of homelessness we relate to factors associated with an individual's experience of institutional living; this affects young people living in foster or state care, people who have lived in long-stay hospital or psychiatric care, and people who have been imprisoned. Relationship breakdown can affect young people, people in relationships and older people whose relationship has dissolved as a result of separation or death of a spouse. Individual or personal causes of homelessness are linked to the well-known factors of substance dependency, mental illness or mental capacity. Fitzpatrick et al (2000) describes, from a review of recent research, a series of triggers of homelessness which can be linked to these factors (Table 10).

While it does not provide a complete explanation of the diversity of practice, our description of a continuum of support approaches, shifting from preventative and housing-focused support at one pole, to reintegrative and care-focused support at the other, is suggestive of the manner in which the housing and support dimensions may be integrated to meet the range of perceived needs. At the preventative end of the spectrum, support will be focused (more) on enabling people to sustain a tenancy and will (at most) be linked to employment and training initiatives; this may indicate that services are more prescribed (rather than based on an individualised and negotiated contract) and are more likely to involve a single agency or small number of agencies. At the reintegrative end of the spectrum, support involves more individualised care (and housing) plans and a more diverse range of services involving health, personal care, counselling, and housing support, as well as those services linked to labour market reinsertion where this is appropriate or feasible. At this end of the continuum, the required services will probably involve a number of agencies and hence issues of partnership or

Table 10: The causes and triggers of homelessness

Causes	Factors	Triggers	Support focus
Structural	Poverty Unemployment Housing	Debts Financial crisis Eviction (arrears) Eviction (behaviour)	**Prevention**
Institutional	Institutional living Foster/state care Prison experience Armed forces	Leaving care Leaving care Leaving prison Forces discharge	**Housing focus**
Relationship	Abusive relationship (childhood) Abusive relationship (with a partner) Family breakdown (death or separation)	Leaving family home Fleeing violent relationship Coping with living alone	**Care focus**
Personal	Mental illness Learning difficulty Drug dependency Alcohol dependency	Deterioration/illness episode Support breakdown Substance misuse Substance misuse	**Reintegration**

coordination (or joined up procedures) will be more of an issue. We stress that this continuum is introduced as a heuristic device to suggest the range of support needs and the distinctive contributions which supported housing initiatives may play as a solution to the problems of homelessness.

We began this discussion by considering the relationship of supported housing to other homelessness services, and concluded that supported housing will probably involve more than a simple stepping stone from traditional low threshold homeless hostels to permanent housing. Our consideration of the causes of homelessness confirms that the nature of support provision will need to be diverse to respond to the diversity of needs. We now consider the role of supported housing in meeting the diversity of needs of different types of homeless people. Sahlin (1999), describing the objectives of the municipalities in Sweden in the provision of supported housing, distinguishes between normalising lifestyles and normalising housing conditions (see Figure 2). Adapting her approach, and the concepts of normalisation which underpin it, we distinguish four categories of people in relation to the dimensions of accommodation and support (Table 11).

The characteristics of each group are conceptualised here in relation to the FEANTSA working definition of homelessness rather than Sahlin's perception of normalising housing condition and normalising lifestyles. The reason for this revision of Sahlin's model is to posit the needs of homeless people clearly in terms of housing and support requirements. We also suggest that this approach reflects more explicitly the causes of homelessness for different groups of homeless people, as identified in Table 10. The characteristics of each group of homeless people are described in relation to their risks of institutional living and their need for accommodation and support. In this way we attempt to reflect the distinction between roofless (or no abode) homeless, those who are houseless (because of their experience of institutional living), and those who are at risk of homelessness (due to insecurity of tenancy, inadequate, or inappropriate, accommodation, debt or relationship difficulties).

Table 11: Typology of target groups for supported accommodation

		Support dimension	
		Need is for permanent support	Need is for transitional Support
Accommodation dimension	High risk of institutional living	1 Learning disability Frail older people Mentally ill *	2 Ex-offenders
	Low risk of institutional living	3 Physically disabled HIV/AIDS	4 Vulnerable single parents Women fleeing domestic violence
		Alcohol/drug abusers*	Young people

*These groups may have a permanent need for support which will fluctuate over time, as distinguished from groups who may have a transitional need for support.

The first group of people (group 1 in Table 11) will generally have a need for permanent support arising from their dependency needs. This support may often involve high level support with intensive staff involvement or, especially in the case of people with a mental health problem, may involve periods of hospitalisation combined with periods in the community. The requirements of support delivery may often predicate residential or institutional forms of accommodation or at least mean that these people have experienced institutional living or are at risk of doing so. To the extent that institutional living occurs in an inappropriate manner (ie contrary to the needs or wishes of the individual) then these people may be regarded as 'houseless'. Those with a mental health problem face the greatest risk of 'homelessness' in this category. It has been estimated (Bhugra, 1996) that perhaps as much as one third of homeless people have a mental health problem. The support needs of these categories of people will involve personal or healthcare needs as well as support in managing their housing situation.

The second group mainly includes ex-offenders who present a particular case of people who may have hostel accommodation available through the criminal justice system (for example bail hostels or probation hostels), but whose support needs are not specifically provided for by social care and social protection systems. Their support needs will relate specifically to their resettlement needs. This will include reintegration into the labour market but it may also include need for counselling and support to re-establish social networks. Ex-offenders may also have needs arising from drug or alcohol dependency or mental illness which have been associated with their offending behaviour.

The third group include people with a physical (or sensory) disability who have specific housing requirements, have a low risk of institutional living, and are likely to have specific social care services provided by the welfare system. People with HIV/AIDS may have difficulty accessing ordinary housing and have particular healthcare needs which are often not well recognised by traditional systems. However, those with a drug or alcohol dependency are at the greatest risk of homelessness and have support needs related to a chaotic lifestyle. While they may not be at risk of institutional living, they nevertheless have needs for housing and support to sustain a tenancy and independent lifestyle; the nature of their dependency means that people in this category have support needs of a personal or healthcare nature.

The fourth category of people generally have support or housing needs resulting from their relationship situation. The accommodation dimension is important because it is a condition for the protection and development of an integration programme or because risk is strongly determined by the housing situation. The support dimension is related to their relationship situation and involves counselling (women fleeing domestic violence) or is associated with their acquisition of skills to sustain a tenancy or occupation (vulnerable young people or vulnerable single mothers).

It will also be apparent that the process (or trajectory) of homelessness may vary for each client group, hence the access to supported housing will be different for each group. People in group 1 (Table 10) will be defined as homeless if they are living in institutional settings as a result of insufficient housing or support in the community; they may also become roofless following a move into the community from a long-stay institution. People in group 2 may become homeless as a result of the breakdown in housing or familial relationships following a period of incarceration related to their offending behaviour. In group 3, people with a drug or alcohol dependency become homeless while living within the community – their housing circumstance may involve living in the family home, living with friends and relations, temporary accommodation, hostel accommodation and rooflessness. Group 4 people are at risk of homelessness because of their relationship or family circumstances; this may involve a progression from care homes or foster homes for young people, or from the family home following a relationship crisis which may be accompanied by temporary accommodation or protected accommodation. This typology is suggestive of the nature of the relationship which may exist between accommodation and support for different client groups.

The following section, drawing on the above typology (Table 11), examines the contribution of supported housing for four groups of homeless people. These groups have been chosen partly because they represent a large proportion of the composition of the (single) adult homeless population, and partly because they illustrate different aspects of the contribution of supported housing to the prevention of homelessness.

People with a mental health problem are representative of a group of homeless people who are at risk of institutional living and who have a continuing need for support. This group, our typology suggests, illustrates a range of challenges to housing and support providers because of their fluctuating support needs. Intuitively, we may assume that these challenges are also linked to the tension between empowering the individual to live independently and the 'duty of care' obligations which providers owe to other tenants and neighbours. People with a drug or alcohol dependency represent a group whose risk of institutional living may be low but who require long-term, and often specialised, support in the community if they are to sustain independent living. Vulnerable young people, according to our typology, are typical of a group who have a need for transitional support to facilitate their integration following a period of institutional, residential or foster care, or who require a temporary period of support to enable them to sustain independent living.

Ex-offenders are an important category because of their risk of institutional living and their need for transitional (and sometimes specialised) support to ensure their reintegration. This is also an important group of people to consider because of the insights they may provide about the level of official awareness of the need for support in the prevention of homelessness (and possible recidivism), and the interaction between criminal justice, social welfare and housing systems to provide it. However, there is insufficient empirical evidence available to provide a detailed analysis of these issues. This lack of evidence, in our opinion, reflects a gap in service provision for this group rather than a limitation of research. If this perception is correct then it also indicates a weakness in 'joined-up action' between the prison, welfare and housing sectors in meeting this need.

The typology in Table 11 is limited in at least one important respect in that it does not identify immigrants as a distinct population group at risk of homelessness. Evidence from the national reports of the correspondents of the Observatory, however, reflects the (growing) importance of this heterogeneous group and identifies their distinctive support needs.

People with mental health problems

It has been argued that, for people with mental health problems, the most striking departure with past tradition "is the attempt to move away from reliance on psychiatric hospitals as the core of the mental health services in Western Europe. While West European countries differ in the pace, range and depth of change, this change of direction can be detected in all countries" (Ramon, 1996, p 26).

It has been estimated that between one quarter and one third of all homeless people suffer from serious mental illness (Scott, 1993; de Feijter and Blok, 1999; see Bhugra and Leff, 1993 for a review). Bhugra (1996, p 99) argues that "the relationship between homelessness and mental illness is complex and mental illness is only one of many interacting factors leading to and perpetuating homelessness". Clearly the percentage of mentally ill among the homeless varies from country to country and is influenced not only by the number of beds in psychiatric hospitals, but also by the quality of 'ambulant' and specialised provision for the mentally ill. However, reductions in institutional care have been particularly acute in psychiatric care (see Ramon, 1996, for a review of the European experience). While this de-institutionalisation is often blamed for the increase in homelessness during the 1980s, the research evidence to support this conclusion is sparse. There does, however, appear to be more consensus that adequate follow-up and support for long-stay psychiatric patients discharged from hospital is critical in preventing homelessness (Dayson, 1992). It therefore follows that there is an increasing need for housing and support services in the community to accommodate the shift to the community delivery of mental health services.

In a recent review article, Scott (1993) suggests that we need to be aware of the existence of three sub-groups of people who are both homeless and suffer from mental illness so that their needs may be recognised and services planned accordingly:

- people with a history of hospitalisation who become homeless some time after discharge from hospital;
- younger people who avoid psychiatric intervention and whose mental illness may have contributed to 'social drift';
- people who became mentally ill due to homelessness or the personal/social problem that led them to become homeless in the first place.

People with mental health problems have particular support needs which often do not fit easily with accommodation provision, and which renders them vulnerable to hospitalisation, imprisonment or homelessness. For example, their support needs are liable to fluctuate and may require periods of hospitalisation and this can place them in a vulnerable position in relation to their housing rights. Additionally, their medical condition may make it difficult to offer them shared accommodation. A general lack of available self-contained housing may then result in institutionalisation or homelessness. Inappropriate placement in shared accommodation can also lead to eviction and hence to homelessness.

We would suggest that it is the fluctuating nature of the support requirements, combined with the difficulties of assessment and allocation and a relative scarcity of appropriate housing, which combines to leave this group of people susceptible to homelessness. The following examples of supported housing, drawn from a range of countries, describe the response to the difficulty of meeting the support needs of this group in order to prevent homelessness, and identify some common themes across Europe.

Finland

In Finland, since 1980, there has been a reduction of 66% in the number of psychiatric beds, to the present level of 6,000, with further reductions planned. However, the evidence suggests that, at least as far as the role of NGOs is concerned, the provision of supported housing is relatively recent. The Finnish Association for Mental Health commenced housing support operations in 1994, in association with the Y-Foundation and two organisations representing psychiatric patients and their families. In this example, supported housing is based on volunteers who complement public services. This involves networking with the municipal authorities in housing, social and mental health services. Clients and apartments are assessed and allocated in collaboration. A concrete service plan is drawn up jointly by the client, a representative of the municipal mental health outpatient clinic and the voluntary support worker. In 1997 the Finnish Association for Mental Health supported 100 people in 14 municipalities, with more than 150 voluntary support workers.

Supported housing is often part of the care and service chain in the case of psychiatric rehabilitation. Working on the rehabilitation of psychiatric patients in Tampere and the neighbouring municipalities, an association called *Sopimusvuori* has established a service chain whereby the client leaves hospital rehabilitation step by step: rehabilitation home, therapeutic community, supported housing and finally independent apartment. This provision is very localised, however, and it is reported that there are considerable shortcomings in the provision of these services (Taipale, 1998).

Sweden

In Sweden too, the development of outpatient care for mentally ill people has developed too slowly compared to the pace of hospital closure (Beijer, 1997; Halldin et al, 1997). In common with Finland, the number of beds in psychiatric hospitals has reduced by 70% since 1980, to the present total of 8,300. Also in common with Finland and Germany, there has been slow and limited planning for the housing needs of ex-patients of psychiatric hospitals. Sahlin (1999) quotes evidence that 14% of people evicted from housing in 1996 had formerly been patients in psychiatric hospitals (NBHSS, 1998, p 85). Sahlin further argues that hospitalisation reduced the chances even for supported accommodation for this group.

According to the Law on Support and Service, from 1994 people who have difficulty managing their daily lives due to mental health problems have a right to personal support and special housing. By 1998 only 2,000 people were supported under this legislation, out of an estimated eligible population of 43,000; 79% lived on their own, 10% lived in special housing and 11% lived in institutions or other forms of accommodation.

People with mental health problems are situated somewhere in between the regulated and the non-regulated sphere of special housing. One reason for the withdrawal of state subsidy for this category relates to the difficulty of establishing group housing for people whose behaviour is often challenging and disturbing for neighbours who have their own mental problems. It is argued that the controlled and collective arrangements in group housing are likely to be experienced as intrusive and humiliating by people at times when their mental health is improved (NBHSS, 1998 p 78).

For the mentally ill, effective support cannot be organised in the same manner as for other groups of the population, partly because their needs are continually shifting, as are their own assessments of their needs and willingness to accept support. However, as Sahlin (1999) has demonstrated, their need for support to sustain a tenancy is evidenced by their increased likelihood of eviction. One approach to delivering social support for this group, which has proved successful in some municipalities, is to use 'mobile teams' which may include psychiatric nurses, psychiatrists and other professionals. A new form of support is emerging, although only indirectly associated with housing. Part of the government subvention of 943 million SEC for the period 1995-97, which was intended to develop outpatient support, has been used to develop the practice of assigning 'personal representatives' to people with mental health disorders. This approach aims to overcome the fragmentation of responsibilities and legislation which makes it difficult for people with mental health problems to access available support. This allocation (of 24 million SEC) has been used to develop projects in 10 municipalities, targeting 350 individuals with severe psychiatric disabilities. An evaluation of the projects, after 18 months, has demonstrated a high level of client satisfaction, with recorded improvements in the level of care and support provided, social networks and quality of life.

Germany

In Germany, it is suggested that the ideal of 'therapeutical communities' (sic) often influences schemes of shared supported accommodation (Brill, 1998). Nevertheless an expert commission of the Federal government proposed:"To enable a self-contained way of living in the familiar home setting, either together with relatives ... or as single resident tenant/ owner should be considered as a priority aim" (Expertenkommission, 1988). However, it has been argued that psychiatric reform has been slow to occur, with the exception of a few urban municipalities (Busch-Geertsema, 1999). Ramon (1996, p31) suggests that "the ongoing difficulty of recognising non-medical initiatives in the community as an integral part of the mental health system in Germany is highlighted by the exclusion of such interventions from the package of services that are reimbursed by insurance companies, while hospitalisation remains a remunerable expense". Therefore, community living and preventative initiatives have, he argues, been slower to emerge, and have to struggle for their financial survival.

The Netherlands

In the Netherlands, a variety of supported living arrangements for people with a mental health problem are available. This may be partly the result of the dual funding system in which local government is responsible only for the social shelter and care sector, while mental healthcare is mainly paid for by health insurance companies. Social boarding houses are intended for people who are not independent enough to live on their own and are therefore a provision between supported living and a shelter. Criteria for access are that the client is homeless, is over 18 years of age, has a history of mental healthcare and needs permanent professional care. People are obliged to sign the house rules and in some cases get a probationary period. For some people the social boarding house acts as a stepping stone to independent (supported) living, while for others it is a permanent way of living.

Greece

Since the mid-1980s a number of rehabilitation and community health services have been established in Greece, in line with the EC Regulation

815/84 which funded psychiatric reform in that country. Rehabilitation programmes have been established in all nine public psychiatric hospitals in the country (Sapounakis, 1996). Implementation of the programmes have generally combined housing rehabilitation with some form of vocational training. Housing is provided, initially, in short-stay guesthouses or in long-stay residential care hostels with the intention of moving people on to private rented supported flats. The rent of the supported flats is covered either by a disability pension or from earnings. Support is normally provided by the community mental health services. An innovative agricultural cooperative was established in 1990 on the island of Leros, in which the employees (approximately 29) are accommodated in a combination of supported flats and guesthouses. Madianos (1994, p 169) suggested that 768 places in supported community-based housing projects would be required to meet the real needs of psychiatric patients in Greece. However, the future of those projects which have been established under the EC regulation is uncertain since their initial funding ran out in 1999.

Denmark

Børner Stax and Nielsen (1996) describe four different types of living situation for the mentally ill in Copenhagen. One project, described as a 'staircase community', consists of 16 self-contained flats where each inhabitant has their own apartment located near a common flat from which the staff team operate. Similar projects in the UK are called 'core and cluster' projects. Access to the project is through the psychiatric services and most tenants continue to receive psychiatric treatment. Different kinds of shared dwellings, provided by the Municipality of Copenhagen, provide supported housing for schizophrenics with a low intelligence for whom the alternative would be institutional nursing home care. Municipal domiciliary support is available combined with short-stay hospitalisation when necessary. Intermediate accommodation is available for patients being discharged from hospital as a stepping stone to permanent housing. Finally, there is a project of 30 private apartments with support from 'home assistants' who supplement the normal home-help and community psychiatric nursing ('home-nurse') service.

Summary

It is difficult to contradict the argument that long-stay psychiatric patients need support in the community, at least for a transitional period, to prevent their homelessness following hospital discharge. Yet it is evident, from all European countries, that the pace of institutional closure has not been matched by an increase in supported housing. This means that some people remain inappropriately housed in institutions while others become homeless some time after discharge from hospital.

Most of the examples of supported housing cited here have referred to projects linked to hospital closure or have catered for people who were formerly psychiatric patients. Access to such accommodation is therefore mediated through formal hospital assessment procedures and referral mechanisms involving health and social services. Thus, in this period of de-institutionalisation, services have been aimed at a population who have moved from institutional living (for the most part) to living in the community. In the future, however, homelessness services and supported housing will have to deal with a population of younger people who may avoid psychiatric intervention altogether, or have periods of infrequent and short-term hospitalisation and whose mental health may have been deleteriously affected by their insecure housing or homelessness. It is difficult to envisage how supported housing, as currently provided, will either be accessible to young people with mental health problems or will meet their fluctuating support needs. It is clear that if the challenge of preventing homelessness among this group of young people both now and in the future is to be met, the coordination of housing, social services and community mental health services will be critical.

We suggested in the introduction to this chapter that examination of the provision of supported housing for people with a mental health problem would give some indication of its effectiveness in providing for, and preventing homelessness among, people who have fluctuating support needs. Our evaluation of the evidence suggests that, because of the fluctuating nature of their support needs, people with a mental health problem are very likely either to fall outside the 'regulated' or funded supported or special housing sector altogether, or to remain trapped in a psychiatric service chain whose end point of independent living is difficult to attain or sustain. Indeed it appears that the nature of the support needs, coupled with the patchy and localised provision, has led to a bifurcation in the form of accommodation provision with highly protected, or controlled, accommodation being provided in some countries (wards in the community in Germany, social boarding houses in the Netherlands and therapeutic communities in Finland); supported accommodation in other countries (special housing in Sweden, staircase housing in Denmark and shared housing or group homes in the UK). In yet other countries and indeed elsewhere in the countries named above, mental health problems are not addressed and people suffering from mental illness end up homeless or living in insecure accommodation with sporadic periods of support or institutional living.

People with a drug or alcohol dependency

It has been argued elsewhere (Edgar et al, 1999) that one indication of the shift in perception of homelessness is the recognition of the multidimensional nature of the causes and of the needs of homeless people. Nowhere is this trait more evident than in relation to people with a drug or alcohol dependency. Retracing the path to housing autonomy and to autonomy *tout court* for people with addiction problems is too often an intractable process.

People with acute addiction problems are often the most seriously marginalised, are more likely to be roofless and to be dependent on emergency or temporary accommodation. Consideration of modes of intervention and of programs of resettlement for people with addiction problems raise important issues and questions about the potential role of supported housing in the reintegration of homeless people. These are considered here, using the empirical evidence available from the reports of the correspondents of the European Observatory on Homelessness.

It has been argued in the case of *Portugal* that the low threshold intervention offered by night shelters is an indispensable part of a wider reintegration strategy which needs to be linked into a network of services (Valentini, 1996). To be effective in linking to specific forms of supported accommodation, night shelters will have to develop beyond the role of emergency provision and containment, to a proactive role which pays particular attention to the life history and needs of the individual and to the drawing up of individual, multidimensional reintegration plans. An example of the integration of shelters and supported housing, or rather of the development of the traditional shelter into an individualised social support role, is to be found in the *Shelter of Graça* in Lisbon. This project represents an integration of the Municipality's temporary shelter (*Abrigo de Xabregas*), the *Assistência Médica Internacional* network of centres and the specialist services of the *Santa Casa da Misericórdia de Lisboa*. It is estimated that around 80% of the service users had an alcohol addiction problem. The project stems from a traditional shelter for a relatively small group of individuals (around 25). It is based on a partnership between the agencies involved, aimed at fostering a convergence of complementary inputs from the partners focused on the social, employment and housing needs of the individuals. The project, as with similar projects in Oporto run by the *Santa Casa da Misericórdia*, thus links the traditional night shelter with transitional supported accommodation. A contractual condition of moving into the supported housing involves accepting a job and agreeing to abide by the rules and conditions of the accommodation. The expectation is that the transitional supported accommodation is limited to a four-month period, although this may be extended, after which a move into independent housing should have been achieved. The project attaches a high degree of importance to the role of the family in this reintegration process.

In *Italy*, where the solution to homelessness is understood more from a social welfare than a housing paradigm, dealing with the multidimensional needs of homeless people with addiction problems involves cooperation between service providers. In Genoa, there is an operational technical group composed of representatives of all organisations that deal with people who are 'marginalised'. The Adult Social Services in Bologna encouraged the establishment of a technical committee, for problems of marginalisation, composed of public and private sector bodies. In Milan, while the *Consulta per l'Emarginazione* (consultative body for the 'emarginated') was ineffective in providing central coordination, a network of cooperation has emerged of which the *Cena dell'Amicizia* is a good example. This cooperates with the Milan *Caritás*, making referrals for places in the association's accommodation, with the Alcoholics Treatment Centre for psychological support, and with the *Aler* (public sector housing agency) to obtain small apartments requiring repair and renovation. The *Cena dell'Amicizia* has a transitional centre and 20 protected apartments, for use by people at the 'pre-autonomy' stage, rented from the *Aler* at below market rents. Occupants, during the period of their stay, remain in close contact with the voluntary associations and continue to be supported by social services. They are not assisted to find their own permanent accommodation until they have completed their reintegration plan. Living in protected accommodation for two years gives occupants the right to six points in public sector housing applications (a high score compared to three points awarded for eviction applicants).

Elsewhere in Europe, the provision of supported accommodation is often linked to the provision of specialist services which deal with addiction and detoxification. In *Sweden*, where there has been a tradition of compulsory incarceration for treatment for alcoholics since the beginning of the century, and for drug addicts since 1982, state subsidies for treatment and prevention were transferred to local social authorities in 1986 to promote the development of non-institutional facilities (Bergmark and Oscarsson, 1998, p 48). A large number of private institutions, established in the late 1980s, offer treatment according to the Minnesota model (which is inspired and associated with the Alcoholics Anonymous movement). Thus the process of treatment has shifted away from compulsory treatment, and from a combination of medical treatment and institutional care to therapy based on day centres and outpatient arrangements. Institutions have often been converted into group homes for alcoholics in which residents pay full rent, although they may still be evicted for rule breaking. In 1994, the Commission for Alcohol Policy recommended that municipalities develop more outpatient support and 'protected housing' for chronic addicts. Support is aimed at control and regulation more than personal assistance since sober addicts are assumed to be able to live independently. Although policy has aimed to replace institutional care with support and supported accommodation, it is difficult to assess the extent to which these policies have actually changed practice (Bergmark and Oscarsson, 1998, p 51).

The *Communidade Vida e Paz* (Life and Peace Community) in *Portugal* has also developed specialist services for addicts, employing a different process. Addicts (restricted to men aged 18 to 45) will undergo group and individual therapy for an initial period (8 to 10 weeks) in the *Centre of Alvalade* after which they transfer to the *Centre of Fatima* which specialises in drug addiction. The project is self-sufficient with respect to drug therapy which is based on the Minnesota (twelve steps) model. The centre develops its work in three stages – the primary unit (for up to three months), which is effectively an assessment period, is followed by the secondary unit (for 10 months), which focuses on therapy and occupational training, and the final stage (for one year), concentrates on occupational and social reinsertion. The Community has five homes to support the initial phase of reintegration and provides six months' rent for people moving into normal housing. Those moving on to permanent accommodation are monitored for at least one year with regular review.

In *Finland*, where the number of homeless people was decreasing up to the early 1990s, a decision was made to close the homeless shelter in Koupio (a medium-sized town in eastern Finland) and turn it into a centre for intoxicant abusers. Terraced houses, complete with support dwellings, were constructed around the main building. The centre also has a place where addicts can sober up and find crisis help. In addition, one floor in a tenement was converted into a community for previous homeless people who are trying to pursue intoxicant-free lifestyles.

Examples of the use of a 'staircase of transition' have been described in a number of countries including Sweden (Sahlin, 1998), the Netherlands (de Feijter, 1998) and Germany (Busch-Geertsema, 1999). Busch-Geertsema suggests that in Germany, as in Sweden, there are many examples where the 'staircase of transition' has turned into a 'staircase of exclusion' (Busch-Geertsema, 1999, p 47) because the lower steps of the system are used as negative sanctions for the misdemeanours of residents (especially in relation to supported housing). Particularly in relation to homeless people with drug addiction, Busch-Geertsema (1999, p 47) demonstrates considerable downward mobility, revolving door effects and periods of stay in special housing which exceed the intended duration of stay. This experience is also reflected in the empirical findings in Sweden and the Netherlands, quoted above.

While supported accommodation may be necessary to meet some of the needs of people with a drug/alcohol dependency, there is also a need to enable them to access permanent housing while they are undergoing therapeutic support or during their reintegration into society. Often this involves both personal support and guarantees to private and social landlords that the tenancy obligations will be observed. In this respect social rental guarantee schemes have proved to have an important role to play in their own right and in association with supported housing initiatives for people with a drug or alcohol dependency. Social Rental Agencies are described in countries which have high proportions of privately rented housing (Belgium, Luxembourg, Germany) as a method of securing permanent accommodation for homeless people who have a drug or alcohol addiction.

It might be argued that, especially for people with a long-term or chronic drug or alcohol addiction, autonomy and reintegration must be considered as relative, acknowledging the positive nature of partial reintegration (Aldridge, 1998). Tosi and Ranci (1999) argue, for example, that "for many of the no abode partial reintegration may be an appreciable objective" (p 29). This argument suggests that in many cases more realistic objectives such as the reduction or containment of hardship and the improvement of the quality of life – rather than reintegration – must be considered. Aldridge (1998), in describing projects in the *UK*, describes the case of Wernham House in Aberdeen as an example of a project which meets the needs of people with an addiction problem while not aiming at full integration in permanent housing. Wernham House is described as a 'wet hostel', near the centre of Aberdeen, which provides accommodation for 18 people; the project has a stable population, with relatively little turnover during the last 15 years. Thus its inhabitants are described as integrated into a community in which they are 'valued' and have a role. If people have privacy, control over their own room, a stable or secure occupancy and social relationships then, asks Aldridge, does this not meet the basic criteria of 'normalisation'?

It is apparent from the description of these projects that there is tension between the normalisation objectives associated with de-institutionalisation and the delivery of care in the community, and the reality of containment and control policies and procedures employed by initiatives aimed at the reintegration of people with a drug or alcohol dependency. Many of the initiatives described above involve a negotiated personal contract which binds the individual to particular modes of behaviour or makes the acceptance of support conditional on the occupancy of the accommodation. It is apparent in Sweden, for example, that sobriety or detoxification is a necessary pre-condition to entry to supported housing or group homes. The move to individualised approaches of determining and planning support are controlling as well as empowering. Negotiated individual contracts thus involve an acceptance by the individual of the regime of sobriety or detoxification in return for support and accommodation.

In this context there are different perceptions of the meaning of normalisation (which we discuss in Chapter 3) and these are reflected in the distinction in approach or philosophy between 'wet' and 'dry' projects. Wet projects, which tolerate the consumption of alcohol or drugs, accept that the defeat of addiction may be a long-term aim. Projects of this type may aim to contain the addiction while providing the individual with the personal skills, occupational skills, relationships and personal confidence necessary to combat the addiction. They may also, as in the case of Wernham House, contain the addiction sufficiently to improve the quality of life of the individual (measured in terms of the social relationships of the individual). Dry projects, on the other hand, resolve from a paradigm of compulsion and medical treatment. Access to such projects presupposes a stage of detoxification or non-consumption. There is an assumption in such situations that successful reintegration in permanent housing is only possible if the (medical) condition of addiction is solved. The approach in this type of project is often to link the stages of therapy (for example in the Minnesota model) to specific forms of accommodation. Access to supported housing is thus conditional on the individual proving their intention to abstain.

It is also evident from the empirical evidence of the projects described here that there are defined time-scales for different stages of the process of reintegration. There is no evidence to suggest that these time-scales are appropriate to the stages of reintegration or that they are adequate to meet individual needs. Rather they tend to reflect the funding and procedural constraints of the provider agency.

Summary

From the selected examples described above, it is possible to identify a number of factors which may act to constrain (or enhance?) the effectiveness of the role of supported accommodation in meeting the needs of homeless people who have a drug or alcohol addiction. The evidence suggests that its effectiveness is conditioned both by organisational factors and by external constraints in relation to the housing market and social services.

It has been argued, with reference to homeless people who have an addiction problem, that housing provision is not the solution to their homelessness. In this view supported housing, seen as a step to reintegration, will only be effective in so far as the complex support needs (health, counselling, financial, employment, relationships) of the individual are met. Meeting such complex needs means that the coordination of support is a necessary context, even precondition. In the Portuguese example the Church-organised project employs a range of workers (59), and provides the opportunity to integrate the more traditional shelters with supported housing. In the Italian context, on the other hand, support provision relies on the coordination of public and voluntary support agencies. Such coordination has occurred both through formal, top-down, structures as well as informal, bottom-up, forms of cooperation.

Because of the trajectory into homelessness taken by people with an addiction, access to supported housing will often be through referral from more traditional homelessness shelters. Thus, as evident in the Portuguese example, it is important to integrate or link supported housing to these low threshold (more traditional) shelters. This integration will involve organisational and funding decisions as well as operational procedures in relation to referral.

Where supported housing is provided as part of a 'staircase of transition', for example in Belgium, Germany, the Netherlands and Sweden, the approach is criticised both in terms of its philosophy and its operation. The major concern centres on its efficacy in terms of the small proportion of people who manage to move through all stages into permanent housing. Concern is also raised about the effects on people who move down the ladder.

Although more research evidence would be necessary to provide corroboration, it is our impression, from the national reports, that the reintegration phase of transitional supported accommodation is generally time-limited by funding constraints and that these time limits are not appropriate or realistic. It is also apparent that funding for outreach support and continuing (low-level) support is uncertain or absent. For example, many projects are recently established (such as Lisbon) or funded as special projects:"The day centre activities and supported housing has been financed by the Slot Machine Association as a special project, and thus their continuity is not guaranteed" (Kärkkäinen, 1999, p 27 – Finland).

The efficacy of supported accommodation provided as specialist transitional housing for people with addiction problems is often constrained by the fact that either there is a shortage of suitable accommodation to move people on, or there is a need to mediate access to permanent housing through SRA guarantees for which there is limited funding. An example of the shortage of appropriate housing is given in Finland: "residence at Aamurusko is temporary. When living in a supported dwelling is no longer necessary, ordinary housing, usually council-owned rental apartments, are provided; this is, however, hampered by a shortage of small apartments" (Kärkkäinen, 1999, p 27). An example of the need for funding for social rental guarantees is given in Belgium, Luxembourg and Spain.

It is clear from some evidence (for example France, Italy, Austria) that the desire to provide flexible support is achieved by the use of individual, negotiated, contracts. Such an approach is necessary and, in theory at least, provides a mechanism to specify the responsibilities of the user and the service provider and should therefore empower the stakeholders (clients and the agency's staff). However, concern is sometimes evident in the descriptions of such approaches that negotiated contracts are controlling as well as emancipating.

Young people

Harvey (1999) suggests that the age of homeless people is falling: "the principal age range is now 30 to 39 years, with the young homeless teenager as an identifiable subset" (Harvey, 1999, p 60). While on average one fifth of the population in European countries is aged under 30, we may expect that only a small proportion of young people will be at risk of homelessness or literally homeless at any one time. Fitzpatrick and Clapham (1999) argue that the pathway which young people take in the process of leaving home is in itself a key to understanding how some young people become homeless. Avramov (1998) suggests that young people "at a high risk of homelessness during their early adulthood are those who have had an experience of substitute care, who live in a hostile family environment or have experienced an episode of family homelessness during their childhood" (Avramov, 1998, p 63). The key risk factors of exclusion and the composition of the risk groups do not, she argues, vary substantially between countries. Indeed there is empirical evidence to substantiate her view that these groups of young people embark on independent living at a particularly young age (Jones et al, 1993; Fitzpatrick and Clapham, 1999). It is evident also that such young people will lack family support to make the transition to independent living and they will have either to possess particular resilience or to find support from elsewhere if they are to successfully make the transition without falling into homelessness.

In some countries, welfare legislation for young people (and especially young people leaving care) provides a framework of responsibility and funding within which support services and supported accommodation have developed.

The 1983 Child Welfare Act (amended in 1990) in *Finland* provides for an after-care obligation for the municipality for young people aged 18 to 21. The municipality must provide housing and the most common form of housing provided is supported accommodation. Under this legislation, the young person has a right of appeal if the municipality fails to meet its statutory duty to provide adequate housing. The development of supported housing thus dates from the period of this legislation. A typical procedure is to assign the young person a support family who live nearby. In many cases the support family lives in a council-owned rental apartment, a section of which is occupied by the young person. This annex has a bathroom, cooking facilities and separate entrance and thus constitutes an almost self-contained unit. The concept of a 'family home' consisting of a semi-detached house, part of which is occupied by three young people and part by a support worker (social educator), has been used in Hamina (a town in south-eastern Finland). More recently the voluntary sector has initiated a project to expand the development of supported accommodation launched by an association called *EHJÄ*.

Germany has perhaps the most developed legislative framework for the provision of supported housing for young people. The Welfare Act for Children and Young People (KJHG), which was fundamentally reformed in 1991, explicitly provides not only for pedagogical support in children's homes but also for "other forms of supported housing" (Section 35, KJHG) as well as "intensive individual pedagogical care" (Section 35, KJHG) for young people with special problems. Young people who are of age but under 27 years old still have a legal right to support in developing their skills and leading an independent life (Section 41, KJHG). Within the framework of this legislation a great variety of housing schemes for young people have emerged. The majority of schemes involve groups of young people sharing dwellings as residents groups (*Wohngruppen*). However, the provision of support to individuals living independently is gaining in importance and is second in importance only to that provided for older people (Blath, 1998). Places in shared supported housing, in external residents groups belonging to institutions (*Außenwohngruppen*) and self-contained housing with support (*betreutes Einzelwohnen*) have been created while places in traditional homes have been reduced. Busch-Geertsema (1999) argues that, although supported housing now has a high priority in social work provision for young people, places in homes are still predominant not least because it has been difficult to acquire adequate housing during the last decade.

In the *UK* an estimated 12% of all supported accommodation is occupied by young people (at risk or leaving care). In 1997/98, 2% (800) of the 39,000 homeless households entering supported accommodation in England were young people who were referred to housing associations under the terms of the Children Act 1989 (Pleace et al, 1999, p 51), while a further 6% (2,200) were young people at risk. However, for all homeless households entering supported accommodation in that year, the median age of the head of (the predominantly lone-person) household was only 25 years; while the median age of the 55% of female-headed households was five years lower than male-headed households (at 22 years of age). In both England and Scotland the provision of supported accommodation for young people is relatively concentrated in the metropolitan centres (mainly London and Glasgow). As described in other countries, the support is generally confined to intensive housing management and help in resettlement into more permanent housing. However, in some situations (for example, the Glasgow supported tenancy projects), the housing is intended to be permanent after the transitional support period, when the support will 'float off'. Support is provided for a transitional period related to the initial tenancy period (normally a six-month tenancy).

In the *Netherlands*, by contrast, social security entitlements of young people operate to deter the development of supported living projects aimed at this group. In most supported living projects, clients pay both for rent and for support services. However, young people aged below 18 have no entitlement to supplementary benefit, while those aged between 18 and 21 have only partial entitlement. Therefore, responsibility for funding young people in supported living falls to the municipal social security agency. Since this is exceptional, payments will normally only be made where agreements have been entered into before a supported living project starts. Nevertheless, some supported accommodation for young people has been provided by NGOs such as the Help the Homeless (HVO), which is a private non-profit welfare organisation based in Amsterdam. The Residential Support division (BWA) of HVO focuses support solely and directly on the residential problems of the client. Their clients include young people who have left their parental home, juveniles who work, homeless youth and young immigrants who have left their parental home as a result of conflicts arising from growing up between two cultures. In most cases the young people have had a long history of institutions and welfare programs and have therefore not lived independently before in their lives. BWA cooperates with a variety of Amsterdam-based housing associations from which they rent accommodation and sub-let to their young clients. Normally the accommodation is shared housing but the BWA has developed separate group housing projects for young immigrants specialised to their particular needs. Because the young people generally live in shared housing, during the last months of the residential support trajectory, each client starts looking for suitable housing with the help of their social worker. The nature of the support provided is differentiated to the individual needs of each client but will normally include housing management, finance and social skills training.

In *Belgium*, following legislation in 1990 lowering the age of adulthood, a hundred places have been created in seven initiatives offering support services to young people in dispersed housing. The upper age limit of 21 was recently raised to 25 years of age (de Decker and Serriën, 1997). This change, mirroring a similar change in Germany, reflects the perception that the transition to adulthood and independent living (whether the young person is leaving care or leaving the family home) is a protracted process. It has been suggested that this process has become more difficult and elongated in recent years as a result of housing and social security policies as well as adverse labour market conditions (Jones, 1995). Therefore, such shifts in statutory definitions are necessary to bring support more into line with the needs of young people.

Support for young homeless people in *Italy* occurs within a context in which transitional services are differentiated for different service users. The main tendency followed by services for the no abode in Italy in recent years has been to differentiate between emergency and transitional accommodation and support services. The objective of transitional services is the (partial) reintegration of the individual into society through the use of personalised reintegration plans. Transitional supply makes use of purpose-built facilities that reflect the philosophy of de-institutionalisation. On the one hand, the size of the facilities is reduced to provide a more homely (less communal or institutional) environment. On the other hand, the supply is differentiated or specialised providing different types of facility for different types of user as well as for the different degrees of autonomy reached by occupants. Transitional solutions can be broadly classified into two basic forms of accommodation – community lodgings and protected apartments. Community lodgings are larger facilities for 10 to 30 people with communal living areas, while protected apartments are genuine apartments for two to three people, and are run by the occupants with regular visiting support and supervision. Community lodgings have been established in Turin aimed specifically at young homeless people (18 to 30 years of age). The *Cena dell' Amicizia* has 20 protected apartments, for use by people at the pre-autonomy stage, rented from the *Aler* (local public housing agency) which are for use by men from 18 to 45 years of age.

By contrast, Sapounakis points to "the lack of localised statutory social services in *Greece* which young people falling through family and social safety nets can turn to for help" (Sapounakis, 1998, p 217). He argues that, in the context of this lack of statutory services and the limited provision by voluntary agencies such as *Arsis* and *Onissimos*, there is an urgent need for "supported housing projects for young people in need of housing which are community-based and distinct from child care institutions" (Sapounakis, 1998, p 217).

Summary

The importance of legislation protecting the welfare of children and young people in providing a framework for the provision of supported housing for young people is highlighted in many countries. However, as the UK case illustrates, the link between leaving care and supported housing as a transitional support to independent living is only weakly developed. Busch–Geertsema (1999) describes a similar situation in Germany but identifies the lack of adequate housing as a key cause in the failure to expand this form of provision for young people. It is significant that the eligible age for support has been raised in Belgium and in Germany in recognition of the difficulty of transition to independent living caused by uncertainty in the labour market and constraints in the housing market. Defining the obligation to provide support to the age of 26 is significant in that half of all people in supported housing in the UK were under that age and that they comprised the second largest segment of supported housing in Germany. The concept, in Finland, of linking support to a support family living nearby raises an important issue regarding the perception of the skills and values included in supporting independent living. The emphasis on family values and the family home may be appropriate in the context of supporting young people leaving care. However, where the main reason for accessing supported housing is the need to leave the family home (see the evidence in Britain), this approach may be less appropriate or acceptable to the young person. Equally, the support needs of young people involve more than the attainment of life skills which this approach tends to emphasise.

Immigrants

Fitzpatrick (1998) argues that immigrants run a higher risk of homelessness than the rest of the European population, while Daly (1993) suggests that illegal immigrants face the greatest difficulties of all. It has been estimated that between 10 and 20% of homeless people are migrants, refugees or asylum seekers, and they are a significant proportion of the homeless population in countries such as Italy and Greece, which have experienced high levels of immigration (Harvey, 1994). Tosi and Ranci (1999) argue that difficulties of a specifically housing nature are of fundamental importance to the problems of immigrants and their chances of insertion into the destination society. A large proportion of immigrants face housing difficulties, hardship or exclusion, and for them housing is a priority problem to solve. Housing exclusion also acts as an important factor in the processes of marginalisation that affect immigrants. It is for this reason that immigrants, according to Tosi and Ranci (1999), need supported housing.

There were approximately one million immigrants from developing countries and Eastern Europe with valid stay permits in Italy at the beginning of 1998 and, it is estimated, a further 300,000 illegal immigrants (Tosi and Ranci, 1999, p 40). The scale and increase in the volume of immigration is becoming a problem for many other countries of the EU. In particular, Germany, the Netherlands, France, Britain and Spain can all refer to an increase in scale of economic immigration. Other countries exhibit particular issues of migration, such as the returning migrants to Greece from Pontos.

Immigration, according to Tosi and Ranci (1999), involves two distinct requirements for supported housing. First, there are the problems of initial housing and social insertion that arise upon arrival – reception needs. Second, there is a need for support to assist immigrants with housing integration in the face of the specific or additional difficulties that immigrants may encounter in the housing market.

In *Italy*, the response to the needs of immigrants has occurred by the development of first reception centres (*Centri di accoglienza*) and transitional centres. Inevitably, in the absence of an adequate social housing supply and therefore of housing chains, the reception centres have tended to become a more permanent surrogate for insertion into normal social rented housing. The transitional centres aim to focus on issues of social exclusion or at-risk situations providing both accommodation and welfare support. Unlike the first reception centres, the accommodation more often consists of ordinary housing. Non-profit associations and municipalities have also developed a number of projects aimed at rental guarantee schemes and at increasing the supply of non-public sector social housing.

In the *Netherlands*, the Help for Homeless (HVO) non-profit organisation has a division – *Jonker* – which specialises in care, housing and support for refugees and asylum seekers. *Jonker* manages over 400 houses in Amsterdam, providing accommodation and support to people who have a provisional permit to stay in the country (the so-called VVTV group) and who can remain in their houses for up to three years. In 1997 *Jonker* offered assistance to over 1,000 clients. In 1994 HVO *Jonker* started the AMA project, designed to provide housing and support for young asylum seekers aged 14 to 18 years old. A number of special projects for this group have been established, where they live together in a small-scale living unit (normally four people) with a social worker. The project currently offers housing, support and care to 96 young people in 24 houses dispersed throughout Amsterdam.

There are 8,000 officially recognised refugees in *Greece* today. The influx of people seeking asylum in Greece is constant and has, in fact, increased in recent years. Yet only a small portion of the nearly 800,000 immigrants who are estimated to be in the country have applied for asylum. Thus, only a tiny fraction of the immigrant population are considered as political refugees who, for this reason, may enter the relevant integration programme. The UN High Commissioner for Refugees supports three NGOs, the Foundation of Social Service, the Greek Council for Refugees and the International Social Service which provide legal and practical assistance as well as social support to asylum-seekers and refugees. The Greek government provides accommodation for up to 350 refugees in the Lavrion Refugee Camp, as well as education and healthcare in all public services in the country. It is estimated that approximately 75% of the refugees stay in Greece after leaving the camp. The organisation *EIYAAPOE* (Greeks from Pontos) promotes the social integration of Greek repatriates from the Pontos region. The support organised by *EIYAAPOE* includes provision of accommodation as well as of other forms of support (practical assistance, psychological support and training). They provide a number of services aimed at achieving social integration, including medical care, Greek language lessons, assistance with initial registration procedures, vocational training or retraining wherever that is required, preparation of children for joining the Greek educational system, general information about life in Greece, customs, social organisation, and assistance in the process of seeking employment.

Summary

The Italian situation illustrates the need for specific approaches to ensure the adequate supply of social housing and the changing role of reception and transitional centres. Clearly the risks of social exclusion, and community conflict, may be greater if reception centres become surrogate permanent housing because of the lack of support to enable people to move quickly into ordinary housing. The particular issues in countries such as Greece may suggest the need for specific approaches linked to international funding sources. The evidence from the Netherlands and from Britain raises the need to consider the intergenerational impact of immigration and the sustainability of policies. In the Netherlands, the example was given of accommodation provided for young people, born to immigrant parents, leaving home. In Britain, a tenth of the places in supported housing for women fleeing domestic violence were occupied by women of Asian origin, while men of Caribbean origin were over-represented in supported housing for ex-offenders.

Conclusions

Even on the most conservative estimate it is evident that there is an apparent lack of provision of supported housing in relation to need in all European countries. This may partly be explained by the fact that supported housing is a relatively recent innovation in most countries, and has been slow to develop even in the context of institutional closure. Yet there is a general consensus that the solution to homelessness must involve the provision of support as well as the provision of housing; overall, the evidence recorded in this study indicates a clear positive contribution by supported housing in this respect. However, the sustainability of supported housing, and its longer-term contribution to the prevention and eradication of homelessness, requires that present weaknesses and shortcomings are identified and addressed. In this respect three issues seem to be of particular importance: clarity of objectives, the restrictive nature of regulations concerning referral and allocation, and the limitations imposed by some forms of management and funding.

From the examples provided in this study, it is evident that the objectives of supported housing are not always clearly identified and articulated. For example, where supported accommodation forms part of a therapeutic regime (for people with a mental illness or drug/alcohol dependency), there is often clear tension between the therapy, control or containment objectives of provision and broader principles of empowerment and individualised support. Equally, where supported accommodation forms part of a 'continuum of care' or 'staircase of transition', there is a danger of creating a secondary market which may act to trap and exclude people rather than liberate and reintegrate them successfully into the community. There is a need in most countries for more research to evaluate the sustainability of outcomes from supported housing, and resettlement, projects and good practice would further suggest that procedures of monitoring and evaluation should form an integral part of the implementation and funding of projects.

The form of provision as well as referral and allocation procedures can act to constrain the role which supported housing plays in meeting the needs of different groups of homeless people. The fact that a high proportion of supported accommodation involves shared living arrangements may not be appropriate to the needs of some client groups and may even act to exclude some people. In particular, people with a chaotic lifestyle, substance dependency or challenging behaviour may be vulnerable to exclusion or eviction and thus remain more dependent on traditional forms of shelter provision or more vulnerable to roofless living. There is also evidence that the efficacy of specialised supported accommodation may be compromised by the lack of affordable rented housing for people to move on to. The relative lack of self-contained housing is a reflection of both housing market constraints, historic patterns of provision and current funding constraints for support provision.

Referral and allocation mechanisms can act to exclude people or to limit the role of supported housing in a variety of ways. Some supported accommodation, for example, has been specifically provided as part of a programme of hospital closure and institutional reprovisioning, and is therefore not generally available to people who are self-referred (the majority in the UK), but limited mostly to people referred by social work or other agencies. In other cases allocation rules can be restrictive. For example, abstinence may be a precondition for entry to accommodation for drug/alcohol users, while labour market participation is often a requirement for entry to supported housing; this is especially the case for entry to low-threshold homelessness hostels, and leads us to question how sustainable this option may be for some people. It may also be the case that formal referral mechanisms are not sensitive to certain needs – for example, young people with a mental illness who have not been in psychiatric care.

Factors of management and funding may constrain the role of supported housing, particularly for three of the groups discussed in this book – people with a mental health problem, drug/alcohol dependency and young people. Systems of funding and management are commonly based on a time-limited period of support. Funding structures rarely recognise that lengthy periods of support are often required for the reintegration of homeless people; nor do they cope well with the type of fluctuating support needs of some groups. The effective delivery of supported housing involves coordination between traditional homelessness services, between different support providers and between housing and support providers. While we identify in this study different approaches to coordination, it will require further research to assess the long-term effectiveness of these approaches. There is evidence in a number of countries that the link between young people leaving care, supported housing and independent housing is often weakly developed. Indeed in some cases, for example in the Netherlands, social protection systems actually operate to constrain the development of supported housing for this group.

These shortcomings should not detract from the evidence of this study, which indicates that, where it is provided, supported housing has made a positive contribution to the solution of the problems of homelessness. While not wishing to claim that supported housing provides *the* solution to the prevention of homelessness and the reintegration of already homeless people, we would argue that the defects of supported housing, as it is currently delivered, are surmountable and that supported housing can build on its record and continue to make a positive contribution into the foreseeable future.

SEVEN

Empowerment: choice and control in the reintegration process

This chapter assesses from a user perspective the extent to which policies and practices in supported housing facilitate empowerment and social inclusion. It builds on discussions in the previous chapters of social exclusion in the context of the European Union and the principle of empowerment underpinning community care provision. It argues that the effectiveness of supported housing in encouraging social inclusion for homeless people rests not only on its ability to provide housing and support for reintegration, but also its ability to empower individuals to make choices, influence structures and take control over their lives. The discussion considers the nature of empowerment and examines the extent to which policies and practices in supported housing affect homeless people's ability to make choices, influence and take control over their lives.

The user perspective in supported housing has all too often been a neglected or at least marginalised dimension. The limited research that exists on the user perspective tends to be client group or project specific in which service providers become the filters for understanding the views of service users. There is clearly a need for more systematic and critical evaluation of service delivery which directly involves users in assessing processes and measuring outcomes. These issues need to be borne in mind in interpreting the following account which, in drawing on the 15 reports from the national correspondents of the Observatory, is also largely reliant on a service provider's perspective.

It is worth noting at the start of this chapter that terms such as 'service user', 'client' and 'user perspective' are themselves problematic. These terms raise issues about the nature of the relationship between the service and the people who live in the housing and use the support. Their use implies a consumerist approach which may be incompatible with citizenship rights in relation to housing and support. Describing people who live in supported housing as 'clients' or 'service users' sets them apart from mainstream tenants. Some people living in supported housing are actually tenants, often long-term tenants. Others may only live in supported housing for short periods and their stay may or may not be regulated by legal tenancy arrangements. Regardless of their tenancy status, the fact remains that the vast majority of people living in supported housing view it as their primary home and as such they should be referred to as tenants or residents.

The importance of empowerment

Homelessness is an extreme form of social exclusion which can involve exclusion from normal rights of citizenship: housing rights, political rights, rights to actively participate in the community and social rights to fully benefit from welfare systems. The process of becoming homeless and the state of homelessness itself weaken an individual's ability to fully exercise his/her social, political and legal rights of citizenship. The importance of empowerment can be seen in terms of supporting the individual to redress this diminution of their rights. Barnes and Walker (1996) define 'empowerment' as a "process enabling excluded and marginalised individuals and groups to exercise greater autonomy in decision making" (p 380). In their discussion of the status and practice of citizenship, Prior et al (1995) argue that "empowerment must be concerned ... with strengthening the position of those who lack the power of influence or control" (p 81). Choice, influence and control are thus central planks of the process of empowerment and effective empowerment is central to processes of social inclusion.

Empowerment is generally regarded as a key principle of supported housing in most EU member states. Behind this seemingly simple term lies a gamut of concepts and practices, reflecting differences in national constructs of citizenship rights, professional attitudes, organisational structures and perceptions of client groups. Based on Prior et al's (1995) argument that empowerment is a process of enabling people to exercise their rights of citizenship, we broadly distinguish four different concepts of citizenship, closely linked to welfare regime types: within a social democratic model between the individual and the state, in a liberal regime between the individual and the market, in a continental welfare system between the individual and labour market or community and in a Mediterranean/formative regime between individual and the family (Table 12).

To illustrate this relationship between rights of citizenship and empowerment, we draw on selective examples from each welfare regime

Table 12: Concepts of empowerment within different welfare regimes

Welfare regime	Concept of empowerment	Legislation
Social Democratic	Citizenship	Explicit rights for all Rights to choice within social care legislation
Liberal	Consumer	Implicit rights for most Explicit rights for certain groups (eg 'priority need' homeless in the UK) Rights to choice within consumer legislation
Continental	Community/labour market	Implicit rights Explicit for certain groups (eg young people in Germany) No explicit rights to choice
Mediterranean/ formative	Family	Weak implicit rights or no rights at all No right to choice

type. The social democratic formulation of citizenship in Sweden guarantees individual rights to support, to choice in support and to refusal of support (for some client groups, see below). In practice, pressures on scarce resources, and the emerging tendency towards quasi-markets, have sometimes necessitated court involvement to safeguard the exercise of these rights. Empowerment may thus involve supporting individuals to fully exercise their rights of citizenship by challenging service providers to meet their legally defined obligations. In Britain, market-oriented welfare provision has lent a consumerist interpretation to empowerment (Prior et al, 1995). Such an interpretation stresses the importance of the *presence of individual choice*, without recognising the structural and organisational obstacles to the *exercise* of such choice, particularly for very vulnerable people (Prior et al, 1995). The interpretation of citizenship in terms of consumer rights also ignores the important role of influencing in empowerment processes. The French construct of citizenship rests on the notion of solidarity. Within this construct, empowerment may be understood in terms of enabling individuals to exercise both rights and responsibilities, particularly in relation to reinsertion into the labour market and reintegration into the community. In formative welfare regimes, citizenship may be constructed in terms of freedoms and family responsibility rather than specific rights.

In Greece and Portugal, for example, empowerment has yet to emerge as a significant principle within supported housing.

In some countries, the emergence of politicised pressure groups lobbying for the rights of certain community care client groups has, to some extent, led to differentiated notions of empowerment, a process encouraged by changing societal and professional perceptions of the differentiated abilities and potential of clients. For example, strong pressure group movements have been instrumental in shifting the focus of empowerment for disabled people from a protection model to a rights-based approach (Barnes and Walker, 1996), while the degree of self-determination and choice offered to young homeless people often differs substantially to that offered to elderly homeless people or to people with learning difficulties. In Sweden, people with learning difficulties have a right to refuse support, while mentally ill people, people suffering from dementia and those with substance abuse problems, are denied such rights. Similarly, concerns over the behaviour of mentally ill people in Britain and the potential risks involved in their care have led to a culture of professional control over their lives which is markedly different from that experienced by people with learning difficulties.

The processes of empowerment may also differ according to service level factors related to the organisation of provision and professional attitudes. Organisational frameworks for the delivery of services, interagency relationships and service level philosophy all impact on the individual's ability to make choices, influence structures and take control. The move from institutional care to community based services has brought with it a relative shift in power relationships at least insofar as the individual, as opposed to the group, has become the centre of provision. Professional training and culture can also directly affect the interpretation of 'empowerment'. The continued role and authority of medical professionals in community based hostels for ex-psychiatric patients in Greece, for example, has effectively transferred the medical model of care from the institution to the community. Social and welfare workers may be trained to encourage choice and self-determination but may still be hampered by their professional culture and organisational structures. At a fundamental level, Hutson (1999) and others have argued that the growing emphasis on support in provision for homeless people is a consequence of the involvement of social workers and welfare workers with specific skills in care and support, rather than arising from the expressed need or choice of homeless people.

The above discussion shows that empowerment is far from being a consistent notion. It varies between states, between professionals, between client groups and between service providers. Despite these variations, three central tenets can be distinguished: choice, control and the potential for influencing. Each of these in turn can be examined in relation to three 'person-centred' dimensions – a physical dimension (housing), a personal dimension (support), and a social dimension (daily life) (see Table 13). We now consider the relevance of each of these tenets of empowerment.

Table 13: Empowerment in the physical, personal and social spheres

	Physical	Personal	Social
Choice	Accept/reject housing Type of housing Location of housing Type of landlord	Accept/reject support Nature of support Level of support Duration of support Type of provider Key worker	Who shares daily routines Social association Participation in activities Selection of meals, clothes, etc
Control	Over private space Over tenancy	Over level of support Over duration of support	Over daily routines Over use of time Over finances
Influencing	House rules Use of common space Type of tenure	Methods of working Allocation processes Interagency relationships Perceptions of client group	Relations with community Daily routines Group activities

Choice

Choice is not about an open-ended set of possibilities, but rather about an exercise of some level of decision making by the individual with regard to their own lives. Homeless people are at the extremes of marginalisation both socially and economically. Their lack of choice is affected by and in turn impacts on their economic and social position. Enabling them to make choices appropriate to their needs is likely to encourage their sense of dignity, control and inclusion in wider society. Most people in mainstream housing can exercise a degree of choice in relation to housing, albeit within market constraints. People who are able to directly purchase support in their own homes can choose between different providers and are likely to have some control over the nature and level of support provided. In everyday life, people exercise choice in relation to their daily routines, the food they eat, how they spend their money, who they associate with and where they work. It should be remembered, however, that individuals do not always want to exercise choice. Some people may prefer to depend on others for decision making. Even this is a matter of personal preference.

Within supported housing, choice may be exercised, at the physical level, in relation to the type of housing, its location, the duration of stay and the type of landlord. At the personal level, choice may be exercised in relation to the type of provider, the nature and intensity of support, the duration of the support programme and the specific key worker (where applicable). At the social level, choice can relate to daily routines including social association, participation in activities and selection of meals and clothes.

According to Prior et al (1995), the growing emphasis on consumer choice in increasingly market-led welfare provision is misleading. Users of welfare provision seldom have real choices in deciding between providers. Processes of assessment and allocation by professionals in various fields act to negate direct purchasing of services by the people using them and create, instead, a hierarchy of power relationships from which the ultimate consumer is most often excluded. The limited range of service providers in specific areas and structural and organisational constraints on provision limit the exercise of choice even by purchasers. On this basis we may surmise that choice is most common at the social level and, to a lesser extent, at the personal level, while in housing-related matters choice remains restricted.

Control

An understanding of 'empowerment' necessarily requires an examination of power relationships within supported housing and the processes which encourage or redress them. Power relationships exist in all parts of society. They exist between individuals, between individuals and organisations, between organisations, between groups, between social classes and ultimately between the state and the individual. No individual, group of individuals or organisation is free from the effects of power relationships on their lives. The degree and effects of power relationships are exaggerated for people living in supported housing. This is partly due to the fact that service providers take on multiple roles: landlord, mediator, advisor, advocate, support worker, personal carer, filter to other services, filter to social contacts, conflict manager, financial manager, even organiser of daily activities and daily routines. These, often conflicting, roles give service providers considerable power over people living in supported accommodation unless mediated by an organisational philosophy and culture which gives primacy to the principles of empowerment.

Supported housing is often distinguished from traditional hostels or reception centres by its emphasis on autonomy and the shifting of control to the individual. However, both the organisation of provision and the attitudes of professionals may limit the individual's control over their life. The evidence from the national reports suggests that in supported housing control is exercised primarily at the social level and, to some extent, at the personal level. By contrast, there is very little evidence that people living in supported housing have control over their housing circumstances or their finances, arguably two key areas where individual control is critical to the process of empowerment. In Belgium, welfare workers act as facilitators, supporting rather than directing the individual in decision making. The French concept of 'mediation' places the welfare worker in a similar position, acting as a go-between on behalf of the individual. Facilitation and mediation relate primarily to personal support and social issues.

Influencing

Homeless people may have had little opportunity to influence their life circumstances and may perceive themselves as victims of events that have spiralled out of their control. These self-perceptions may be re-enforced by professional attitudes which underscore the individual's negative rather than positive agency in his/her life circumstances. Such attitudes accentuate a sense of powerlessness and futility. Lack of self-confidence and self-esteem are common experiences for homeless people. For people living in supported housing, the possibility of influencing is likely to encourage a sense of belonging, identification and participation. Adapting Sahlin's (1999) analysis, we can identify three dimensions of influencing: the sphere of influencing (personal, in practice and in policy), the method of influencing (formal and informal), and the nature of influencing (individual or collective).

Influencing differs from choice and control in that it extends beyond the personal to encompass the possibility of shaping practice within the project and policy both within and beyond the service. Influencing can also take place either formally (for example through care plan reviews, regular house meetings, voting rights, formal consultations, membership of user pressure groups, etc) or informally through individual or group discussions. Additionally, influencing offers the possibility of collective voice and collective action which may help individuals to feel valued within a group, improve communication skills and build a sense of community based on common interest rather than mere location or forced sharing. The possibility of influencing can help to build self-confidence, self-esteem and self-worth. As with choice and control, the opportunities for influencing appear to be restricted to the personal (support) and social spheres, with little or no input from residents on crucial issues such as housing type, co-residents, methods of working and staffing levels.

This discussion has shown that both the national and the service level contexts impact significantly on the ways in which the principle of empowerment is put into practice. Notions of citizenship shape national level conceptualisation of the principle of empowerment. Perceptions of client groups, professional biases of service providers and service level organisational structures create a complex and interlinked backdrop against which the individual's ability to make choices, take control and influence services is played out. Service-defined and service-led notions of empowerment and independence are not necessarily the same as user-led perspectives on these principles. The balance between them may ultimately depend on the possibilities available to residents to influence the working methods and policies of service providers. Enabling homeless people to exercise greater autonomy in decision making is a process of gradual and appropriate power sharing between the service provider and the individual living in supported housing.

The impact of policies and practices on empowerment

In this section we consider the extent to which policies and practices in supported housing encourage or discourage empowerment and social inclusion. We examine these policies and practices within the three person–centred dimensions described above (physical, personal and social; see Table 13).

In each dimension we ask what choices individuals have, how much control they can exert, and the extent to which they are enabled to influence their environment.

The physical dimension

This section considers the extent to which people living in supported housing are empowered to make choices, exercise control and influence their surroundings in relation to the type of housing (choice), the type of tenancy (control) and the influence over personal and communal space.

Type of housing

Shared living arrangements are the dominant form of supported housing provision in most EU member states. This dominance may be attributed to historical development, the demands of management efficiency, funding practices, housing market influences or, more commonly, a combination of all four. Thus the existence and continued use of shared housing is a direct result of the structure and organisation of supported housing rather than the preferences of residents. Research in Germany (Ruhstrat et al, 1991; Evers and Ruhstrat, 1994, cited in Busch-Geertsema, 1999) shows that the vast majority of single homeless people expressed a preference for self-contained dwellings over shared group living arrangements. Yet, as Busch-Geertsema points out, shared housing in Germany remains the norm with self-contained dwellings used primarily in model projects.

Shared living offers both advantages and disadvantages; it may be desirable and appropriate for some people but not for others. The social environment can alleviate loneliness and isolation and support the individual to re-establish social bonds and redevelop social skills. On the other hand, shared living arrangements can lead to conflict between residents, highlight any problems associated with challenging behaviour and, especially in larger-scale provision, impose limitations on individual choice and control. Busch-Geertsema (1999) summarises the negative effects of shared living arrangements as follows:

> ... residents ... learn strategies of behaviour to survive in enforced communities with an institutional structure which strengthen their capacity to adapt to group pressures and a life under social work control with obvious restrictions on self-reliance and individual responsibilities instead of building up competence for coping independently in individual housing. (p 46)

In a number of countries, shared living arrangements are more common for certain client groups. In the UK and Finland, for example, there is evidence that shared living is most common for people with learning difficulties and less so for young people, people with mental illness and families. The differentiation of housing type according to client groups suggests that preconceived notions of group needs and group management operate to minimise individual preferences. Policies and practices which consign whole groups of people to specific forms of housing run counter to concepts of individualisation so often articulated in relation to supported housing provision.

Within shared living, it is possible to differentiate between large-scale provision and smaller-scale more homely types of accommodation where household bonds may be encouraged (Edgar and Mina-Coull, 1999). In most member states, a shift from larger-scale shared housing to small-scale provision has been evident over the past decade. However, the re-emergence of homelessness as a significant problem in some countries is threatening to reverse this trend in order to meet the growing demand for provision.

Larger-scale shared provision is less conducive to the empowerment of the individual, not least because its effective management is likely to suppress the choices of the individual in favour of the needs of the group. Smaller-scale provision (two or three people sharing), with its closer resemblance to mainstream family living conditions, may represent a more normative model. Possibilities for social cohesion, individual choice and control are arguably greater in such models, while working methods in small-scale shared provision are more clearly oriented towards facilitating choice and control. De Decker (1998) notes that, in Belgium, the 'small-scale' ideology forms a key feature in the growth of housing with accompaniment. The small-scale nature of the provision facilitates the use of ordinary housing in ordinary streets. Unlike large-scale provision, which is physically intrusive in the neighbourhood and thus easily identified and stigmatised, ordinary housing can provide a step towards breaking down the barriers of exclusion.

Supported housing is also organised in self-contained dwellings (ie single-person housing or sharing only with family members). It is possible to distinguish three different strands in the development of self-contained supported housing. The dominance of self-contained dwellings in supported housing in some countries (for example Belgium and Luxembourg) reflects the historical reliance on private sector landlords for the supply of housing. In other countries (for example UK, Austria, France and Germany) the more recent shift from shared to self-contained housing may be understood in relation to principles of normalisation, empowerment and independence. In the Mediterranean countries the dominance of owner-occupation influences the use of short-term transitional accommodation and protected housing, while support and advice centres focus on the reinsertion of people into ordinary apartments in the housing market (for example Spain, Portugal, Greece and parts of Italy).

Self-contained housing has a number of advantages over shared living arrangements. First, individual choices do not have to be balanced against group needs. Second, families do not have to be separated as may be the case in shared housing. Third, self-contained housing can offer stability and a sense of permanence, especially where the accommodation is offered on a long-term or indefinite basis. Fourth, issues of privacy and control over physical space are less problematic in self-contained housing. This is especially important in relation to the management of challenging behaviour. For some people, however, self-contained accommodation may contribute to social isolation and loneliness. In Belgium, dispersed supported housing units are therefore sometimes linked through neighbourhood communal lounges and cafes that give people opportunities to meet and to develop social relationships.

Tenancy issues

Tenancy issues in supported housing are important for two reasons. First, the offer of mainstream tenancy conditions (ie tenancies which are common to all tenants in the specific sector) imparts a normative dimension to supported housing. Second, for homeless people, it is precisely their lack of housing security and their vulnerability in the cycle of revolving door services which marginalises them and leads to social exclusion. Security of tenure can encourage a sense of commitment, ownership and belonging to both the home and the community which, in turn, may facilitate social inclusion.

None of the member states has specific legislation governing tenancy rights in supported housing. Legally, the types of tenancy agreements possible are determined by the status of the landlord: private sector tenancies for housing rented from private landlords and public sector tenancies for housing rented from social landlords. Nevertheless the evidence indicates that the vast majority or residents in supported housing have some form of occupancy or tenancy agreement. Only a small minority of residents in supported housing lack any form of written contractual agreement. For example, in Belgium, research has shown that 7% of supported housing providers offer no form of written agreement (de Decker, 1998), while in the UK only 4% of residents do not have a written agreement (Edgar and Muirhead, 1998).

In practice, three overlapping structural and organisational issues appear to be minimising housing security and housing rights for people living in supported accommodation. First, there is some evidence to suggest that, in some countries (for example UK, Sweden, Denmark and Finland), the type of housing (ie self-contained, small-scale shared or large-scale shared) may affect legal tenancy entitlements. While the information on tenancy rights in shared living arrangements is limited to a small number of countries, the evidence does indicate that shared housing affects the individual's legal right to hold normalised tenancies. In Scotland, Edgar and Mina-Coull (1999) have shown that shared housing arrangements, while not legally incompatible with full tenancy rights, nevertheless raise a number of complex practice-based issues which often result in a minimisation of housing security and increase the individual's vulnerability to discretionary eviction. In Sweden, Denmark and Finland, rights to support and 'special housing' enshrined in the Social Services Acts constrain the use of ordinary tenancies.

Second, the practice of sub-letting arrangements can affect the resident's security of tenure. In several member states, the concerns of private and even public sector landlords over the risks of offering tenancies directly to vulnerable households is promoting the use of sub-letting arrangements. In this context the support provider acts as a buffer between the property owner and the resident. These arrangements guarantee landlords regular rent payments by tenants who are receiving support to ensure their 'good behaviour'. For residents, sub-letting often translates into lesser housing security, a situation which Busch-Geertsema (1999) describes as discriminatory. Nevertheless, in some cases, the resident can eventually accede to the principal tenancy. However, more recently there has been concern that landlords, accustomed to the safeguards offered by supported sub-letting arrangements, may be reluctant to use direct tenancies or to eventually transfer the tenancy to residents. De Gouy (1998) notes that, as a condition of accessing housing, French landlords, in both the public and private sectors, are increasingly requesting intervention from support providers who would hold the principle tenancy and provide support. This trend may result in households being forced to accept support in order to access housing. Service charges for unnecessary support, which may be added to rents, further disadvantage households with low incomes.

In Sweden, recent changes in VAT legislation are persuading some municipalities to abandon direct tenancies altogether in favour of sub-leases in order to reclaim their 18% VAT discount. Housing enterprises in Germany frequently refuse to transfer sub-letting contracts into full tenancies, despite regular rent payments and good neighbour relationships, preferring instead the security offered by the mediation of social offices.

Third, the integration of housing management and support provision may be one reason why some purchasers and providers are favouring lesser forms of housing contracts in supported accommodation, especially where legal ambiguity over tenancy rights exists. Most people living in supported housing have some form of written contractual agreement either with the landlord, with the support provider or with both. The circumstances under which housing agreements are integrated into or separated from support agreements are unclear. Even where two different contracts are concluded, their interdependence may not be spelled out explicitly. While good practice would suggest that security of tenure should be independent of a support contract, in practice, tenancies in supported housing are often contingent upon acceptance of and compliance with a support package. This form of linkage between housing and support exists in both self-contained and shared housing. By implication, even in self-contained housing, individuals who no longer need or want the support offered, would be obliged to move. Such a rupture in the individual's life is an example of the dominance of organisational needs over individual choices. In other cases, however, the support contract allows sufficient freedom for the tenant/resident to select alternative sources of support or terminate the support altogether while remaining in the accommodation. This form of contractual arrangement gives people greater choice in their support provider while, at the same time, enabling them to benefit from housing stability.

Normal tenancy rights are less likely to be offered in situations where the supported accommodation is intended to be for a limited or transitional period. They are also less likely to occur where the support provider both owns and manages the accommodation. De Decker comments that "this can be seen as inappropriate, since the contractual relationship between provider and client can be seen as a structuring feature of the process towards independence" (1998, p 48). In Greece, people with mental illness living in hospital-linked supported housing have no written or verbal agreements with the service providers. The combination of close physical and organisational proximity to the institutional hospital setting, and the view that the accommodation is only transitory, have led to the conclusion that tenancies were a non-issue (Sapounakis, 1998).

The 'staircase of transition' approach to support provision combine features of transitional accommodation, shared living and contractual rules and has been particularly criticised for failing to provide normalised living conditions which empower individuals. Holding out the dual possibilities of eventual full tenancy rights and discretionary eviction for non-compliance, their use severely limits resident control and increases resident vulnerability. Busch-Geertsema (1999) argues that, in the absence of housing security, the staircase of transition can turn into the staircase of exclusion as "the lower steps of the system are used as negative sanctions for misdemeanour". There is a concern that the growing use of these types of housing contracts may lead to the expansion of a secondary, marginalised, housing market.

Personal and communal space

Privacy, the ability to control private space and the potential for influencing the management of shared space are likely to contribute to the individual's identification with their home. Most people living in shared housing have their own bedrooms and the reported incidence of dormitory type sharing is very low. Single bedrooms offer a measure of autonomy and the possibility of retreat into private and safe space. People living in shared supported housing are often required to comply with house rules and regulations governing their conduct. Breaches of behavioural rules and regulations which are linked to tenancy agreements can result in eviction. To the extent that such rules of conduct extend beyond the normal expectations of a mainstream tenancy, these requirements limit normalisation. In shared living arrangements, the rationale for behavioural rules and regulations tends to be embedded in the duty to protect all residents. In this respect, the nature of the accommodation itself may be imposing behavioural restrictions which do not encourage independence. According to Schoibl, "failure in supported housing – for whatever reason – results then in a decline into very precarious structures of actual homelessness or into very precarious accommodation, with uncertain prospects and for indefinite periods of time" (Schoibl, 1999, p 17).

The personal dimension

It is perhaps in its approach to individualised support packages that supported housing is most successful in encouraging choice and flexible working. The real extent to which individuals are involved in determining the level of support they want, the nature of it and, importantly, who delivers it, remains unclear. This section considers the extent to which the individual is empowered to make choices and exercise control with respect to the nature, level and duration of support.

Nature of support

In supported housing, individual choice and control is relevant in relation to access to support, accepting or rejecting support and determining the nature of support. In some EU member states, certain client groups have a legally recognised right to support. In Sweden, Finland and Denmark, for example, these rights are enshrined in Social Welfare Acts. The existence of these legal rights gives individuals the power to legally challenge providers to meet their support needs with the most appropriate provision. In countries where no such rights exist (for example Portugal, Greece, Spain), people with support needs may be forced to rely on family, informal networks or inappropriate provision.

Whether or not legal rights to support exist, there is evidence to suggest that in most member states, some client groups or individuals with particular support needs are less likely to access support. Assessment processes often take into account the individual's willingness to participate in support programmes and the likelihood that s/he might benefit from it. People with chaotic lifestyles may be most vulnerable to exclusion from supported housing. In Greece, for example, the very limited existing supported housing denies access to people with drug/alcohol problems, refugees and asylum seekers and people with mental illness.

Rights to accept and, more importantly, reject support are less common. In Sweden, these rights are legally recognised for people with learning difficulties and elderly people, but not for people with mental illness. In the absence of such rights and given the scarcity of affordable housing, people with little or no support needs may be forced to inappropriately agree to supported housing as the only route to temporary or permanent housing. Once in supported housing, residents may have little control over the length of time they receive support. Time limitations on stays in supported housing and lack of exit routes to permanent resettlement minimise the individual's control over the duration of support they require.

Individualised care plans are intended to tailor the nature and intensity of the support programme to the individual's needs. Individualised care plans are common in countries where supported housing has developed out of a planned process of de-institutionalisation. In Belgium, welfare workers support individuals to define the nature and level of support required. The individual is at the centre of provision and is regularly consulted on the appropriateness of the support package. The focus on the individual does not necessarily imply open-ended choice in the nature and level of support. The expertise of support staff, the philosophy and orientation of the project and the available resources often predetermine the range of options open to the individual. In France, reinsertion philosophies in supported housing tend to link housing and support to employment training or protected work projects. Homeless people accessing these types of services have little choice with regard to participation in work programmes. Similarly, many supported housing projects in the UK and elsewhere require participation in drug or alcohol rehabilitation programmes as a condition of entry. Thus, even where the concept of individualised support packages has been embedded into supported housing provision, individuals may have only partial choice and control over the nature and level of support they receive.

Individualised care plans may be less common in countries where supported housing has developed out of innovations within traditional homelessness services. Until recently, generic provision for mixed client groups has been the norm in Austria. Support programmes have traditionally been defined by the service provider with little reference to the specific and individual needs of residents. This type of care provision clearly limits any individualisation of support packages and any individual choice in the type and intensity of support provided. Schoibl (1999) concludes that the type of support provided "depends less on the situation and/or the needs of the users [than] on the available accommodation and the funding of individual support" (p 8). The recently emerging trend towards diversification of services and targeting at particular client groups is giving greater primacy to the concept of individualised support packages.

Level and duration of support

The structure of support delivery in most member states allows few, if any, choices with regard to the support provider. Much of supported accommodation is accessed through a gating system where reception houses and other first contact providers filter people through into supported housing. The matching of client need with support provider appears, in most cases, to be based on available space and interagency links.

Choice and control over the level of support provided may be strongly influenced by purchasing methods in supported housing. In this respect, the financial stability of projects may be at odds with the principle of individualised funding packages. In the UK, block funding of entire projects safeguards the service providers long-term planning and financial security. However, such funding mechanisms can constrain flexibility by predetermining staff time and the nature of support. Individual funding packages based on assessment and review of support needs allow greater flexibility, choice and control for residents but may increase service providers' financial risks.

In most member states, support is only available within the scope of the supported housing project itself. Once resettled into permanent accommodation, outreach support offered on a flexible and needs-led basis is largely unavailable. Particularly in the context of short- to medium-term supported housing provision with resettlement into widely dispersed areas, the absence of outreach support may be a barrier to the integrative process in the new housing environment. It may be argued that discontinuity and rupture disrupt the processes of social inclusion and undo the efforts undertaken within the context of supported housing.

The social dimension

This section considers the extent to which people living in supported housing have choice and control over their daily lives with reference to their daily routines, social association and control over finances.

Principles of empowerment in supported housing are most commonly operationalised in terms of enabling residents to make choices relating to their daily routines. The focus on 'independent living' translates into supporting people to choose their own food, cook their own meals, decide on daily activities, participate in community activities, take responsibility for budgeting and household expenditures and, in some circumstances, take on paid employment. To the extent that these activities form an integral part of mainstream life, facilitating choice and control in these areas represents both normalisation and empowerment.

Over the past decade, academics and service providers have come to recognise that social rupture and social isolation are key contributory factors in processes leading to homelessness. In principle, methods of working in supported housing are intended to facilitate social integration. In practice, three obstacles to effective and normalised social integration arise directly out of the organisation of supported housing: the physical location of supported housing, the dominant use of shared housing and house rules. The physical location of supported housing on the periphery of neighbourhoods, in hard-to-let areas or in stigmatised large structures creates barriers to wider community participation by residents. Physical isolation promotes a sense of exclusion and separation. On the other hand, the simple location of supported housing amidst ordinary housing does not in itself guarantee integration within the social setting. Building community relations, encouraging shared use of community facilities and helping people to become involved in everyday community life and activities are essential elements in social integration. For many people, supported housing is a transitional step towards long-term resettlement. Transitional stays in accommodation tend to be characterised by a sense of instability and a lack of vested interest in establishing deep roots. This is particularly true if, in the end, there is little chance of resettlement within the same community or neighbourhood as the supported housing project. Exit routes from supported housing into mainstream housing are increasingly limited by the combination of tight housing markets and weak interagency links. In Belgium, eligibility criteria for accessing social rental housing are being redefined with the aim of minimising risks to social landlords. 'High risk' households (for example previously homeless households) are increasingly less likely to gain access to the sector. Welfare agencies have no choice but to rely on partnerships within the private rental sector, which itself may be reluctant to provide permanent resettlement opportunities. In this environment, supported housing becomes less a temporary stepping stone to permanent housing and more a permanent revolving door of provision. Individuals facing such a system are unlikely to have choice or control over their housing security. In Italy, on the other hand, living in supported housing gives residents significant additional points in accessing social rented housing.

The dominant use of shared living minimises residents' choice of social contacts. Assessment and allocation processes are increasingly taking into account issues of social compatibility when placing new residents in shared living environments. There is some evidence to suggest that service providers with a strong commitment to empowerment principles have introduced formal processes for consulting existing tenants with regard to the suitability of new placements. However, the extent to which objections of existing tenants influence placement decisions has not been evaluated. Moreover, these practices are the exception rather than the norm. Scarcity of resources and the primacy of professional assessment have generally tended to concentrate choice of flat-mates and control over shared housing in the hands of service providers.

Shared living can affect an individual's control over their daily lives in other respects. We identified above that the majority of residents of supported housing have their own bedroom; however, having one's own room does not always imply control over that private space. As Busch-Geertsema (1999) reports, the fact that residents in shared supported housing have a legal right to refuse entry to their room does not necessarily prevent staff from entering without permission. This example illustrates the gap between rights and practice. The evidence with respect to collective decision making and collective action on the management and use of common space in shared housing is less clear. Anecdotal evidence from the UK and elsewhere suggests that wide variations exist between service providers, between client groups and between long-term and short-term projects. Such variations underline the dominant role of the service provider in determining the extent to which residents are supported to function collectively in shared supported housing.

Finally, particularly in shared supported housing, opportunities for continued or renewed association with family and friends may be curtailed by rules and regulations on visiting. Restrictions on visiting times and overnight visits, lack of appropriate space for private visits, a sense that common areas are not personal and restrictions on staying out all night clearly limit individual choice in social association. In self-contained dwellings, the absence of such rules and regulations is more likely to encourage choice in and control over social contacts.

In order to exercise effective choice in relation to daily routines and activities, people living in supported housing need not only sufficient financial resources but also control over those finances. In the UK, meagre personal allowances paid to people living in registered supported housing (registered with social work departments) have been the subject of considerable criticism. Variable and seemingly discriminatory requirements for registration of provision are seriously restricting individuals' ability to make consumer choices.

Conclusion

Empowerment is a key principle underpinning supported housing in most EU member states. While acknowledging variations in the interpretation of the concept both between countries and between services within a single state, we have nevertheless identified three key elements of empowerment: choice, control and influencing. Enabling people to make choices, take control and exercise some influence in relation to their housing, support and social environment is critical to the process of social inclusion and integration. In the longer term, the effectiveness of supported housing in preventing (repeat) homelessness and reintegrating homeless people will depend as much on the extent to which it enables people to regain their confidence and self-esteem as it does on housing and support provision.

This chapter has shown that, in most member states, support providers are increasingly prioritising empowerment within their working methods, particularly in relation to choice and control over the nature of support and the routines of daily life. On the other hand, the evidence also suggests that the wider structure and organisation of supported housing has been slower to adjust to the requirements of such an evolution. In particular, the dominance of shared living arrangements, lack of choice in housing, residualisation of tenancies, constraints in the housing market and the ways in which supported housing is funded appear to be minimising individual choice and control in critical areas. If supported housing is to fully play a role in the prevention of homelessness and the reintegration of homeless people, then clearly the structure and organisation of provision will need to become more flexible in order to enable greater individual choice and control over both housing and support. In this respect, systematic research on the user perspective would be useful in guiding both structural and service level changes while, at the same time, enabling people living in supported housing to influence services.

EIGHT

Problems, issues and debates

Introduction

Supported housing and support in housing exist, to a greater or lesser degree, in all the member states of the European Union and are expanding, albeit slowly. This trend reflects the now generally accepted view that, to meet the multidimensional causes of homelessness, housing provision, while necessary, is not sufficient. However, this study has also demonstrated that the development, organisation and approach to the provision of supported housing varies across the member states and that there is considerable variation in availability both between and within countries. It is also apparent that there exist strong structural and, in some countries, policy constraints which act to hinder the development and effectiveness of supported housing. In addition, despite a widespread acceptance that there is a need to coordinate support with housing, there remains some ambivalence in some countries concerning the role which supported housing can play in the reintegration of people into society. This ambivalence is apparent whether we view the sector from a social welfare or housing perspective.

Our analysis has demonstrated the contribution which supported housing currently makes to meeting the needs of different groups of homeless people and the extent to which it may impinge on the processes leading to homelessness among vulnerable individuals. This has led us to the conclusion that, while housing provision alone is not the solution to homelessness, neither is the provision of housing with support a simple or total solution to reintegration for all people who are homeless or at risk of homelessness. A range of factors have been identified, in the course of this study, which currently constrain the effectiveness of supported housing in tackling the problems of homelessness. This chapter focuses on these issues and examines the associated debates and dilemmas. It concludes by considering those issues which need to be addressed if supported housing is to empower homeless people to lead (more) independent lives in the community.

Context of the emergence of supported housing

We have suggested that there are three broad groupings of countries in which supported housing has a distinctive genesis, relationship to social welfare and housing policy. We distinguished these groupings of countries on the basis of three broad parameters linked to the development of supported housing: social policy objectives, the legislative framework, and the role of the state.

In the first group of countries, supported housing has emerged within the context of a process of de-institutionalisation and a shift to the community delivery of care services. These countries tend to have a legislative basis for the provision of support defining statutory obligations and, often, personal rights. The instruments of legislation may specify the types of arrangements linking support and housing which are eligible for financial subsidy. Within this group of countries there is a range of forms of provision, often including purpose-built supported accommodation, group homes or special housing on the one hand, and support (ambulatory or floating) to people in ordinary housing on the other. In most instances the responsibility for provision is decentralised to the municipal level of government and the state acts as a purchaser of services from the private or NGO sector. This group of countries includes Denmark, Finland, Germany, the Netherlands, Sweden, and the UK.

The second group of countries shares some of the characteristics of the first group, at least insofar as the process of de-institutionalisation is concerned. They tend to be distinguished by the fact that the development of supported housing has emerged more from a social exclusion policy framework, and from measures, directives and legislation targeted specifically at those most marginalised in society, rather than policies related to the community delivery of care services. Insofar as there is a legislative basis to the development of support services, this may derive from housing policy as much as from welfare policy and is likely to be regionally diverse. This approach is probably most fully developed in France, where the *Loi Besson* introduced the right to housing and remains one of the key legislative instruments in the field of public and social action for households in need. A primary purpose of the measures developed in this legislation is to finance the provision of social care in access to and maintenance of housing. Belgium (at least the French-speaking part) and Luxembourg can also be said to share similar characteristics.

While other countries in this group do not have a legislative basis, they share a similar approach in developing support aimed at integrating the most marginalised groups in society. Austria and Italy, while they do not fit readily into any of the three groups we have identified, sit most easily within this social exclusion and reintegration group. Both countries are characterised by regional disparity in approaches to social assistance, reflected in the nine *Bundesländer* of Austria and in the regional laws of Italy. In Austria the absence of overall guidance, legislation and regulation has given rise to widely disparate approaches, differentiated pace of development and lack of coordination. While supported housing has emerged from localised social services responses, their development has often been linked to labour market reintegration projects (Kofler, 1998). In Italy, regional diversity is a key feature of provision and there is an apparent lack of coordination of housing and social services throughout the country. Hence supported housing has tended to be associated either with adults in difficulty or with people who are seriously marginalised. Provision for the former group is linked to social welfare provision and social assistance aimed at preventing social exclusion, while provision for the latter group tends to emerge from more traditional projects for homeless people. In this respect Italy, although it has had a long history of de-institutionalisation, shares some features with our third group of countries.

The third group of countries is characterised by limited de-institutionalisation; here the family and civil society (especially the church) are important actors in the provision of care. In these countries, supported accommodation projects have been predominantly set up by non–profit organisations, often connected with church organisations operating in the community. They are therefore initiatives planned, at least initially, completely independently by these organisations, often based on previous, more traditional, welfare work (night shelters, emergency help, counselling/advice centres, etc). The religious origin of many of these initiatives has facilitated the connection between supported accommodation and community networks of services already provided by religious institutions (for example *Caritás*). The purpose of the accommodation and support is, generally, to provide a transitional step between traditional homelessness services and ordinary housing. This group of countries includes Portugal, Spain and Greece. However, Ireland and Italy also share many of these characteristics.

Structural constraints

In most EU countries factors linked to the operation of the housing market, housing policy and social policy, either singly or in combination, act to constrain the expansion and implementation of supported housing projects. The most common, and obvious, housing market constraint centres on the shortage of suitable housing. The reasons for this shortage include both basic supply issues as well as tenure structure. A number of countries, including Germany, Sweden, Finland, the UK and the Netherlands, all report a lack of suitable social housing or self-contained housing as a factor limiting the expansion of supported housing. In a number of countries the dominance of the private rented sector requires the development of particular mechanisms of support (for instance, Social Rental Agencies) to guarantee the provision of a supply of housing in which support can be provided for vulnerable people; these countries include Belgium, Luxembourg and Germany. However, the reluctance to allocate housing for the use of people with support needs is not restricted only to the private rented sector. There is evidence from Germany, the Netherlands and the UK that social landlords (including housing associations) are only willing to work with homelessness NGOs in providing supported housing for homeless people. In the UK the implementation of specific performance standards by the regulatory agencies (The Housing Corporation and Scottish Homes) may even act as a disincentive to housing associations becoming involved in this specialised form of housing provision (Edgar and Mina-Coull, 1998). It is also apparent that in those countries where home ownership is the dominant tenure (for example Greece, Ireland, Portugal and Spain) supported housing is significantly less well developed as a solution to homelessness.

Housing policy may also, either directly or indirectly, affect the provision of supported housing. In those countries where there is a statutory basis for the provision of supported housing (the first group of countries identified above), funding priorities have often been slow to respond to assessments of need. Often in these countries, supported housing projects associated with an institutional reprovisioning programme gain higher priority than similar housing for homeless people. In the second group of countries the reliance on the public/social rented sector provides the main source of constraint. There is also evidence that, at least in Italy and possibly also in Austria, a lack of policy coordination between housing and social services agencies has proved to be a major constraint. In these, as in all the countries which make up our third group, the lack of a national legislative basis for the development of supported housing results in a diversity of policies and unevenness in practice across these countries. In our third group of countries there is a lack of a coherent national (or even local) housing policy regarding the development of supported housing or the implementation of services for homeless people. In these countries innovation in support provision has relied on the actions of individual voluntary organisations.

Social policy and social protection policies also affect the development or implementation of supported housing. In our first group of countries – Denmark, Sweden, Netherlands, Finland, Germany and the UK – the main constraint relates either to the lack of adequate revenue funding for support or the restrictive time limits attached to its provision. Uncertainty concerning revenue funding can limit not only the development of supported housing projects but also the provision of adequate outreach or follow-on support for people moving from transitional accommodation to permanent housing. In the Netherlands, for instance, restrictions on social assistance limit the development of supported housing for young people in particular. In the second group of countries – France, Belgium, Luxembourg, Austria and Italy – one of the major constraints relates to the lack of coordination and integration of funding arrangements for support between housing and social welfare services. In the third group of countries – Greece, Spain, Portugal and Ireland – finance for the provision of support is predominantly reliant on the voluntary sector combined with limited, and uncertain, public sector input. Where public sector funding is available it is often prescribed in relation to particular poverty programmes (Portugal) or refugee programmes (Greece).

However, there is evidence that in some countries the framework of funding is changing to a more flexible or a more coordinated approach. In Denmark, for example, recent legislation uncouples the link between particular forms of accommodation provision and financial support for individuals regardless of their housing circumstances. In Italy recent legislation aims to integrate financial support for individuals to ensure the coordination of services aimed at the reintegration of people into society. In the UK, an interdepartmental review group has met to develop proposals for more coordinated financing arrangements, between social care, housing and health. Similarly, in Flemish-speaking Belgium, a single welfare budget aims to allow greater flexibility in funding.

In all countries there is clear evidence of an uneven spatial variation in the distribution and availability of different forms of supported accommodation. The dominant pattern is between metropolitan areas (relatively well provided) and other, non-metropolitan and rural areas (poorly provided). This distinction occurs across all countries regardless of the stage of development of supported housing. In Britain, for example, provision is concentrated in London and Glasgow and, overall, the majority of provision is concentrated in a very few local authority areas. In Finland, Sweden, and Denmark, as well as in Portugal, provision is concentrated in the (major) urban areas. In some countries, for example the Netherlands and Germany, provision has been skewed by the implementation of pilot projects (for example the TWSSV project in the Netherlands and the EXWOST project in Germany) towards particular cities or regions. Elsewhere (in Austria, Belgium, Italy and Spain for example), differences in legislative frameworks between administrative areas of the country have resulted in and perpetuate variation in provision and practice.

Ambivalence of roles

While supported housing is generally regarded as a positive response to the needs of vulnerable people, it is clear that there is an ambivalence in some situations concerning the role of supported housing as a solution to the needs of homeless people. This ambivalence is manifest both in respect to the perception of the objectives of supported housing (the inputs) and with respect to its achievements (its outcomes).

From a care perspective, the end objective of supported housing is to enable independent living while, from a social exclusion perspective, the goal is understood in terms of reintegration into society by enabling re-engagement with the economic and social spheres of life. However, paradoxically it is clear that, for some people, independent living (ie living in the community rather than in an institution) is only achievable with continued and permanent support. Equally, the attainment of complete reintegration or autonomy is, for many, a chimera. In very different contexts, Sahlin (1999) in Sweden, Busch-Geertsema (1999) in Germany and Tosi and Ranci (1999) in Italy, all point to the risks that this ambivalence raises. Sahlin and Busch-Geertsema suggest that long-term dependency on support services may lead to the creation of a secondary housing market, perpetuating rather than preventing exclusion. Tosi and Ranci, in turn, point to the ambivalence of the objective of supported housing for the social integration of marginalised people, since services combine (and move between) protection (and hence control) and the promotion of autonomy. They argue that these conflicting objectives are only reconciled by the acceptance of a concept of partial integration. In supporting this view, Tosi and Ranci argue that even the status of permanent semi-autonomy produces a result which considerably improves the quality of life of many people and can prevent them from progressing towards full and irreversible homelessness. This argument therefore suggests a continuity between reintegration objectives and those of improving the quality of life, and confirms the wisdom of combining different types of intervention (supported accommodation and low threshold support) in service networks.

There is some evidence to suggest that the relatively high costs of support provision, in itself, creates an ambivalence of roles in relation to outcomes. Because of their expense, support costs tend to be regarded as an 'investment' and hence only people who may be perceived as 'good risks' become eligible. There is evidence from all EU countries, regardless of welfare regime, that access is directed to those who can demonstrate a positive attitude, motivation or ability towards achieving integration or independent living. Yet the aim of supported housing is to prevent the social exclusion and homelessness of the most marginalised people, that is people, given their circumstances and life experiences, least likely to display such positive attitudes.

This ambivalence of role is also manifest in the very nature of the provision of supported housing in that it may act to exclude some from access or have a negative effect on the desired goal of inclusion. In all countries, the majority of supported housing occurs within shared dwellings; yet the requirements of shared living may be inimical to the attainment of inclusion and autonomy. For example, if the service provider is to exercise a duty of care to all residents, the challenging behaviour of some individuals needs to be controlled by regulations and procedures which serve to protect the shared living environments by excluding the unruly. A range of factors can account for the predominance of shared living approaches and these vary between countries. In Germany, for example, it occurs despite the expressed intention of the legislation to provide self-contained accommodation. In this case, housing market constraints, support costs and the role of voluntary sector ownership of supported housing coalesce to produce this particular form of accommodation provision. Similar factors are in evidence in other countries.

Where supported housing is provided by means of 'special housing' (for example Sweden) or group homes (for example Finland and the UK) the intention of normalisation, for example in relation to the granting of normal tenancy rights, are often circumscribed. In Sweden,

Sahlin (1999) discusses the need to protect the tenancy rights of those living in 'special housing'. In the UK, Edgar and Mina-Coull (1998) describe a range of factors which lead to less than a fifth of residents in supported accommodation schemes possessing tenancies. Hence in this respect there appears to be an ambivalence between empowerment and normalisation objectives, on the one hand, and the actual outcomes for individuals on the other.

Contribution to the problems of homelessness

In the preceding chapters we have identified that there are different forms and approaches to the provision of supported housing. We have also demonstrated that the distinctive needs of people for support, in order to normalise housing conditions or lifestyles, predicate the requirement for this diversity in approach. We have argued that the contribution of supported housing, and therefore the method of its delivery, may be quite different for people whose route to homelessness or risk of homelessness vary. Making a broad distinction, we suggest that the type, intensity and permanency of support required may be quite different, for example, for people leaving long-term institutional care (people with a learning disability, people with a mental health problem, ex-offenders, young people leaving care), for people at risk of homelessness following a relationship crisis (women fleeing domestic violence, vulnerable young women with children, young people forced to leave home), and for people who are roofless or living in insecure conditions in the community (people with a drug or alcohol dependency, long-term vulnerable homeless, young people).

Within this categorisation of needs, it is apparent that are some people (and groups of people) who have a demonstrable need for permanent support. In this context supported housing performs a preventative role either in relation to the risk of institutional living or of rooflessness. Given the capacity problems identified earlier in the report, in relation to existing provision and the inelasticity of supply, then it is logical to assume that there is a proportion of people who are living in institutions or on the streets because of a lack of adequate permanent supported housing. Equally there are groups of people who have a need for support for a transitional period in their lives. For some this period may be quite short, linked to a crisis or emergency and facilitating a readjustment in their housing, employment and/or relationship circumstances. For others the period may be quite long-term, during which the nature and intensity of support required may vary. Reviewing the evidence, it seems to be the case that supported housing is better at meeting the needs of those with short-term requirements for support rather than those whose needs may be long-term or are fluctuating.

The contribution which supported housing can make to ameliorating an individual's life situation will often depend on whether it is available to them at the time they most require it. Concern is expressed in many of the national reports that the availability of such support is often 'too little too late' for the most marginalised in society. The point of intervention comes too late in the trajectory of exclusion to guarantee a high level of success in the social inclusion or reintegration of (especially long-term) homeless people. Despite this critique of the level of successful outcomes, it is apparent that supported housing does provide a vital intervention for some of the most marginalised in society. In this respect, it is worth reiterating the argument made elsewhere in the report, that we need to view the contribution of supported housing to the problems of homelessness in terms of relatively limited objectives. The ideal objective of normalising housing conditions and normalising lifestyles is not achievable for all and needs to be bounded by more limited criteria.

It is clear that a key distinction in the approach to the provision of support services between countries (and within countries) is that between 'ambulatory' and 'stationary' support or, put another way, between support in housing and supported housing. While the aim, and the ideal model preferred in most countries, is for the provision of support to people in ordinary (self-contained) housing, funding and housing market constraints often prevent the achievement of this model. However, to meet the needs of the different types of people at risk of homelessness it is also recognised that there is a need for a range of forms of provision: supported housing, housing with support, self-contained housing with ordinary tenancies and shared living arrangements. To the extent that housing and support policies and practices in Europe has served to provide such a range of provision, they can be seen as having made a valuable contribution to a solution to the problems of homelessness.

Constraints on effectiveness

The effectiveness of supported housing can be measured on the basis of three basic criteria: whether it is accessible to those who require these services, whether the support and housing provided are appropriate to the needs of the people using the service, and whether the outcome from the service is judged to have achieved the stated objectives of that service (eg resulting in permanent rehousing, improvement in quality of life, prevention of institutional living). The evaluation of supported housing, according to these criteria is exceptional rather than routine and there is, as a consequence, very little hard evidence available with which to address such questions. Nevertheless, it is possible to identify a number of specific factors which act as constraints limiting the effectiveness of supported housing. At the broadest level, we have already argued that the lack of provision, together with the largely urban bias, is itself a constraint on the effectiveness of supported housing. We have also argued that access to support services may be constrained for homeless people either because the services are linked to institutional reprovisioning programmes, or because allocation rules are structured to exclude the most marginalised or difficult people. While there is little direct empirical evidence relating to the source of referral of people in supported accommodation, the evidence which does exist demonstrates different scenarios. Where supported housing is linked to traditional homelessness hostel accommodation, it is to be expected that people have spent time there *en route* to supported housing and that this is part of a reintegration process. In Belgium, de Decker (1999) demonstrates that more than half of people spent time in homelessness reception houses, while a fifth were self-referred and a tenth were referred by the social services authority. In the UK, on the other hand, where housing associations are the main providers of supported housing, linking with voluntary managing agencies to provide the support, access is perhaps less prescriptive. Self-referral or direct application is the most common method of accessing supported housing (28% of all households) and is the most common mode of referral for single homeless people. Almost a fifth of people were referred by voluntary organisations, and these people were more likely to be single homeless, women fleeing domestic violence or refugees. Local authority nominations (12%) were more likely to be made for frail older people, vulnerable women with children, physically disabled people or people with AIDS/HIV. Social services referrals (10%), on the other hand, tended to be made on behalf of young people leaving care, people with a learning difficulty or physical disability as well as frail older people.

We have identified that support falls broadly into three types: housing support (obtaining and managing a dwelling), social support (providing skills, information and counselling to re-enter the employment market and maintain social contacts) and personal support (meeting personal, health and related care needs). The availability of appropriate support in meeting people's needs – housing, social and/or personal – can be constrained by the legislative basis under which services are provided, in particular by funding constraints or by organisational factors.

In those countries which have a legislative basis for the provision of supported housing, the form of support and the eligibility for funding is generally defined in the legislation or in related guidance. However, as financing arrangements and criteria change and become more flexible, such constraints on support provision may be lessening. In the UK, for example, recent attempts have been made to improve coordination between departments by clarifying the distinction between housing support and social care, and between social and healthcare to clarify confusion over funding responsibilities. In Denmark, legislative change has removed the distinction between institutional and non-institutional support. In Italy legislative change, by creating an integrated system of social assistance and social services, aims to promote active intervention by creating a 'social protection network' coordinating public and private sector social welfare agencies. Thus we can perceive that different approaches to financial constraints – more 'joined-up' responsibilities, more flexible eligibility criteria and attempts to promote proactive intervention – are all in evidence. However, Busch-Geertsema (1999) reflects a widespread concern when he questions whether changes in Germany, which could allow more flexibility in the type and intensity of the support which can be provided, will be undermined by the pressure to reduce overall expenditure.

In Finland, there is a similar split between municipal housing support services and state funding for social and health service support; however, there is also a heavy reliance on the funding from the Slot Machine Association and on charitable donations. In Mediterranean countries the funding of supported housing is almost exclusively reliant on the innovative capacity of charitable organisations.

However, it is not only the type of support which is available which is critical to changing the life circumstances of homeless people. The process of provision is also a significant factor influencing its effectiveness. Particularly for single homeless people, and for those who have experienced lengthy periods of homelessness or of institutional living, intensive and extensive outreach support is essential. It is necessary at the reception phase and may be required for a lengthy period until a reintegration strategy can be implemented. It is equally necessary at the autonomy phase of involvement as people move on to independent living. However, the evidence from all countries suggests that this is the area of work which is least likely to be funded and where time-limited, or uncertain, funding acts as a major constraint affecting successful outcomes.

There is evidence from all welfare contexts that support provided to an individual is time-limited. This limited arrangement is generally determined in a prescriptive manner or from funding restrictions rather than on the basis of the individual's needs or in negotiation with the person concerned. In Germany, for example, the regular duration of support is defined in national guidelines to be not longer than 12 to 15 months (BAG ueoe Tr, 1995, p 163). In the Netherlands, a study of 31 supported living projects identified the duration of support to vary from a period less than six months (for 21% of clients) to a period of around two years (27% of clients). In a different context, support in the Portuguese projects is intended to be for a period of four months. In all countries, it is possible to vary this time period in specific instances, but it is clear that exceptional circumstances are measured against such benchmarks.

The effectiveness of support arrangements also relies heavily on organisational factors, especially if the support is to be flexible in approach and individualised in focus. The integration of housing and support, as well as the provision of different forms of support, will generally involve coordination of action both within and between agencies. Examining the variety of management and coordination arrangements, which are described in Chapter 5, we can identify a number of factors which may act to constrain such coordination. First, coordination tends to arise from the cooperative effort of individual agencies driven by mutual needs. There is little evidence of the state providing a strategic focus or platform for such coordination or establishing funding mechanisms to encourage or support it. There is, however, evidence of agencies evolving to provide services (in a primary–secondary relationship) for smaller, specialist or locally based agencies (for example the Y-Foundation in Finland and the SWH in Germany). Second, the purchasing role of municipal authorities, together with the tendering approach adopted in many instances and the restrictions on budgets, may all act to constrain and frustrate efforts of coordination in the interests of flexible service provision. Finally, coordination requires a shared understanding of problems, solutions and professional responsibilities. While most studies report a consensus of professional perspective on the multidimensional causes of homelessness, it does not follow that this is easily translated into procedures for action and service delivery. Mechanisms for assessment and review are needed to improve the effectiveness of service delivery. There is a need for further research to establish the effectiveness of such mechanisms.

Although the general view is that practice should aim to move towards an individualised and flexible form of supported housing focused on the individual's needs, it is uncertain how far such approaches are actually implemented. The financial and organisational factors outlined above may act to constrain the implementation of this mode of operation. However, since the majority of supported housing is provided in shared living environments, the suspicion remains that planned programmes of support provided for all residents may be a closer reflection of reality rather than individualised support packages. To the extent that this is the case, then supported housing is likely to provide too much support for some and not enough for others. For example, there is reference in a number of the national reports to people having to accept social support when their need is for support to enable them to sustain a tenancy.

We have already referred to the dilemma involved in measuring the effectiveness of supported housing for homeless people solely in terms of reintegration in permanent housing. Partial autonomy or improvements in the quality of life may equally be viewed as successful outcomes for people with enduring dependency needs or chaotic lifestyles. Nevertheless the success of supported housing, in meeting the needs of some groups of people, will be measured by the extent to which it has enabled a more normal housing situation or lifestyle. Different scenarios have been described in this respect: on the one hand, people may become trapped in a secondary market of dependency and exclusion; on the other, the proportion of people moving on to independent living or a better living situation are generally lower than anticipated. This lower than expected resettlement rate may be linked to procedural constraints in the provision of supported housing – for example, the time limits for follow-on support are simply unrealistic. However, they also reflect the enduring nature of the structural factors leading to homelessness in the first place. For example, de Decker reflects that while two thirds of people leaving supported housing in Antwerp moved on to a better living situation, only one fifth had a higher or more secure income than when they entered supported housing.

The study has also examined the effectiveness of supported housing from the user's perspective by considering whether and to what extent it empowers individuals. While support is a necessary component in changing the life circumstances of homeless people, the evidence from across Europe suggests that, in the variety of forms of provision which exist, supported housing can have a controlling as well as an emancipating influence on people's lives. The control emerges from the structural factors associated with the provision of support which we have identified: the shared nature of the accommodation, the restricted and time-limited nature of the support funding, and the management arrangements between housing and support agencies which involve the sub-letting of accommodation. Such control can be ameliorated by the implementation of, for example, individualised care plans and by appropriate organisational culture and philosophy which prioritises the goal of empowerment.

Conclusion

There is a widespread consensus that the reintegration of homeless people requires the combination of both appropriate housing and support. Our analysis has demonstrated that the integration of housing and support to achieve the aims of social inclusion of homeless people is a complex process, involving a range of interrelated structural and organisational factors. Those involved in service delivery understand that reintegration can also be a lengthy process. In this chapter we have therefore highlighted those factors which act to constrain the effectiveness of supported housing as a solution to the problems of homelessness. While these factors operate to determine a more restricted role for supported housing than some would claim, they do not undermine the now widely recognised need for support in achieving the objectives of social inclusion. The provision of support is a relatively recent innovation and one which is evolving in response to identifiable constraints as well as to organisational experience and to users' needs. The expansion of the sector is to be encouraged by removing constraints and by targeting provision appropriately.

The constraint factors we have identified have important policy implications which need to be tackled if the effectiveness of supported housing is to be enhanced. We would suggest that there are three policy issues that are of crucial importance in this context. First, in relation to housing provision, the extensive use of shared accommodation needs to be combined with more self-contained and smaller shared accommodation. In this respect an understanding of the needs of particular client groups is essential. Second, while funding restrictions constrain the level and nature of support, it is the mechanism of funding allocation rather than simply the level of funding which needs to be addressed. In particular, the unrealistic time-scales assumed in funding regulations and the lack of funding for outreach support are major obstacles to effective implementation of reintegration strategies. Third, we have described a certain ambiguity with regard to the objectives for supported housing, at least for some client groups. Good organisational practice, however, demonstrates the need to clarify overall objectives as well as performance targets for supported housing services. By its very nature the integration of housing and support involves interagency coordination at all levels, including planning, implementation and management. Coordination between agencies in relation to the provision of supported housing has tended to occur more from the bottom–up rather than to be facilitated by commissioning, funding or policy processes. Indeed, while there are examples of excellent organisational initiatives involving voluntary, welfare and housing agencies, it would appear that public sector arrangements for purchasing services from voluntary sector agencies may impede effective coordination.

Our discussion of the role of supported housing, throughout this study, has been set in the context of social inclusion policies and objectives and has reflected the principles of normalisation and empowerment which underpin the development of the community delivery of care services. The effectiveness of support in housing in realising these objectives will depend in large measure on the extent to which it meets the users' needs and aspirations. Organisations which seek to embrace a user perspective need to develop procedures which engender a culture or philosophy or normalisation and empowerment and to develop techniques and procedures which allow the realistic evaluation of outcomes. Such organisations will need to be a learning organisation sensitised and responsive to the needs and requirements of users.

References

Abrahamson, P. (1992) 'Welfare pluralism: towards a new consensus for a European Social Policy?', in L. Hantrais, S. Mangen and M. O'Brien (eds) *The mixed economy of welfare*, Loughborough: Cross-National Research Papers, Loughborough University, pp 5-22.

Alcock, P. (1993) *Understanding poverty*, Basingstoke: Macmillan.

Aldridge, R. (1998) *National report − Services for homeless people: United Kingdom*, Brussels: FEANTSA.

Aldridge, R. (1999) *National report − Support in housing: A solution to homelessness: United Kingdom*, Brussels: FENTSA.

Atkinson, A.B. (1998) 'Social exclusion, poverty and unemployment', in A.B.Atkinson and J. Hills (eds) *Exclusion, employment and opportunity*, CASE, paper 4, London: Centre for Analysis of Social Exclusion, London School of Economics.

Avramov, D. (1996) *Exclusion from housing: Causes and processes*, Brussels: FEANTSA.

Avramov, D. (ed) (1998) *Youth homelessness in the European Union*, Brussels: FEANTSA.

Bank-Mikkelsen, N. (1980) 'Denmark', in R.J. Flynn and K.E. Nitsch (eds) *Normalisation, social integration and community services*, Austin, TX: Baltimore University Park Press..

Barnes, M. and Walker, A. (1996) 'Consumerism versus empowerment: a principled approach to the involvement of older service users', *Policy & Politics*, vol 24, no 4, pp 375-93.

Bauman, Z. (1998) *Globalisation: The human consequences*, Cambridge: Cambridge Univeristy Press.

Beijer, U. (1997) *Psykiskt störda hemlösa − uppsökande verksamhet vid Kammakargatans planeringshem*. FoU-rapport 10, Stockholm stad.

Berghman, J. (1995) 'Social exclusion in Europe: policy context and analytical framework', in G. Room (ed) *Beyond the threshold*, Bristol: The Policy Press, pp 10-28.

Bergmark, A. and Oscarsson, L. (1998) 'Hur styrs missbrukarvården? Om utvecklingen under 1990-talet', *Socionomen*, no 4, pp 47-53.

Bhugra, D. (1996) *Homelessness and mental health*, Cambridge: Cambridge University Press.

Bhugra, D. and Leff, J.P (1993) *Principles of social pyschiatry*, Oxford: Blackwell Scientific.

Blath, A. (1998) 'Betreutes Wohnen in Sachsen Anhalt', in *Jugendhilfe* no 1.

BMFSFJ (Bundesministerium für Familie, Senioren, Frauen und Jugend) (1998) *Zweiter Altenbereicht wohnen im Alter* (Drucksache 13/9750), Bonn.

Børner Stax, T. and Koch Nielsen, I. (1996) *National report 1995: Denmark*, Brussels: FEANTSA.

Børner Stax, T., Kæmpe, J. and Koch Nielsen, I. (1999) *National report 1998: Denmark*, Brussels: FEANTSA.

Boyne, G.A. (1998) 'Public services under New Labour: Back to bureaucracy?', *Public Money and Management*, July–September, pp 43-50.

Brill, K.E. (1998) 'Betreutes Wohnen', *Neue Wege in der psychiatrischen Versorgung*, Munchen.

Bruto da Costa, A. (1999) *National report 1998: Portugal*, Brussels: FEANTSA.

BAG ueor TR (Bundesarbeitsgemeinschaft ueeberoertlicher Traeger der Sozialhilfe) (1995) 'Rahmenempfehlungen der ueberoertlichen Traeger der Sozialhilfe zur Gestaltung der Hilfe fuer alleinstehende Wohunglose', *Wohnungslos*, April.

BAG (Bundesarbeitsgemeinschaft) Wohnungslosenhilfe (1998) 'Zur organsiatorischen Gestaltungen der ambulaten persönlichen hilfe nach §72 BSHG für Menschen in wohnungen', *Empfehlungen der BAGF Wohngslosenhilfe e V, Wohnungslos*, January.

Busch-Geertsema, V. (1998) *National report 1997: Germany*, Brussels: FEANTSA.

Busch-Geertsema,V. (1999) *National report – 1998: Homelessness and support in housing in Germany*, Brussels: FEANTSA.

Byrne, D. (1999) *Social exclusion*, Buckingham: Open University Press.

Castellani, P. (1996) 'Closing institutions in New York State', in T. Mansell and K. Ericcson (eds) *Deinstitutionalisation and community living*, London: Chapman Hall.

Censis (1993) *Indagine sulla condizione abitativa in Italia. Analisi della domanda marginale*, Roma.

Chapman, M. and Murie, A. (1996) 'Housing and the European Union', *Housing Studies*, vol 11, no 2, pp 307-18.

Clapham, D. and Munro, M. (1994) *A wider choice: Revenue funding mechanisms for housing and community care*, York: Joseph Rowntree Foundation.

Coates, K. and Silburn, R. (1970) *Poverty, the forgotten Englishman*, Harmondsworth: Penguin.

Corden, A. and Duffy, K. (1998) 'Human dignity and social exclusion', in R. Sykes and P. Alcock (eds) *Developments in European social policy: Convergence and diversity*, Bristol: The Policy Press, pp 95-124.

Council of Europe (1993) *Homelessness*, Strasbourg: Council of Europe.

Cousins, C. (1998) 'Social exclusion in Europe: paradigms of social disadvantage in Germany, Spain, Sweden and the United Kingdom', *Policy & Politics*, vol 26, no 2, pp 127-46.

Daly, M. (1993) *Abandoned: Profile of Europe's homeless people*. Synthesis report of the European Observatory on Homelessness, Brussels: FEANTSA.

Dayson, D. (1992) 'The Taps project: crime, vagrancy and re-admission', *British Journal of Psychiatry*, vol 162 (supplement 19), pp 40-4.

de Decker, P. (1998) *National report – Services for homeless people: Belgium*, Brussels: FEANTSA.

de Decker, P. and Hardouin, G. (1999) *National report 1998: Support in housing between control and emancipation: Belgium*, Brussels: FEANTSA.

de Decker, P and Serriën, L. (1997) *Trends in housing, housing policy and youth homelessness*, Brussels: FEANTSA.

de Feijter, H. (1998) *Between housing and care in the Netherlands, National report 1998,* Brussels: FEANTSA.

de Feijter, H. and Blok, H. (1999) *National report 1998: Netherlands,* Brussels: FEANTSA.

de Gouy, A. (1998) *National report 1997: France,* Brussels: FEANTSA.

de Gouy, A. and Damon, J. (1999) *National report – Support in housing: France,* Brussels: FEANTSA.

DSS (Department of Social Security) (1998) 'Supporting People', Government Consultation paper, London: The Stationary Office.

Deutsches Bundestag (1998) *Bericht der Bundesregierung über Maßnahmen zur Bekämpfung der Obdachlosigkeit,* Bundestagsdrucksache 13/10141.

Douglas, A., MacDonald, C. and Taylor, M. (1998) *Living independently with support: Service users' perspectives on 'floating' support,* York: Joseph Rowntree Foundation.

Edgar, W. and Doherty, J. (1996) *Scotspen – Supported accommodation database,* research report 45, Edinburgh: Scottish Homes.

Edgar, W. and Mina-Coull, A. (1999) *Supported accommodation: The appropriate use of tenancy agreements,* Edinburgh: Scottish Homes.

Edgar, W., Doherty, J. and Mina-Coull, A. (1999) *Services for homeless people: Innovation and change in the European Union,* Bristol/Brussels: The Policy Press/FEANTSA.

Edgar, W. and Muirhead, I. (1998) *Tenancy rights in supported accommodation in Scotland,* Edinburgh: Scottish Homes.

Ely, P. and Samà, A. (1996) 'The mixed economy of welfare', in B. Munday and P. Ely, *Social care in Europe,* London: Prentice Hall, pp 96-126.

Emerson, E. (1992) 'What is normalisation?', in H. Smith and H. Brown (eds) *Normalisation: A reader for the 1990s,* London: Routledge, pp 1-18.

Engberg, M. (1982) 'Afdelningernes selvstaendiggörelse', *Psykisk Utvecklingshämning,* vol 84, no 4, pp 10-4.

Ericsson, K. and Mansell, J. (1996) *De-institutionalisation and community living,* London: Chapman & Hall.

Esping-Andersen, G. (1990) *The three worlds of welfare capitalism,* Cambridge: Polity Press.

Esping-Andersen, G. (1999) *Social foundations of post-industrial economies*, Oxford: Oxford University Press.

European Commission (1991) *The regions in the 1990s*, Directorate-General for Regional Policy, Brussels.

European Commission (1991a) *Final report of the recent European Poverty Programme 1985-89*, Brussels: EC Commission.

European Commission (1992) *Council Recommendations of 24 June 1992 on Common Criteria concerning sufficient resources and social assistance in social protection systems* (92/441/EEC).

European Commission (1993) *Action programme to combat social exclusion and to promote social solidarity*, Brussels: DGV.

European Commission (1994) *European social policy – The way forward for the Union*, Com 994 333, Brussels.

European Commission (1994a) *The perception of poverty in Europe: Poverty 3*, Brussels: EC Commission.

European Commission (1997) *Promoting the role of voluntary organisations and foundations in Europe* Com/97/0241.

European Commission (1999) *Communication from the Commission: Concerted Strategy for Modernising Social Protection*, Com/99/347.

European Commission (2000a) *Social trends: Prospects and challenges*, Com 2000/82.

European Commission (2000b) *Building an inclusive Europe*, Com (2000) 79.

Evers, A. (1993) 'The welfare mix approach. Understanding the pluralism of welfare systems', in A. Evers and I. Svetlik (eds) *Balancing Pluralism*, Aldershot: Avebury.

Evers, J. and Ruhstrat, E.U. (1994) 'Wohngsnotfaelle in Schleswig-Holstein', in Ministerin fuer Arbeit, soziales, Jugend und Gesundheit des Landes Schleswig-Holstein (ed) *Im spanungsfeld zwischen Sozial-, Ordnungs- und Wohnungpolitik*, Keil.

Expertenkommission (1988) *Empfehlungen der Expertenkommission der Bundesregierung zur Reform der Vorsorgung im psychiatrischen und psychotherapeutischen/psychosomatischen Bereich auf der Grundlage des Modellprogramms Psychiatrie der Bundesregierung*, Bundesminister für Jugend, Familie, Frauen und Gesundheit, Munich.

FEANTSA (1999) *Europe against exclusion: Housing for all*, London: FEANTSA and Shelter.

FO (Federatie Opvang) (1998) *Decentralisatie maatschappelijke opvang*, monitor 1997, Utrecht: FO.

Fitzpatrick, S. (1998) 'Hidden homelessness amongst young people', *Youth and Policy*, special edition, 'Youth homelessness and social exclusion', no 59, pp 8-22.

Fitzpatrick, S. (1998) 'Homelessness in the European Union', in M. Kleinman, W. Matznetter and M. Stephens (eds) *European integration and housing policy*, London: Routledge, pp 197-214.

Fitzpatrick, S. and Clapham, D. (1999) 'Homelessness and young people', in S. Hutson and D. Clapham (eds) *Homelessness: Public policies and private troubles*, London: Cassells.

Fitzpatrick, S., Kemp, P. and Klinker, S. (2000) *Single homelessness: An overview of research in Britain*, Bristol/York: The Policy Press/Joseph Rowntree Foundation.

Folketingets Forhandlinger (1995) Folketinget Forhandlinger, #13, Copenhagen: Schultz Grafisk A/S, preliminary publication.

Goldsmith, M. and Newton, K. (1988) 'Centralisation and decentralisation: Changing patterns of intergovernmental relations in advanced western societies', *European Journal of Political Research*, vol 16, no 4, pp 359-63.

Goodwin, S. (1990) *Community care and the future of mental health service provision*, Aldershot: Avebury.

Gore, C. (1995) 'Introduction: markets, citizenship and social exclusion', in G. Rodgers, C. Gore and J. Figueiredo (eds) *Social exclusion: Rhetoric, reality, responses*, Geneva: International Institute for Labour Studies, UN Development Programme, pp 1-42.

Greengross, S. (1992) 'Europe: a rich map of change', in R. Anderson et al, *The coming of age in Europe*, London: Age Concern, pp 7-13.

Hadjimichalis, C. and Sadler, D. (eds) (1995) *Europe at the margins: New mosaics of inequality*, Chichester: Wiley.

Halldin, J., Åhs, S. and Sundgren, M. (1997) 'Hemlösheten i Stockholm med fler kvinnor och psykiskt sjuka', *Socialmedicinsk tidskrift*, årg 74, häfte 10, 452-61.

Hantrais, L. (1995) *Social policy in the European Union*, Basingstoke: Macmillan.

Harvey, B. (1994) 'Homelessness in Europe', European Network for Housing Research Conference, University of Glasgow, 29 August–1 September.

Harvey, B. (1999) 'The problem of homelessness: a European perspective', in S. Hutson and D. Clapham (eds) *Homelessness: Public policies and private troubles*, London, Cassell.

Heinonen, J. (1997) *Tukiasuminen. Sininauhaliitto* (Finnish Blue Ribbon), Jyväskylä.

Hyde, M. and Ackers, L. (1997) 'Poverty and social security', in T. Spybey (ed) *Britain in Europe*, London: Routledge, pp 343-58.

Hutson, S. (1999) 'The experience of homeless accommodation and support', in S. Hutson and D. Clapham (eds) *Homelessness: Public policies and private troubles*, London: Cassell.

James, S. (1998) 'Labour markets and social policy in Europe: the case of the European Union', in R. Sykes and P. Alcock (eds) *Developments in European social policy: Convergence and diversity*, Bristol: The Policy Press, pp. 29-54.

Jamieson, A. (1990) 'Informal care in Europe', in A. Jamieson and R. Illsley (eds) *Contrasting European policies for the care of older people*, Aldershot: Avebury.

Jones, G. (1995) *Leaving home*, Edinburgh: Centre for Educational Sociology, Briefing No 2, University of Edinburgh, June.

Jones, G., Gilliland, L. and Stevens, C. (1993) *Young people in and out of the housing market*, Edinburgh: Working Papers 1-5, Centre for Educational Sociology, University of Edinburgh and Scottish Council for Single Homeless.

Kahn, A.J. and Kamerman, S.B. (1976) *Social services in the United States: Policies and programmes*, Philadelphia: PA Temple University Press.

Kärkkäinen, S.-L. (1999) *National report 1998: Finland*, Brussels: FEANTSA.

Kazepov, Y. (1996) *Le politiche locali contro l'esclusoine sociale*, Roma: Commissione d'indagine sulla poverta' e l'emarginazione.

Kleinman, M. (1996) *Housing, welfare and the state in Europe*, Cheltenham: Edward Elgar.

Kleinman, M. (1998) 'Western European housing policies: convergence or collapse?', in M. Kleinman, W. Matznetter and M. Stephens (eds) *European integration and housing policy*, London: Routledge.

Kofler, A. (1998) *National report 1997: Austria*, Brussels: FEANTSA.

Kugel, R.B. and Wolfensberger, W. (1969) *Changing patterns in residential services for the mentally retarded*, Washington DC: Presidential Committee.

Leal Maldonado, J. and Laínez, I. (1999) *National report – Support in housing: Spain*, Brussels: FEANTSA.

Madianos, M. (1994) *Psycho-social rehabilitation – From the asylum to the community*, Athens: Greek Letters.

Mallander, O., Meeuwisse, A. and Sunesson, S. (1998), 'Normalisering', in V. Denvall and T. Jacobson (eds) *Vardagsbegrepp i socialt arbete*, Stockholm: Norstedts Juridik, pp 159-206.

Marcuse, P. (1996) 'Space and race in the post–fordist city: the outcast ghetto and advanced homelessness in the United States today', in E. Mingione (ed) *Urban poverty and the underclass: A reader*, Oxford: Blackwell, pp 176-216.

Marques, C. and Bras Gomes, V. (1993) 'Social action and local government in Portugal', Lecture for Kent County Council, Maidstone Kent quoted by B. Munday (1996) *Social care in Europe*, London: Prentice Hall.

Marshall, T.H. (1950) *Citizenship and social class and other essays*, Chicago, IL: University of Chicago Press.

Means, R. and Smith, R. (1994) *Community care: Policy and practice*, Basingstoke: Macmillan.

Mitchell, M. and Russell, D. (1998) 'Immigration, citizenship and social exclusion in the new Europe', in R. Sykes and P. Alcock (eds) *Developments in European social policy: Convergence and diversity*, Bristol: The Policy Press, pp 75-94.

Morris, J. (1993) *Independent lives?: Community care and disabled people*, Basingstoke: Macmillan.

Muenstermann, K. (1996) *Entstehung, Gegenwart und Perspektiven des betreuten Wohnens* – pädagogische, psychologische und soziologische Grundlagen, in Landesshauptstadt Dresden (ed).

Munday, B. (ed) (1993) *European social services*, European Institute of Social Services, University of Kent at Canterbury.

Munday, B. (1996) 'Social care in the member states of the European Union', in B. Munday and P. Ely (eds) *Social care in Europe*, London: Prentice Hall.

Munday, B. and Ely, P. (1996) *Social care in Europe*, London: Prentice Hall.

Munn, D. (1996) *Out of the ordinary*, Edinburgh: Scottish Council for Single Homeless.

National Housing Federation (1996) *Supported housing CORE*, London: National Housing Federation.

NBHBP (National Board of Housing, Building, and Planning) (1994) 'De bostadslösas situation i Sverige', *Socialstyrelsen föier upp och utvärderar 1994:15, Stockholm*: Socialstyrelsen och NBHBP.

NBHBP (National Board of Housing, Building, and Planning) (1998) *Bostadsmarknadsläge och förväntat bostadsbyggande 1998-99. Kommunernas bedömning*, NBHBP rapport 1, Karlskrona: NBHBP.

NBHSS (1998) *Reformens första tusen dagar. Årsrapport för psykiatreformen 1998*, NBHSS följer upp och utvärderar 4, Stockholm.

Neale, J. (1997) 'Homelessness and theory reconsidered', *Housing Studies*, vol 12, no 1, pp 47-62.

Negri, N. and Saraceno, C. (1996) *Le politiche contro la povertà in Italia*, Bologna: Il Mulino.

Nirje, B. (1969) 'The normalisation principle and its human management implications', in R.B. Kugel and W. Wolfensberger (eds) *Changing patterns in residential services for the mentally retarded*, Washington DC: Presidential Committee.

Norström, C. and Thunved, A. (1998) *Nya sociallagarna med kommentarer, lagar och författaningar som de lyder den Januari 1998*, Stockholm: Nordetsdts Juridik.

Observatoire Européen des Politiques Familiales (1994) *Evolution des Politiques Familiales Nationales*, Vienna: OEPF

O'Cinneide, S. (1993) 'Ireland and the European welfare state', *Policy & Politics*, vol 21, no 2, pp 97-108.

O'Sullivan, E. (1998) *National report 1997: Ireland*, Brussels: FEANTSA.

O'Sullivan, E. (1999) *National report 1998: Ireland*, Brussels: FEANTSA.

Parkinson, M. (1998) *Combating social exclusion: Lessons from area-based programmes in Europe*, Bristol/York: The Policy Press/Joseph Rowntree Foundation.

Pels, M. (1999) *National report 1998: Luxembourg*, Brussels: FEANTSA.

Petch, A. (1996) *Delivering community care: Initial implementation of care management in Scotland*, Edinburgh: HMSO.

Pinder, D. (1998) *The new Europe: Economy, society and environment*, Chichester: John Wiley.

Pleace, N., Ford, J., Wilcox, S. and Burrows, R. (1999) *Lettings and sales by registered social landlords 1997/98*, York: Centre for Housing Policy, University of York.

Poteri, R. (1997) *Kun pelkkä asunto ei riitä – Erityisryhmien tukiasuntotoiminnan tutkimus – ja kehittämisprojektin loppuraportti.* Sininauhaliitto (Finnish blue Ribbon), Jyväskylä.

Prior, D., Stewart, J. and Walsh, K. (1995) *Citizenship: Rights, community and participation*, London: Pitman.

Race, D. (1987) 'Normalisation: theory and practice', in N. Malin (ed) *Reassessing community care*, London: Croom Helm, pp 62-79.

Ramon, S. (1993) *Beyond community care: Normalisation and integration work*, Basingstoke: Macmillan Press.

Ramon, S. (1996) *Mental health in Europe: Ends, beginnings and rediscoveries*, Basingstoke: Macmillan/Mind.

Randall, G. and Brown, S. (1993) *The move in experience*, London: Crisis.

Rekenkamer, A. (1997) *Decentralisatieproces maatschappelijke opvang.* Tweede kamer, vergaderjaar 1996-1997, 23315, nrs. 1 en 2. 's-Gravenhage: Sdu'.

Rodgers, G. (1995) 'What is special about a "social exclusion" approach?', in G. Rodgers, C. Gore and J. Figueiredo (eds) *Social exclusion: Rhetoric, reality, responses*, Geneva: International Insitute for Labour Studies, UN Development Programme, pp 43-56.

Room, G. (ed) (1992) *National policies to combat social exclusion*, Second Annual Report of the EC Observatory on Policies to Combat Social Exclusion, Brussels: European Commission.

Room, G. (ed) (1995) *Beyond the threshold: The measurement and analysis of social exclusion*, Bristol: The Policy Press.

Room, G. (1999) 'Social exclusion, solidarity and the challenge of globalisation', *International Journal of Social Welfare*, vol 8, pp 166-74.

Ruhstrat, E.U. et al (1991) 'Ohne Arbeit keine Wohnung, ohne Wohnung keine Arbeit!', *Entstehung und Verlauf von Wohnungslosigkeit*, (ed) Evangelischer Fachverband Wohnung und Existenzsicherung, Bielefeld.

Rutter, M. and Madge, N. (1976) *Cycles of disadvantage: A review of research*, London: Heinemann.

Saarenheimo, U. and von Hertzen, H. (1996) *Asunnottoomuus väheni suomessa, Määrätieoinen työ tuo tuloksia, Suomen Ympäristö 49/1996*, Helsinki: Ministry of the Environment.

Sahlin, I. (1993) *Socialtjänsten och bostaden. Redovisning av en enkätundersökning om socialtjänstens metoder och resurser att lösa klienternas bostadsproblem*, Research report, Lund: Sociologiska institutionen.

Sahlin, I. (1998) *National report 1997: Sweden*, Brussels: FEANTSA.

Sahlin, I. (1999) *National report 1998: Sweden*, Brussels: FEANTSA.

Sapounakis, A. (1996) 'Urgent accommodation shelters for homeless people in Greece', Eurohome Executive Report, Workshop 2, *Services for the homeless*, Brussels: FEANTSA.

Sapounakis, A. (1998) *National report: Greece*, Brussels: FEANTSA.

Sapounakis, A. (1999) *National report – Support in housing: Greece*, Brussels: FEANTSA.

Schoibl, H. (1999) *National report – Support in housing: Austria*, Brussels: FEANTSA.

Scott, J. (1993) 'Homelessness and mental illness: Review article', *British Journal of Psychiatry*, vol 162, pp 314-24.

Seligman, A. (1992) *The idea of civil society*, NY: Free Press.

Sen, A.K. (1985) *Collective choice and social welfare*, Oxford: Clarendon Press.

Silver, H. (1995) 'Culture, politics and national discourses of the new urban poverty', in E. Mingione (ed) *Urban poverty and the underclass: A reader*, Oxford: Blackwell, pp 105-38.

Silver, H. and Wilkinson, F. (1995) 'Policies to combat social exclusion: A French–British comparison', in G. Rodgers, C. Gore and J. Figueiredo (eds) *Social exclusion: Rhetoric, reality, responses*, Geneva: International Insitute for Labour Studies, UN Development Programme, pp 253-82.

Somerville, P. (1998) 'Explanations of social exclusion: Where does housing fit in?', *Housing Studies*, vol 13, no 6, pp 761-79.

Specht-Kittler, T. (1998) *Statististikbericht 1996*, Bielefeld: BAG Wohnungslosenhilfe.

Sykes, R. (1998) 'Studying European social policy – Issues and perspectives', in R. Sykes and P. Alcock (eds) *Developments in European social policy: Convergence and diversity*, Bristol: The Policy Press, pp 7-26.

Sykes, R. and Alcock, P. (eds) (1998) *Developments in European social policy: Convergence and diversity*, Bristol: The Policy Press.

Taipale, I. (1998) *Mielen sairaat ja palveluasunnot*, sosiaali- ja terveys ministeriö, Helsinki: Ministry of Social Affairs and Health.

Taylor, P. (1996) *The European Union in the 1990s*, Oxford: Oxford University Press.

Tosi, A. and Ranci, C. (1994) *National report 1993: Italy*, Brussels: FEANTSA.

Tosi, A. and Ranci, C. (1999) *National report 1998: Support in housing: Italy*, Brussels: FEANTSA.

Townsend, P. (1964) *The last refuge: A survey of residential institutions and homes for the aged in England and Wales*, London: Routledge and Kegan Paul.

Townsend, P. (1981) 'The structured dependency of the elderly: the creation of social policy in the twentieth century?', *Ageing and Society*, vol 1, no 1, pp 5-28.

Valentini, B. (1996) 'Introduzione a: Risultati dell'indagine sui servizi a bassa soglia', *TRA*, vol 1, pp 3-5.

Valtakunnallinen asunto-ohjelma vuosille (1976) *1976-1985. Komiteanmietintö.*

van der Meijden, R.R. (1994) *Lokaal thuislozenbeleid. Een handboek voor integraal gemeentelijk beleid*, Rijswijk: Ministerie van WVC.

Vranken, J., Geldof, D. and Van Menxel, G. (1997) *Armoede en sociale uitsluitng. Jaarboek 1996*, Leuven: Acco.

Wendon, B. (1998) 'The Commission and European Union social policy', in R. Sykes and P. Alcock (eds) *Developments in European social policy: Convergence and diversity*, Bristol: The Policy Press, pp 55-74.

Wilson, W.J. (1987) *The truly disadvantaged: The inner city, the underclass and public policy*, Chicago, IL: Univeristy of Chicago Press.

Wolfsenberger, W. (1972) *Normalisation: The principle of normalisation in human services*, Toronto: National Institute on Mental Retardation.

Wolfsenberger, W. (1992) 'Deinstitutionalisation policy: How it is made, by whom and why', *Clinical Psychology Forum*, vol 39, pp 7-11.

Wolfsenberger, W. and Thomas, S. (1983) *PASSING: Programme analysis of service systems' implementation of normalisation goals*, Toronto: National Institute on Mental Retardation.

Index

NOTE: Abbreviations following page numbers: *fig* = information in a figure; *n* = information in note; *tab* = information in a table.

C

care *see* community care; social care
care in the community *see*
    community care
Caritás 127, 129, 152
'catastrophic discontinuity' 21-2
category housing, Sweden 50,
    102*tab*, 103
CECODHAS 31*n*
Cena dell'Amicizia, Italy 109, 152,
    161
Chapman, M. 26, 31*n*
charitable organisations *see*
    voluntary agencies and NGOs
children *see* young people
child welfare legislation 45-6, 47
choice: empowerment characteristic
    170, 171, 173-4, 183, 187-8
church and social care 42, 64, 90,
    91, 122, 123, 156, 191
    see also civil society model of
    social care
citizenship rights 40, 49, 169,
    170-3
civil society social care model 42,
    43, 62-6
    supported housing in context of
    90-2, 109-11, 122-4, 191
    see also voluntary agencies and
    NGOs
Clapham, D. 158
collective housing, Sweden 101,
    102*tab*, 103
Commission Communications 6
communal space 182
Communidade Vida e Paz, Portugal
    153
community care 33-68, 69-70
    legislative framework 43-52, 74-6,
    82, 85, 99, 104-5, 190-1
    principles of 11, 35-40
    see also de-institutionalisation;
    supported housing
'Community Charter for
    Fundamental Social Rights for
    Workers' (1988) 17
Concerted Strategy for
    Modernising Social Protection 7

continuum of care 70-1, 73,
    139-40, 165
contracts 117, 157, 179-80, 181, 182
control: empowerment
    characteristic 40, 170, 174-5,
    183-4, 186, 188, 201-2
Council of Europe
    definition of homelessness 1-2
    'Human Dignity and Social
    Exclusion' study 17-18
    Social Charter 18, 30*n*
counselling support 70, 75, 84,
    113*tab*, 114, 116, 118
Cousins, Christine 23

D

da Costa, Bruto 92
Daly, M. 162
de Decker, P. 106, 119, 137-8, 178,
    181, 198, 201
de-familialisation 66
de Feijter, H. 137
de Gouy, A. 180
de-institutionalisation 11, 33-5
    contributing factors 34, 69
    opposed in Portugal 65
    rate of closure 3-4, 34
    social care model 42-52, 59, 63,
    138
    supported housing in context of
    74-83, 90, 93, 124, 128, 136, 190
    accommodation dimension 99-
    106
    needs of mentally ill homeless
    people 143, 144-51
    support dimension 111-18, 147
    see also community care
Delors, Jacques 18
demographic changes 5-6, 41
Denmark
    de-institutionalisation model 43-
    5, 75, 137
    legislative framework 36-7, 43-5,
    74-6, 104-5
    supported housing in 74-6, 104-5,
    117-18, 131, 149
    structural constraints on 193, 194,
    199

homeless people 140–165
data on 125, 134–5, 165
defining 9–10, 72–4, 82, 93
delivery and provision 95–132,
190
accommodation dimension 9, 71–
2, 96–111, 166, 177–82
coordination and delivery 124–5,
126, 128–32, 166–7, 200–1, 203
management dimension 9, 71*tab*,
124–32
provision in Europe 74–92, 134–5
social dimension 185–8
structural constraints 192–4, 201
support service dimension 111–
24
see also support services
effectiveness evaluation 165, 189,
192–6, 197–202
emergence of concept 29–30, 69–
94, 190–1
funding 51–2, 78, 95, 126–7, 166
constraints on effectiveness 193,
199–200, 202–3
individual needs based funding
52, 114, 185, 201
problematical in UK 51–2, 99,
112, 185, 193, 199
geographical concentration 135,
159, 193–4
legislative framework 43–52, 57–8,
74–83, 114, 130–1, 147
nature of 69–72
resourcing 124, 125–7
lack of adequate housing 8–9, 55,
162, 165, 192, 196
see also funding *above*
social care frameworks *see* civil
society social care model; de-
institutionalisation; reintegration
social care model
support in housing 9–10, 73, 76, 93,
189, 197
see also ordinary housing; self-
contained housing
'Supporting people' report (DSS)
51–2, 112, 113*tab*

support services 9, 111–24,
183–5, 198–9
ambulant/floating support 73, 78,
79, 82, 105, 116, 144, 160, 190,
197
categories of support 70, 111, 112,
113*tab*
duration of support 73, 183–4,
185, 196–7, 200
funding for 52, 125–6, 202–3
in relation to housing 71–2
support workers 54, 116, 127, 172
transitional support 71*tab*, 79,
141*tab*, 143–4
Sweden 31*n*, 101–3
alcohol abusers 39, 115, 153, 155,
172
de-institutionalisation framework
49–50
supported housing in 79–81, 135
accommodation dimension 100–
4, 192, 195–6
empowerment issues 171, 181,
183–4
group housing 50, 80–1, 100–1,
102*tab*, 103, 147
homeless target groups 146–7,
153, 155
normalisation through 38*fig*, 39,
50, 100, 101*fig*, 114–15
structural constraints on 192, 193,
194
support dimension 114–15, 147,
183–4
Sykes, R. 25

T

temporary accommodation 2, 4, 73,
79–80, 109
see also transitional
accommodation
tenancy issues 57, 169–70, 179–82,
188, 196
'therapeutic' care 76, 115–16, 138,
153
Thomas, S. 116